KNIVES
AND SWORDS
A VISUAL HISTORY

Featuring material from *Weapon*

KNIVES
AND SWORDS
A VISUAL HISTORY

DK

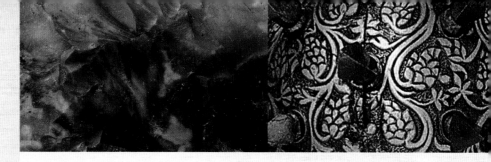

DK

LONDON, NEW YORK, MELBOURNE,
MUNICH, AND DELHI

GENERAL EDITOR Chris McNab

PROJECT ART EDITOR Anna Hall
DK PICTURE LIBRARY Romaine Werblow
PICTURE RESEARCH Frances Vargo, Karen VanRoss
PRODUCTION EDITOR Joanna Byrne
PRODUCTION CONTROLLER Mandy Inness
US EDITOR Margaret Parrish
MANAGING EDITOR Camilla Hallinan
MANAGING ART EDITOR Karen Self
ART DIRECTOR Bryn Walls
ASSOCIATE PUBLISHER Liz Wheeler
PUBLISHER Jonathan Metcalf

DK DELHI

SENIOR DESIGNER Tannishtha Chakraborty
DESIGNERS Rajnish Kashyap, Ivy Roy
EDITORIAL MANAGER Rohan Sinha
EDITORS Garima Sharma, Samira Sood
PRODUCTION MANAGER Pankaj Sharma
DTP COORDINATOR Sunil Sharma
DTP DESIGNERS Harish Aggarwal, Dheeraj Arora,
Jagtar Singh, Preetam Singh
PICTURE RESEARCH Arijit Ganguly, Mahua Sharma
ART DIRECTOR Shefali Upadhyay

First American Edition, 2010

Published in the United States by DK Publishing
375 Hudson Street, New York, New York 10014

10 11 12 13 14   10 9 8 7 6 5 4 3 2 1

175993—March 2010

Published in Great Britain by Dorling Kindersley Limited.

A catalog record for this book is available from the Library of Congress.

ISBN 978-0-7566-5646-1

DK books are available at special discounts when purchased in bulk
for sales promotions, premiums, fund-raising, or educational use. For
details, contact: DK Publishing Special Markets, 375 Hudson Street,
New York, New York 10014 or SpecialSales@dk.com.

Printed and bound in China by Hung Hing

Discover more at
www.dk.com

ANCIENT BLADES
3000 BCE—1000 CE   6

Introduction   8
The first blades   10
Mesopotamia and Egypt   16
Bronze- and Iron-Age blades   22
CELTIC WARRIOR   24
Bronze-and Iron-Age blades (cont.)   26
Ancient Greece   28
HOPLITE   30
Ancient Rome   32
ROMAN GLADIATOR   34
Anglo-Saxon and Frankish blades   36
EARLY ARMOR   40
Viking blades   42
VIKING RAIDER   48
Spears and arrows   50

THE MIDDLE AGES
1000—1500   60

Introduction   62
European swords   64

TOURNAMENT COMBAT   68
European swords (cont.)   70
MEDIEVAL KNIGHT   76
European daggers   78
MEDIEVAL FOOT SOLDIER   84
European staff weapons   86
MEDIEVAL FIGHT BOOKS   92
Aztec blades   94
Japanese and Chinese blades   98
SHAOLIN MONK   104
Japanese and Chinese blades (cont.)   106
Asian staff weapons   108
Arrows and bolts   112
BLADE VS. BOW   114

THE AGE OF SWORDSMANSHIP
1500—1775   116

Introduction   118
Two-handed swords   120
European infantry and cavalry swords   124
DUELING   136

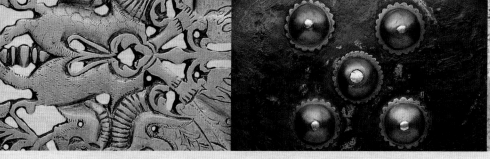

European rapiers 138
European smallswords 142
European hunting swords 146
COSSACK WARRIOR **154**
European daggers 156
LANDSKNECHT **166**
European one-handed staff weapons 168
European two-handed staff weapons 172
PIKEMAN **176**
Indian and Sri Lankan swords 178
Indian staff weapons 184
CUTTING AND THRUSTING **188**
Japanese samurai weapons 190
Wakazashi sword 198
SAMURAI **204**
Asian daggers 206
Combination weapons 214

TWILIGHT OF THE SWORD
1775–1900 218

Introduction 220
European swords 222

BRITISH CAVALRYMAN **226**
European swords (cont.) 228
FENCING **234**
Swords of the American Civil War 236
UNITED STATES CAVALRYMAN **242**
European and American bayonets 244
BAYONET TACTICS **252**
North American hilt weapons 254
NORTH AMERICAN WARRIOR **260**
Ottoman Empire swords 262
OTTOMAN WARRIOR **266**
Ottoman Empire swords (cont.) 268
Chinese and Tibetan swords 272
NINJA **280**
Japanese special weapons 282
KENJUTSU **286**
Indian swords 288
Indian blades 294
Indian staff weapons 300
African blades 304
ZULU WARRIOR **306**
African blades (cont.) 308
Daggers of Oceania 312
MAORI WARRIOR **314**

THE MODERN WORLD
1900 ONWARD 316

Introduction 318
German and Italian blades 320
WWII BRITISH COMMANDO **328**
British, American, and Allied blades 330
GURKHA **338**
Japanese blades 340
Modern African blades 342
Postwar bayonets 350

Glossary 352
Index 356
Acknowledgments 360

ANCIENT
BLADES
3000 BCE—1000 CE

FROM PREHISTORIC TIMES TO 1000 CE, the creation and use of tools with sharp edges was one of the pivotal developments in technology. When exactly early humans started sharpening rocks into cutting tools is unclear, but rudimentary hand axes—rocks with one end sharpened and the other shaped to fit into a hand—were first used up to two and a half million years ago in Africa and the Middle East. Such tools were not only useful for everyday jobs, such as scraping meat off bones, but also served as potential weapons against human adversaries. These blades were made by pressure flaking—a process of hitting a rock with a piece of horn or antler until its edge became jagged—and were surprisingly sharp. Using this simple method, prehistoric man made many practical tools such as stone blades, particularly those made from flint, with smooth or serrated edges. However, a further step was required to transform the stone blade into a true fighting weapon.

The addition of a hilt or a grip to the hand ax launched the prehistoric blade's journey toward becoming a sword. By binding a wooden hilt to the unsharpened end of a hand ax, the user increased both the fighting distance between him and an adversary, and the force with which he could deliver a blow, due to the wider angle of movement the hilt provided. However, early hilts were attached rather crudely and were prone to coming loose in combat. Around 40,000–60,000 years ago, with the invention of bow and arrow technology, small stone blades began to be used as arrowheads. Designed with serrated edges or barbs, these arrows dramatically increased the accuracy and severity of injury when fired from bows, while allowing the warrior to distance himself farther from the enemy. By 10,000 BCE, warriors had a varied arsenal of bows and arrows, as well as hilted blades such as flint daggers, axes, and flint-tipped spears. The use of such weapons meant that warfare began to produce much higher numbers of fatalities.

Although stone blades remained in use in some primitive or tribal societies for centuries to come—blades made from flint, for example, were used by the Aztecs until the 16th century CE—a metallurgical revolution took place during the third millennium BCE. Copper and bronze became the new materials for blade manufacture. These were stronger and more durable than stone, and could be made into a more uniform shape and sharpened more keenly. During the second millenium BCE, daggers were transformed into full-length swords in most parts of the world, except Egypt, which relied upon daggers. Copper and bronze, although responsible for major developments in sword manufacture, were malleable and weapons made from them could be damaged easily in combat. It was the use of iron that truly revolutionized sword production. By 900 BCE, iron began to be widely used to produce more lasting and lethal weapons. Soon pattern welding—a technique in which iron is hammered flat, folded, and welded—was being used to produce stronger and more flexible swords.

Between 1000 BCE and 1000 CE, metal weapons became the fundamental tools of organized armies across the world. However, the high cost of making swords meant that in many societies these weapons were used only by the military elite and the nobility. New techniques such as casting the blade and hilt in one piece solved the problem of broken hilt joints. The design of metal weapons also evolved, and swords featured either thrusting or slashing characteristics. A thrusting sword had a sharp point for penetration, while a slashing sword placed more emphasis on the cutting edge. However, some swords had both qualities. The Roman *gladius*, for example, had a point capable of punching through chain-mail armor, but also had a double-edged blade ideal for slashing attacks. Many swords also featured grooves called fullers along much of the length of the blade; these served to lighten and strengthen the blade. The ricasso—a small, unsharpened section of the blade just above the hilt—enabled the warrior to grip the blade as well as the hilt, providing extra power and control for a thrusting move. New features appeared on the hilt as well during this period. Shaped protrusions at the end of the grip, called pommels, provided counterbalance to the blade, while metal cross-guards—sitting at a right angle to the blade just at the top of the grip—were designed to protect the user's hand from the enemy's sword. In essence, by the end of the first millennium CE, swordsmiths had laid the foundations of sword design for the next 1,000 years.

ANCIENT BLADES

THE FIRST BLADES

The ability of human beings to manufacture tools was an early step toward gaining mastery over their environment. Among the first tools to appear were simple hand blades and axes made from hard rock; they were used to kill and dismember animals, but they also had the potential to be employed against other humans. The distinction between hunting and military weaponry remained blurred for many millennia. With the invention of the handle or shaft, which turned a blade into a viable handheld weapon, a revolution in hunting and fighting was underway.

Rounded area
held by hand

PALEOLITHIC BLADES

DATE	c. 40,000 BCE
LENGTH	4 in (10 cm)

To be able to cut was of prime importance to early humans, and these stone blades—dating back to about 40,000 BCE—would have been used to dismember animals that had been killed by Paleolithic hunters. Such blades were capable of severing sinew and separating the skin from the animal's flesh.

Narrowed
point

HAND AX

DATE   c. 250,000–70,000 BCE

LENGTH 6 in (15 cm)

A key tool of the Paleolithic Age, the hand ax was
shaped to provide both a cutting edge and a point.
Although hand axes were essentially domestic tools,
they were capable of inflicting savage wounds against
both animals and people. Their cutting ability made
them highly valuable implements.

Rough
cutting edge

Serrated teeth
for sawing

SERRATED FLINT KNIFE

DATE   2,500,000–10,000 BCE

LENGTH 8 in (20 cm)

This serrated knife is fashioned from flint, a hard rock,
readily available in areas of chalk downland, which is
capable of taking a sharp edge. The knife's sharp
teeth enabled the Paleolithic hunter to saw through
harder objects such as bone and gristle.

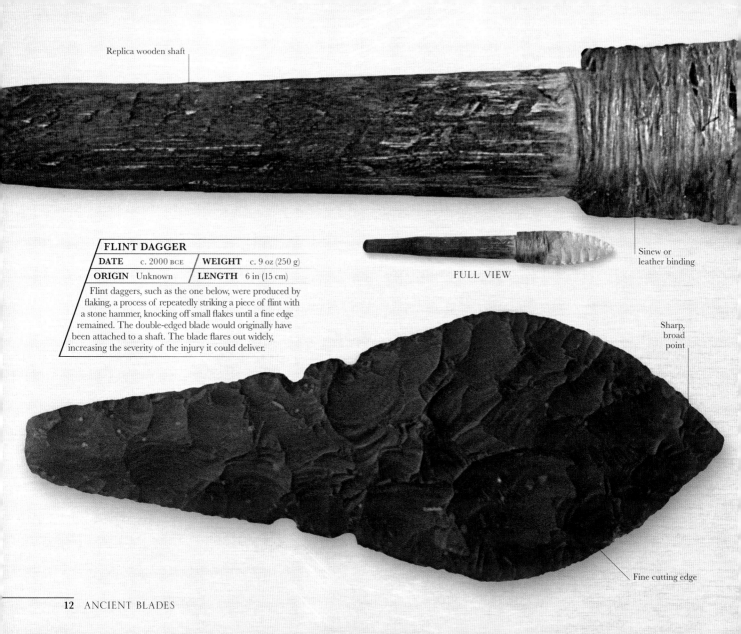

Replica wooden shaft

Sinew or
leather binding

FULL VIEW

FLINT DAGGER

DATE c. 2000 BCE	**WEIGHT** c. 9 oz (250 g)
ORIGIN Unknown	**LENGTH** 6 in (15 cm)

Flint daggers, such as the one below, were produced by
flaking, a process of repeatedly striking a piece of flint with
a stone hammer, knocking off small flakes until a fine edge
remained. The double-edged blade would originally have
been attached to a shaft. The blade flares out widely,
increasing the severity of the injury it could deliver.

Sharp,
broad
point

Fine cutting edge

STONE-AGE DAGGER

DATE	2,500,000–10,000 BCE	WEIGHT	c. 18 oz (500 g)
ORIGIN	Unknown	LENGTH	12 in (30 cm)

By lashing the flint blade to a wooden shaft with a binding of sinew or leather strips, the simple dagger was transformed into a deadly weapon of war. The addition of the shaft enabled the Stone-Age fighter to plunge the blade into his opponent with greater leverage and power.

Narrowed tip

Cutting edge

Area where shaft would have been attached

SMALL CLOVIS POINT

DATE	c. 10,000 BCE	WEIGHT	c. 3 oz (9 g)
ORIGIN	USA	LENGTH	4 in (10 cm)

In 1932, the Ice-Age spearhead shown above was unearthed in Clovis, New Mexico, along with other weapon points. Its broad blade could inflict severe wounds. Binding the spearhead to a long wooden shaft enabled the fighter to throw it with great force, from a relatively safe distance.

THE FLINT WAS FLAKED TO PRODUCE A RAZORLIKE CUTTING EDGE.

STONE AXHEAD

DATE	4000–2000 BCE	WEIGHT	c. 2½ lb (1 kg)
ORIGIN	England	LENGTH	8 in (20 cm)

A dual-purpose tool, the stone ax could have been used for clearing vegetation but would also have been capable of smashing a human skull. The addition of a wooden handle provided greater reach and power. This axhead was dredged from the Thames River in London.

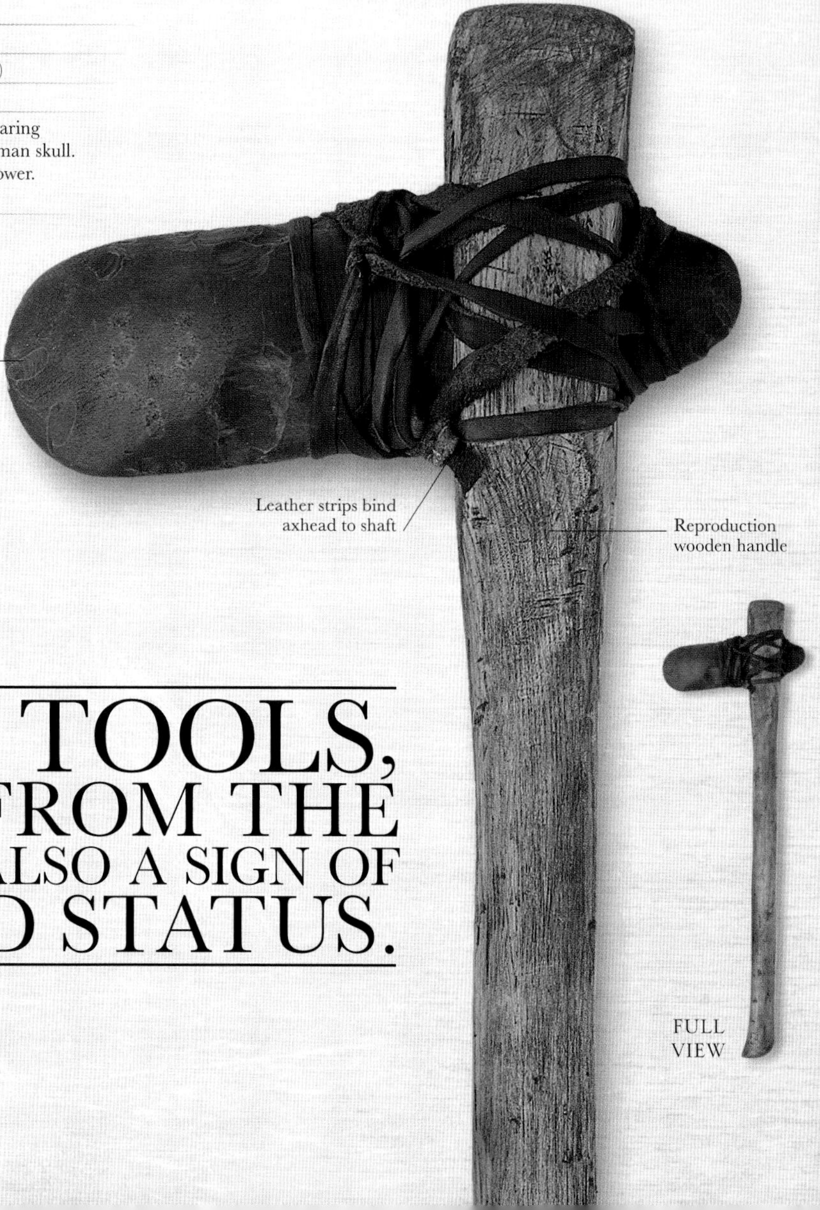

Smooth stone
axhead

Leather strips bind
axhead to shaft

Reproduction
wooden handle

NOT JUST TOOLS,
AXES MADE FROM THE
BEST FLINT WERE ALSO A SIGN OF
WEALTH AND STATUS.

FULL
VIEW

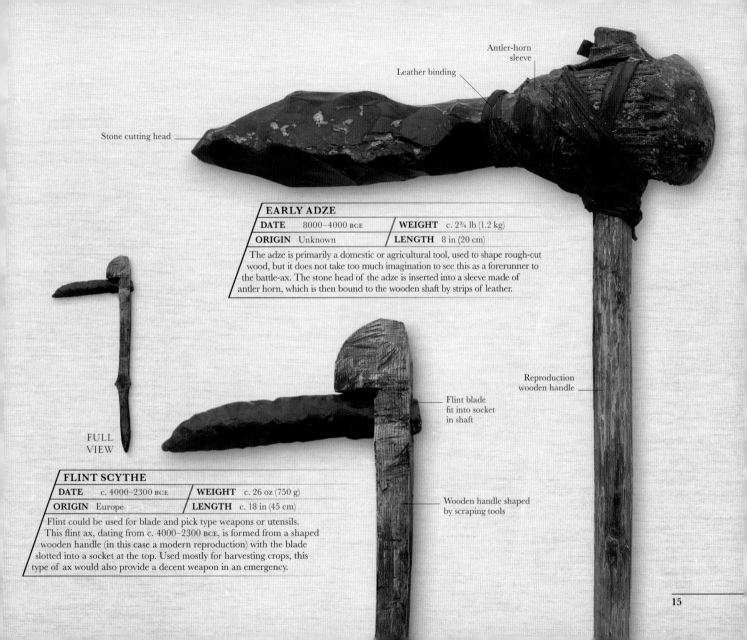

Antler-horn
sleeve

Leather binding

Stone cutting head

EARLY ADZE

DATE	8000–4000 BCE	**WEIGHT**	c. 2¾ lb (1.2 kg)
ORIGIN	Unknown	**LENGTH**	8 in (20 cm)

The adze is primarily a domestic or agricultural tool, used to shape rough-cut wood, but it does not take too much imagination to see this as a forerunner to the battle-ax. The stone head of the adze is inserted into a sleeve made of antler horn, which is then bound to the wooden shaft by strips of leather.

Reproduction
wooden handle

Flint blade
fit into socket
in shaft

FULL
VIEW

FLINT SCYTHE

DATE	c. 4000–2300 BCE	**WEIGHT**	c. 26 oz (750 g)
ORIGIN	Europe	**LENGTH**	c. 18 in (45 cm)

Flint could be used for blade and pick type weapons or utensils. This flint ax, dating from c. 4000–2300 BCE, is formed from a shaped wooden handle (in this case a modern reproduction) with the blade slotted into a socket at the top. Used mostly for harvesting crops, this type of ax would also provide a decent weapon in an emergency.

Wooden handle shaped
by scraping tools

MESOPOTAMIA AND EGYPT

The spear and the bow were the chief weapons of the ancient Egyptian and Mesopotamian soldier. Arrowheads were made at first from flint, then from bronze, and the best specimens were capable of punching through contemporary body armor at close range. Spears were used primarily as thrusting weapons, and battle-axes were also used, the invention of bronze facilitating the development of various shapes for combat use. Swords, due the expense of their production, were more of a rarity, but became increasingly popular during the 1st millennium BCE as Middle Eastern warriors encountered sword-wielding enemies from other territories.

Intricate geometric design

SCABBARD

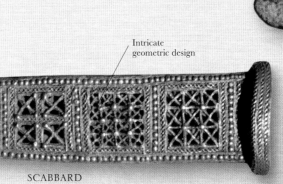

Double-edged blade

CEREMONIAL DAGGER

DATE	c. 2500 BCE	WEIGHT	c. 34 oz (950 g)
ORIGIN	Sumer	LENGTH	c. 10 in (25 cm)

Excavated from the burial site of the Sumerian Queen Pu-Abi (died around 2500 BCE), this ceremonial dagger is of the highest quality—a suitable weapon for a monarch to carry on her journey to the afterlife. The blade and scabbard are made of gold, while the hilt is constructed from lapis lazuli finished with gold decoration.

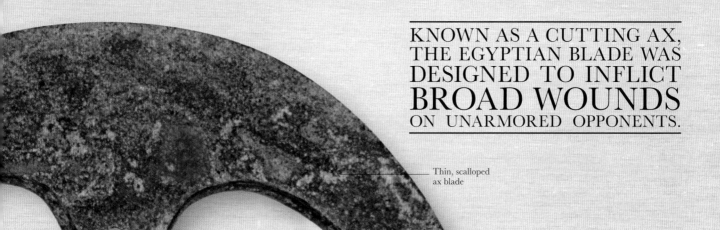

KNOWN AS A CUTTING AX,
THE EGYPTIAN BLADE WAS
DESIGNED TO INFLICT
BROAD WOUNDS
ON UNARMORED OPPONENTS.

Thin, scalloped
ax blade

Attachment hole

BRONZE AXHEAD			
DATE	2200–1640 BCE	**WEIGHT**	c. 18 oz (500 g)
ORIGIN Egypt		**LENGTH**	6¾ in (17.1 cm)

The Egyptian enthusiasm for axes led to the development of a wide
variety of axhead shapes. This broad, scalloped (curved) example has
small holes where the head is bound to the shaft. The distinctive shape
of the blade makes possible a wide slashing action, effective against
unarmored opponents and those wearing light armor.

Blue lapis
lazuli hilt

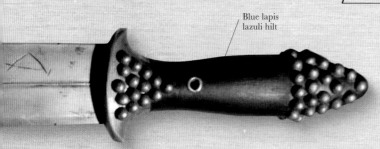

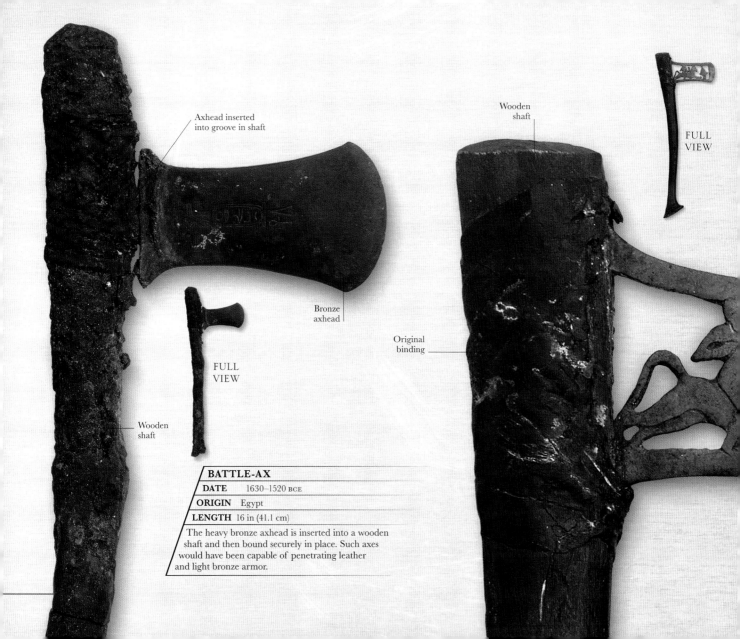

Axhead inserted
into groove in shaft

Bronze
axhead

Wooden
shaft

FULL
VIEW

Wooden
shaft

FULL
VIEW

Original
binding

BATTLE-AX

DATE	1630–1520 BCE
ORIGIN	Egypt
LENGTH	16 in (41.1 cm)

The heavy bronze axhead is inserted into a wooden
shaft and then bound securely in place. Such axes
would have been capable of penetrating leather
and light bronze armor.

CEREMONIAL AX

DATE	1539–1075 BCE
ORIGIN	Egypt
LENGTH	17 in (43.5 cm)

The ax had strong associations with power and prestige, and ceremonial versions were carried by Egyptian rulers. Typically, a scene showing the triumph of the pharaoh would be engraved on the axhead, although in this instance a warrior is depicted on horseback in an open metalwork design.

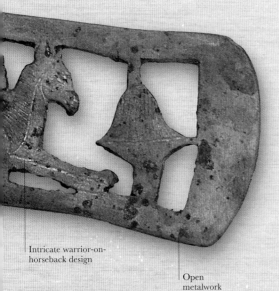

Intricate warrior-on-horseback design

Open metalwork axhead

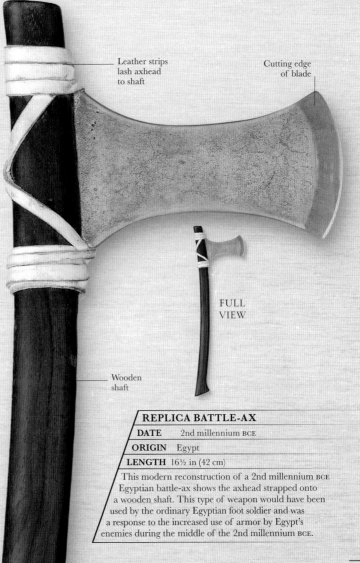

Leather strips lash axhead to shaft

Cutting edge of blade

FULL VIEW

Wooden shaft

REPLICA BATTLE-AX

DATE	2nd millennium BCE
ORIGIN	Egypt
LENGTH	16½ in (42 cm)

This modern reconstruction of a 2nd millennium BCE Egyptian battle-ax shows the axhead strapped onto a wooden shaft. This type of weapon would have been used by the ordinary Egyptian foot soldier and was a response to the increased use of armor by Egypt's enemies during the middle of the 2nd millennium BCE.

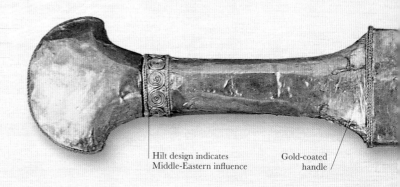

SHORT SWORD

DATE	1539–1075 BCE
ORIGIN	Egypt
LENGTH	12½ in (32.3 cm)

Until the advent of the New Kingdom (1570–1070 BCE), the sword had not been regarded highly by the Egyptians. However, encounters with warlike people from the Middle East encouraged the development of edged weapons that could penetrate armor. This broad-bladed short sword has a gold-coated handle and almost certainly belonged to a member of the Egyptian royal family.

Hilt design indicates
Middle-Eastern influence

Gold-coated
handle

Decorated
gold handle

Double-edged
iron blade

Pommel at top of sword's
grip to provide balance

Gold-coated
handle

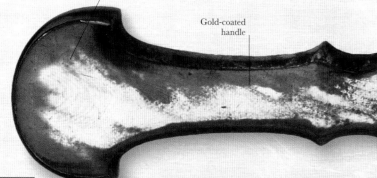

Wide, double-edged
bronze blade

TUTANKHAMUN'S SWORD

DATE   c. 14th century BCE

ORIGIN   Egypt

LENGTH   16¼ in (41.1 cm)

This sword, which belonged to King Tutankhamun (r. 1333–1323 BCE), has an
iron blade, a rarity in this period. The Egyptians did not have direct access to
iron ore and were dependent on supplies from the Middle East—often under the
control of their enemies—which made the production of iron weapons difficult.

LONG SWORD

DATE   1539–1075 BCE

ORIGIN   Egypt

LENGTH   16 in (40.6 cm)

Featuring a large mushroom-shaped pommel, this sword has a copper
blade, while the handle is coated with gold. Although copper was
readily available in Egypt, it lacked the strength of bronze and iron,
and the blade could not be made to take a sharp edge.

Double-edged
copper blade

BRONZE- AND IRON-AGE BLADES

Bronze- and Iron-Age Europe was home to several ferocious warrior peoples. These included the Teutones, Cimbri, Goths, and Celts, and incorporated areas from the Black Sea to Britain. The Celts were renowned swordsmen—heavily armed infantry who, on foot, charged repeatedly at their enemies with little protection other than a helmet and shield. Many of the surviving swords of this period feature decorative hilts and blade engraving.

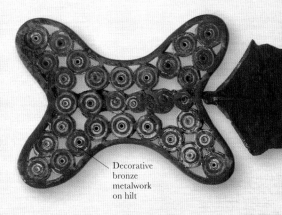

Decorative bronze metalwork on hilt

Hilt was originally wrapped in leather

Extended ricasso (unsharpened part of the blade close to the hilt)

Engraved ornamentation on pommel

BRONZE LEAF-SHAPED SWORD

DATE	c. 1000 BCE
ORIGIN	Britain
LENGTH	22¾ in (57.9 cm)

Until ironworking started in Europe around 600 BCE, bronze dominated weapon manufacture. This leaf-shaped sword, cast in one piece, is typical of Bronze-Age swords in size and shape. Bronze is hard to sharpen and keep sharp, so this blade represents significant metalworking talent.

Hilt plates would have been of wood, bone, or horn

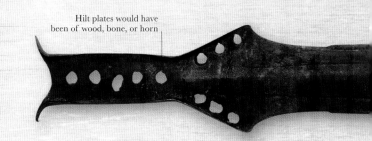

Iron blade

CELTIC DAGGER

DATE	1st millennium BCE
ORIGIN	Britain
LENGTH	c. 11 in (27 cm)

This dagger displays the breathtaking art of the Celts. As with so many pieces of arms and armor, this piece has probably survived because it was used for funerary or display purposes. Knives and daggers were working tools, but this example is so intricate that it may not have been designed for everyday use.

GERMANIC BRONZE SWORD

DATE	1000 BCE
ORIGIN	Germany
LENGTH	26 in (66.5 cm)

One-piece, leaf-shaped swords of the Bronze Age were designed for slashing and required a different style of combat than a spear or thrusting sword. These swords suited the method of fighting the Celts preferred.

Double-edged blade

CELTIC WARRIOR

The Celts were a group of tribal peoples, including Gauls, Iberians, and Britons, who migrated from central Germany to Western Europe around the 1st millennium BCE. They came into conflict with the Romans, whom they fought regularly from the 4th century BCE.

The ancient Greek historian Strabo had this to say about the armory of Celtic warriors in battle: "Their arms correspond in size with their physique; a long sword fastened on the right side and a long shield, and spears of like dimension." Their long swords were initially made of bronze and later, iron, and were double-edged, like the example shown here. Celts also used the *falcatal* (short slashing sword) and long daggers as side weapons. Celtic warriors would typically face the enemy as a mass and make a fearful noise by banging their shields and screaming, attempting to intimidate their opponents. The attack itself was largely a mêlée, the whole mass of warriors—using shields to protect themselves—surging into enemy lines, slashing with their swords and stabbing with their spears.

Tang

Flared hilt acted as hand guard

Bronze double-edged blade narrows toward guard

WEIRD, DISCORDANT
HORNS WERE SOUNDED...
THEY BEAT THEIR SWORDS RHYTHMICALLY
AGAINST THEIR SHIELDS.

"

GREEK HISTORIAN DIODORUS SICULUS DESCRIBING
THE CELTS, 1st CENTURY BCE

CELTIC SWORD		
DATE c. 400 BCE	**WEIGHT**	c. 2¾ lb (1 kg)
ORIGIN Western Europe	**LENGTH**	c. 26 in (66 cm)

The Celts were renowned for their double-edged swords, which had wide blades with thin edges, making them ideal for slashing attacks. The blade's weight was concentrated toward the front, which increased the force at the point of impact.

Blade flares out at
two-thirds of its length

ON THE MOVE

A 1st-century BCE silver vessel from Gundestrup, Denmark, shows Celtic infantry and cavalry, displaying their horns, weapons, and shields. This disciplined formation largely dissolved on the battlefield.

BROAD-BLADED BATTLE-AX

DATE c. 500 BCE

ORIGIN Northern Europe

The head of this ax has been hammered from a
single iron bar. A long wooden handle was wedged
tightly into the socket to make an effective weapon
for hand-to-hand combat.

Edge damaged, as bronze
is too malleable and weak
to hold edge well

Socket for
shaft to be
wedged

Long cutting edge

Decorated guard

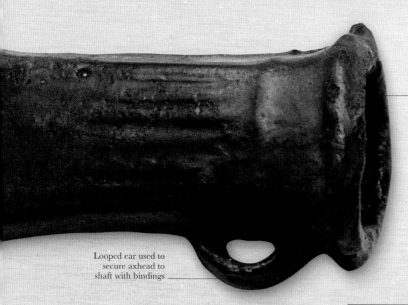

Hollowed-out socket

Looped ear used to
secure axhead to
shaft with bindings

BRONZE AXHEAD

DATE	750–650 BCE
ORIGIN	Europe

Bronze battle-axes, with sockets to take a wooden
shaft, are associated with the Celts from the earliest
times. They were used as tools but they were also
useful in hand-to-hand combat. They became more
effective when made from iron.

AS METALS IMPROVED, THE EDGES BECAME SHARPER AND CUTTING WEAPONS BECAME MORE EFFECTIVE FIGHTING TOOLS.

IRON-AGE DAGGER IN SHEATH

DATE	550–450 BCE
ORIGIN	Britain

This decorated iron dagger would have belonged to
a tribal chief. In this period, iron blades showed status
and were used for everyday functions such as cutting.
In extreme circumstances, they would be pressed into
use as combat weapons.

Wooden sheath
with bronze strips

ANCIENT GREECE

The warriors of ancient Greece used a variety of edged weapons. A classic type was the *xiphos* (*pp. 30–31*), a double-edged blade that swelled out before the point and was intended primarily for slashing attacks against ranks of enemy infantry. The Greek *kopis* was a powerful chopping weapon, with a single-edged, curved blade, set heavily forward to assist the cutting action. Such blades were the principal weapons of hoplites (*pp. 30–31*) for some 600 years and influenced Roman and Middle Eastern designs. Daggers were little known in the Greek world, but axes were sometimes used by heavy infantry (heavily armed or armored foot soldiers) to rupture enemy shields and armor.

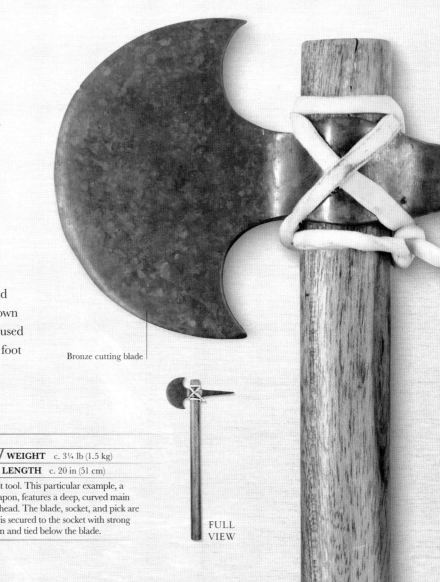

Bronze cutting blade

FULL
VIEW

GREEK HOPLITE AX		
DATE c. 6th century BCE	**WEIGHT**	c. 3¼ lb (1.5 kg)
ORIGIN Greece	**LENGTH**	c. 20 in (51 cm)

The hoplite ax was a powerful combat tool. This particular example, a modern-day replica of the ancient weapon, features a deep, curved main cutting blade balanced by a sharp pick head. The blade, socket, and pick are cast in one piece of bronze, and the haft is secured to the socket with strong rawhide bindings, looped in a cross pattern and tied below the blade.

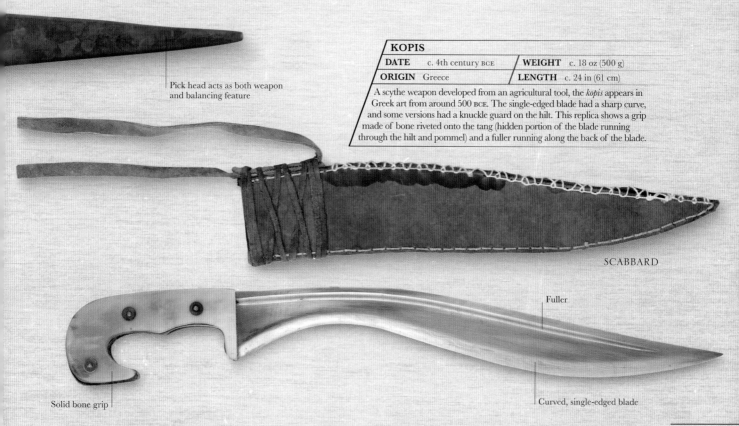

"GO NEAR, STRIKE WITH A LONG SPEAR OR A SWORD AT CLOSE RANGE AND KILL A MAN."

SPARTAN POET TYRTAEUS, 7TH CENTURY BCE

Pick head acts as both weapon and balancing feature

KOPIS

DATE	c. 4th century BCE	**WEIGHT**	c. 18 oz (500 g)
ORIGIN	Greece	**LENGTH**	c. 24 in (61 cm)

A scythe weapon developed from an agricultural tool, the *kopis* appears in Greek art from around 500 BCE. The single-edged blade had a sharp curve, and some versions had a knuckle guard on the hilt. This replica shows a grip made of bone riveted onto the tang (hidden portion of the blade running through the hilt and pommel) and a fuller running along the back of the blade.

SCABBARD

Fuller

Solid bone grip

Curved, single-edged blade

HOPLITE

Hoplites, so named after the *hoplon* shield, were citizen-soldiers—Greeks who would, in times of crisis, break away from their everyday duties to go to war. Hoplites were the backbone of Greek infantry warfare from the 5th century BCE.

Hoplite tactics were disciplined, based on a structure known as a phalanx—an eight-rank-deep formation bristling with spears and swords. The ranks of the phalanx stood tightly in line, each man shoulder-to-shoulder, with shields pressed up against the backs of the men in front. The spears of the first three ranks were pointed forward in the attack, while warriors in the ranks behind angled their spears upward, ready to deploy in action. This presented a powerful battering-ram effect against opposing forces. Hoplites also used a sword called a *xiphos* (below), a double-edged weapon well-suited to close-quarters fighting. The most famous among hoplites were the Spartans, citizens of the city-state of Sparta in southern Greece.

Bronze
hilt cap

Flared
hardwood grip

Replica of double-edged
blade with central fuller

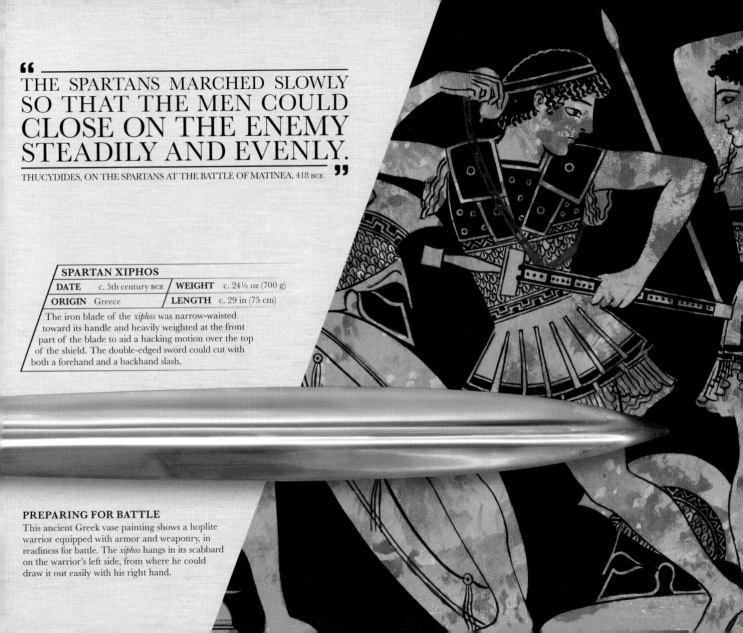

> ## THE SPARTANS MARCHED SLOWLY SO THAT THE MEN COULD CLOSE ON THE ENEMY STEADILY AND EVENLY.
>
> THUCYDIDES, ON THE SPARTANS AT THE BATTLE OF MATINEA, 418 BCE

SPARTAN XIPHOS			
DATE	c. 5th century BCE	**WEIGHT**	c. 24½ oz (700 g)
ORIGIN	Greece	**LENGTH**	c. 29 in (75 cm)

The iron blade of the *xiphos* was narrow-waisted toward its handle and heavily weighted at the front part of the blade to aid a hacking motion over the top of the shield. The double-edged sword could cut with both a forehand and a backhand slash.

PREPARING FOR BATTLE

This ancient Greek vase painting shows a hoplite warrior equipped with armor and weaponry, in readiness for battle. The *xiphos* hangs in its scabbard on the warrior's left side, from where he could draw it out easily with his right hand.

ANCIENT ROME

The Roman army was the finest fighting machine of the ancient world. Highly disciplined and trained, its troops were generally well led. A Roman legionary (armored foot soldier) was fully equipped for close-range battles in densely packed ranks. While archers and javelin-throwing troops would disrupt the enemy, the main battle was invariably fought by the heavily armed foot soldier. Protected by a large rectangular shield, he fought in close formation to overwhelm the enemy with his *gladius*, or short sword.

Gold decoration shows Emperor Tiberius presenting his victories to his stepfather Augustus

Portrait of Tiberius

SCABBARD

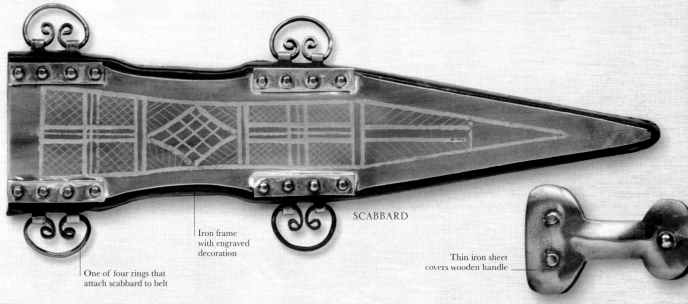

SCABBARD

One of four rings that attach scabbard to belt

Iron frame with engraved decoration

Thin iron sheet covers wooden handle

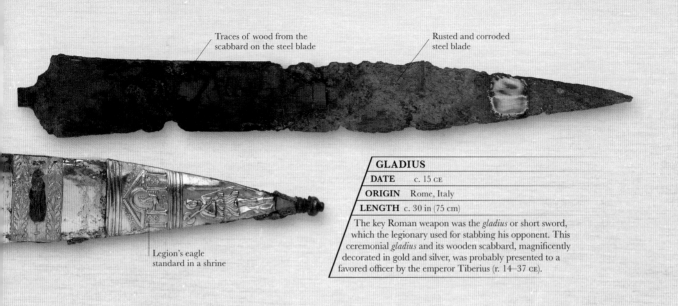

Traces of wood from the
scabbard on the steel blade

Rusted and corroded
steel blade

Legion's eagle
standard in a shrine

GLADIUS

DATE	c. 15 CE
ORIGIN	Rome, Italy
LENGTH	c. 30 in (75 cm)

The key Roman weapon was the *gladius* or short sword, which the legionary used for stabbing his opponent. This ceremonial *gladius* and its wooden scabbard, magnificently decorated in gold and silver, was probably presented to a favored officer by the emperor Tiberius (r. 14–37 CE).

PUGIO

DATE	c. 1st century BCE	**WEIGHT**	c. 24¾ lb (700 g)
ORIGIN	Rome, Italy	**LENGTH**	c. 13 in (33 cm)

In addition to a *gladius*, legionaries carried a *pugio*, or dagger, that was worn at the left hip. A few were richly decorated with bronze handles. The grooves and ridges gave added strength to the blade. The *pugio* acted as a weapon of last resort, but was also applied as a utility tool.

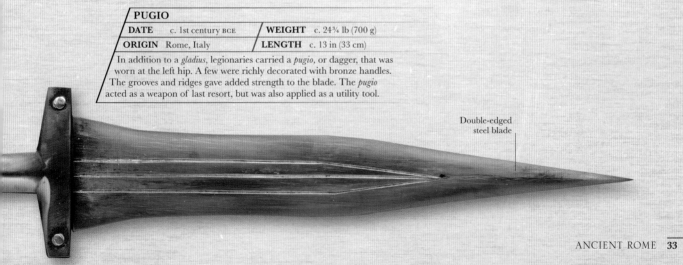

Double-edged
steel blade

ROMAN GLADIATOR

Among the most memorable figures of the Roman Empire, gladiators were volunteers, or prisoners and slaves who fought for public entertainment. Volunteers craved social standing; for the latter, repeated victories could bring freedom.

Gladiatorial fighting began in the 3rd century BCE at private events, but by the 1st century BCE it had grown into an important part of the public games that were played in great arenas at imperial expense. Gladiatorial games were at their peak from the 1st century BCE to the 2nd century CE. The gladiators were rigorously trained and fought as specific types—each type distinguished by the weapons and armor they used and by their manner of fighting. *Retiarii* ("net men") fought with trident, dagger, and net, while *dimachaeri* ("bearing two swords") were armed with a sword in each hand. Usually, gladiators fought one-on-one, in bouts that ended in submission, injury, or death.

Ridged grip

Large rounded pommel provides solid counterweight

Short hand guard

Double-edged blade with central ridge

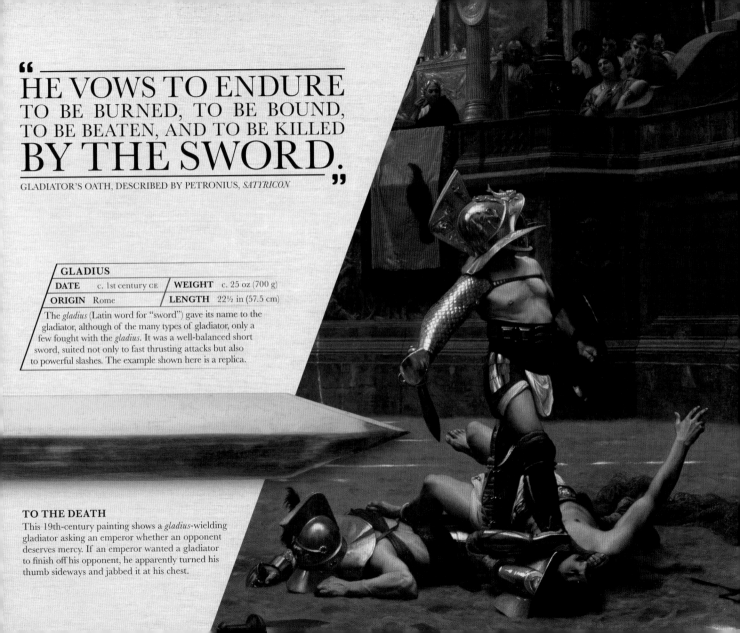

" HE VOWS TO ENDURE
TO BE BURNED, TO BE BOUND,
TO BE BEATEN, AND TO BE KILLED
BY THE SWORD. "

GLADIATOR'S OATH, DESCRIBED BY PETRONIUS, *SATYRICON*

GLADIUS			
DATE	c. 1st century CE	**WEIGHT**	c. 25 oz (700 g)
ORIGIN Rome		**LENGTH**	22½ in (57.5 cm)

The *gladius* (Latin word for "sword") gave its name to the gladiator, although of the many types of gladiator, only a few fought with the *gladius*. It was a well-balanced short sword, suited not only to fast thrusting attacks but also to powerful slashes. The example shown here is a replica.

TO THE DEATH

This 19th-century painting shows a *gladius*-wielding gladiator asking an emperor whether an opponent deserves mercy. If an emperor wanted a gladiator to finish off his opponent, he apparently turned his thumb sideways and jabbed it at his chest.

ANGLO-SAXON AND FRANKISH BLADES

The great majority of Saxon, Anglo-Saxon, and Frankish warriors were infantrymen, who carried a shield and a dagger, often wore a helmet, and fought with spears, axes, and the single-edged weapon variously called the *seax*, *scamasax*, or *scramasax*. More slender double-edged swords were also wielded, although only by the nobility who could afford them. Axes provided both armor-smashing force and, in some cases, throwing weapons.

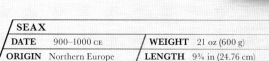

SEAX			
DATE	900–1000 CE	**WEIGHT**	21 oz (600 g)
ORIGIN	Northern Europe	**LENGTH**	9¾ in (24.76 cm)

Swords were extremely expensive weapons, so most people carried a blade that doubled as a fighting dagger and a working tool. Called the *sax* or *seax* (the root of the name "Saxon"), other examples of this weapon have been found from the 5th century onward.

False, unsharpened edge

Blade always single-edged

Tough single-
edged blade

Tapering
tang

BROKEN-BACK SEAX

DATE	900–1000 CE	**WEIGHT**	21 oz (600 g)
ORIGIN	Northern Europe	**LENGTH**	7½ in (19 cm)

In Britain and other parts of Northern Europe, the *seax* was often produced
in this "broken-back" shape, with an angular upper edge and a curved,
sharpened lower edge. Crude and easy to manufacture, these blades
were effective weapons, used until the 15th century CE, providing those
who could not afford a sword with a long blade.

Tang wrapped
in leather

SAXON SWORD

DATE	500–600 CE
ORIGIN	Northern Europe

Swords were expensive and time-consuming to
manufacture by pattern welding. In Saxon society, they
were only used by people of high rank or professional
warriors, and were often objects of great veneration.

Tip less sharp
than many *seaxes*

Slightly tapering,
double-edged blade

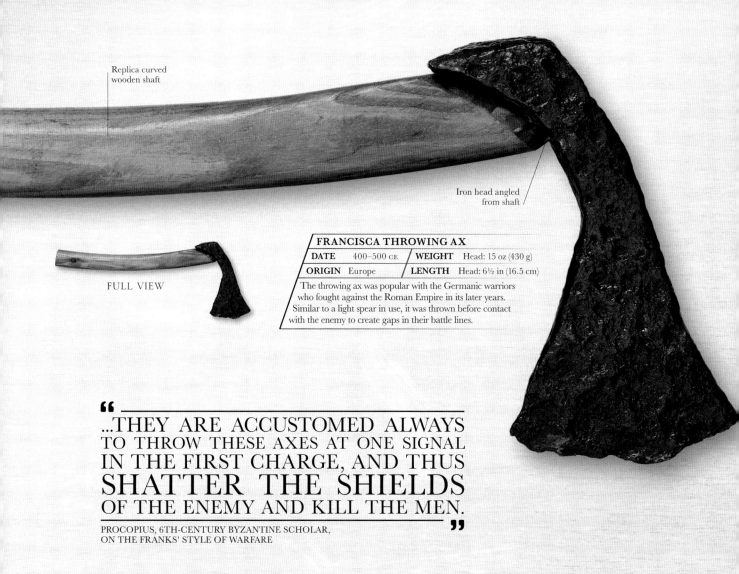

Replica curved
wooden shaft

Iron head angled
from shaft

FULL VIEW

FRANCISCA THROWING AX			
DATE	400–500 CE	**WEIGHT**	Head: 15 oz (430 g)
ORIGIN	Europe	**LENGTH**	Head: 6½ in (16.5 cm)

The throwing ax was popular with the Germanic warriors
who fought against the Roman Empire in its later years.
Similar to a light spear in use, it was thrown before contact
with the enemy to create gaps in their battle lines.

> "
> ...THEY ARE ACCUSTOMED ALWAYS
> TO THROW THESE AXES AT ONE SIGNAL
> IN THE FIRST CHARGE, AND THUS
> SHATTER THE SHIELDS
> OF THE ENEMY AND KILL THE MEN.
> "

PROCOPIUS, 6TH-CENTURY BYZANTINE SCHOLAR,
ON THE FRANKS' STYLE OF WARFARE

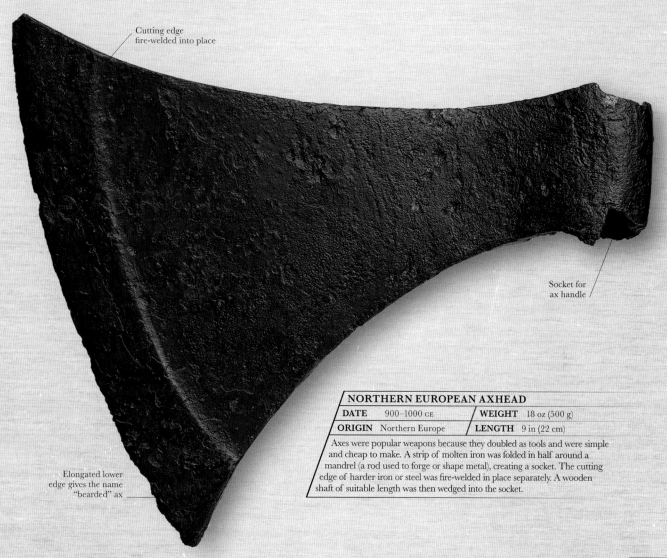

Cutting edge
fire-welded into place

Socket for
ax handle

Elongated lower
edge gives the name
"bearded" ax

NORTHERN EUROPEAN AXHEAD		
DATE 900–1000 CE	**WEIGHT**	18 oz (500 g)
ORIGIN Northern Europe	**LENGTH**	9 in (22 cm)

Axes were popular weapons because they doubled as tools and were simple
and cheap to make. A strip of molten iron was folded in half around a
mandrel (a rod used to forge or shape metal), creating a socket. The cutting
edge of harder iron or steel was fire-welded in place separately. A wooden
shaft of suitable length was then wedged into the socket.

EARLY ARMOR

From ancient times, warriors sought ways to protect themselves from swords and spears. Shields provided handheld protection, while thick animal hide jackets or suits offered some resistance to sword slashes. Far more advanced armor, however, came in the form of chain mail, which was flexible and provided the superb protective qualities of metal.

The earliest example of chain-mail armor is from a Celtic chieftain's grave in Romania, dating to the 4th century BCE. Mail was difficult to penetrate, although some heavy thrusting swords could split poor-quality links. The impact from a sword blow could also injure the wearer, who continued to use a shield to defend himself against blows. Chain mail became popular among European armies, including the Anglo-Saxons, whose armor and shield feature here.

MAIL COAT			
DATE	c. 10th century	**WEIGHT**	c. 22 lb (10 kg)
ORIGIN	Britain	**LENGTH**	c. 30 in (76 cm)

This Anglo-Saxon mail coat is made from riveted, interlocked iron rings. Worn like a jacket, it provided a flexible armor that allowed the wearer free movement in combat, although its weight tested the soldier's endurance. The example shown here is a replica.

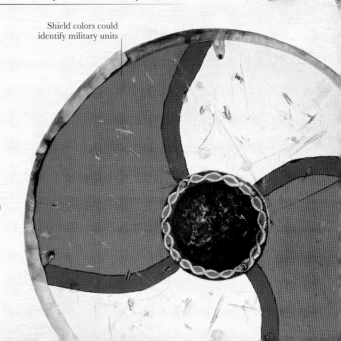

Shield colors could identify military units

ANGLO-SAXON SHIELD			
DATE	c. 10th century	**WEIGHT**	c. 5½ lb (2.5 kg)
ORIGIN	Britain	**LENGTH**	c. 36 in (90 cm)

An Anglo-Saxon shield, of which a replica is shown here, was made from planks of wood riveted together, the whole then covered with leather. The wood types used were those that did not split easily on impact, such as lime and poplar.

NORMAN ARCHERS

The Bayeux tapestry is a long, embroidered cloth that tells the story of the Norman conquest of England. This section of the tapestry depicts armed and armored Norman soldiers at the Battle of Hastings (1066). The soldiers are portrayed wearing thigh-length chainmail suits, and using small shields to protect themselves from spears and arrows.

VIKING BLADES

The seafaring Scandinavians known as Norsemen or Vikings have a special place in European history. From the British Isles to the Varangian Guard in Kievan Rus (modern-day Ukraine), they came to symbolize the quintessential Dark-Age warrior. Striking from the sea in their longboats, they plundered the coasts of Europe, as well as settling possibly as far afield as Nova Scotia, Canada. The Vikings were well armed, in particular with swords and axes, but also with spears and bows. They carried round shields and most wore helmets; many wore chain-mail armor as well.

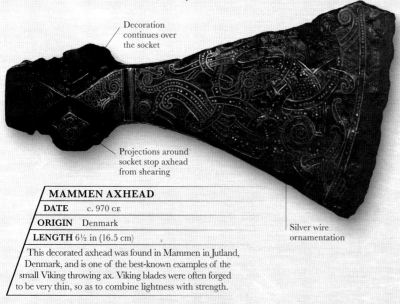

Decoration continues over the socket

Projections around socket stop axhead from shearing

MAMMEN AXHEAD

DATE	c. 970 CE
ORIGIN	Denmark
LENGTH	6½ in (16.5 cm)

This decorated axhead was found in Mammen in Jutland, Denmark, and is one of the best-known examples of the small Viking throwing ax. Viking blades were often forged to be very thin, so as to combine lightness with strength.

Silver wire ornamentation

Long handle to allow two-handed blow

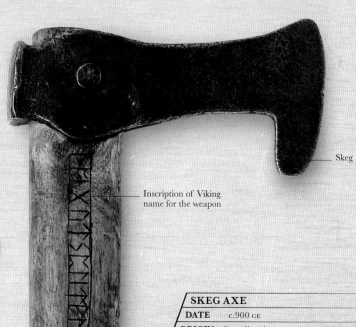

IN BATTLE, VIKINGS THREW AXES AS WEIGHTY MISSILES, AND USED THE BLADE CURVES TO HOOK NECKS AND ANKLES.

Cutting edge made
of hardened steel

Broad, crescent-
shaped blade

Skeg

Inscription of Viking
name for the weapon

FULL
VIEW

SKEG AXE

DATE	c.900 CE
ORIGIN	Scandinavia
LENGTH	Head: c. 6½ in (16.5 cm)

This axe is named after the blunt overhanging hook, or
skeg, at the bottom edge of the blade. A Viking warrior
used the hook to pull down the shield of the enemy, and
then attacked him with the sharpened axe blade.

DATE	900–1000 CE
ORIGIN	Scandinavia
LENGTH	35½ in (90 cm)

This iron sword is typical of Viking weapons, being straight-sided and about 35 in (90 cm) long. It has a two-piece pommel and guard, both of which are decorated with a crisscross pattern in brass inlay. The blade has a figure-eight mark on one of its faces.

Typical
double-edged
iron blade

Large,
decorated
pommel

Straight guard

FULL VIEW

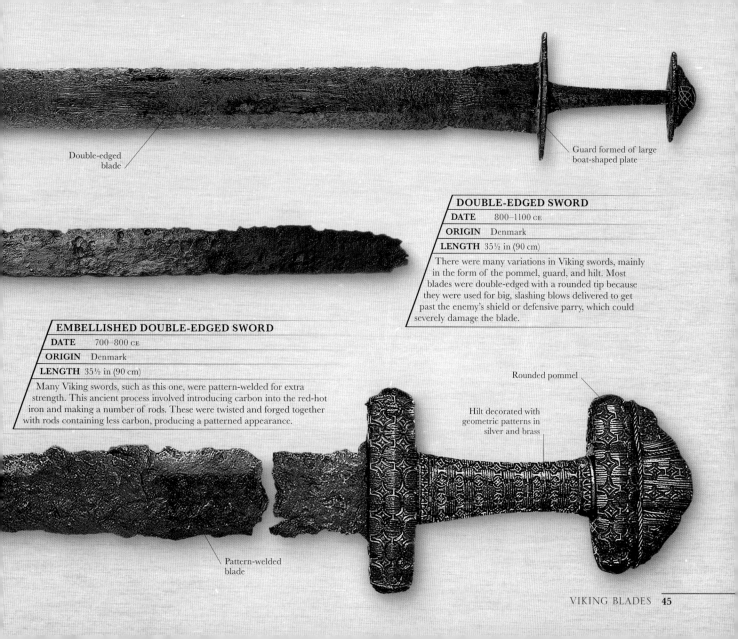

Double-edged
blade

Guard formed of large
boat-shaped plate

DOUBLE-EDGED SWORD

DATE	800–1100 CE
ORIGIN	Denmark
LENGTH	35½ in (90 cm)

There were many variations in Viking swords, mainly
in the form of the pommel, guard, and hilt. Most
blades were double-edged with a rounded tip because
they were used for big, slashing blows delivered to get
past the enemy's shield or defensive parry, which could
severely damage the blade.

EMBELLISHED DOUBLE-EDGED SWORD

DATE	700–800 CE
ORIGIN	Denmark
LENGTH	35½ in (90 cm)

Many Viking swords, such as this one, were pattern-welded for extra
strength. This ancient process involved introducing carbon into the red-hot
iron and making a number of rods. These were twisted and forged together
with rods containing less carbon, producing a patterned appearance.

Rounded pommel

Hilt decorated with
geometric patterns in
silver and brass

Pattern-welded
blade

FULL VIEW

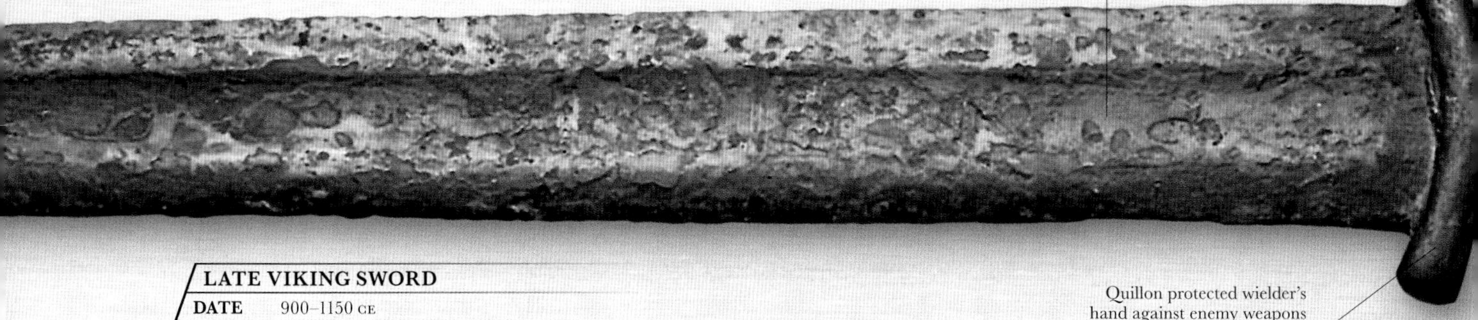

Fuller to
lighten blade

LATE VIKING SWORD

DATE	900–1150 CE
ORIGIN	Scandinavia
LENGTH	35½ in (90 cm)

This broad, straight, double-edged blade retains traces
of an inlaid inscription, now indecipherable, and a
scroll-design pommel; the grip is missing. The sword is
more tapered than earlier Viking swords (*pp. 44–45*).

Quillon protected wielder's
hand against enemy weapons
that slid down the blade

VIKING SWORD

DATE	900–1000 CE
ORIGIN	Scandinavia
LENGTH	31–39 in (80–100 cm)

This Viking sword blade is much corroded, as are so many
found on various archeological sites. Their wooden scabbards
and hilts have almost completely rotted away, making it difficult
to interpret the inscriptions present on them.

FULL VIEW

Tapering blade, a feature
of later Viking swords

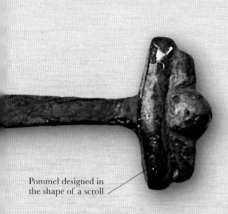

Pommel designed in
the shape of a scroll

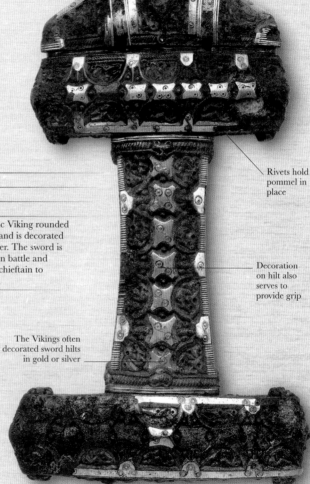

Rounded pommel

Rivets hold
pommel in
place

Decoration
on hilt also
serves to
provide grip

The Vikings often
decorated sword hilts
in gold or silver

VIKING SWORD HILT

DATE   c. 700–1050 CE

ORIGIN   Northern Europe

This sword hilt has a characteristic Viking rounded
pommel—it is made from copper and is decorated
with inlaid geometric designs in silver. The sword is
too finely crafted to have been used in battle and
would have been carried by a Viking chieftain to
show his status or to use in ceremonies.

Iron tang terminates
in broad pommel

VIKING RAIDER

From the 8th to the 11th centuries, the Scandinavian Vikings, traveling in their now-famous longboats, explored, raided, and often wreaked havoc over large parts of Europe. Over time, they voyaged as far as North America and the Black Sea. Viking warriors perfected their own brand of infantry, cavalry, and amphibious warfare.

The typical Viking warrior's body armor consisted of a padded leather or caribou-hide jacket or, if he was wealthy enough, a chain-mail coat. A close-fitting steel helmet (without the horns often depicted in popular culture) protected the skull, nose, and cheeks. For hand-to-hand fighting, Vikings preferred battle-axes and double-edged swords. If they were forced to fight against an organized enemy, however, they would typically stand shoulder-to-shoulder, forming a protective wall with their shields and spears. They threw javelins and throwing axes, and fired sling shots at the enemy as a prelude to a spirited charge, in which their swords, as well as handheld axes, came into play in a vicious, hacking mêlée. They held their shields in the left hand during the fight, using the shield with its boss (the bulge at the center of the shield) as a battering weapon.

Wound leather grip

Short cross-guard

Double-edged blade with broad fuller

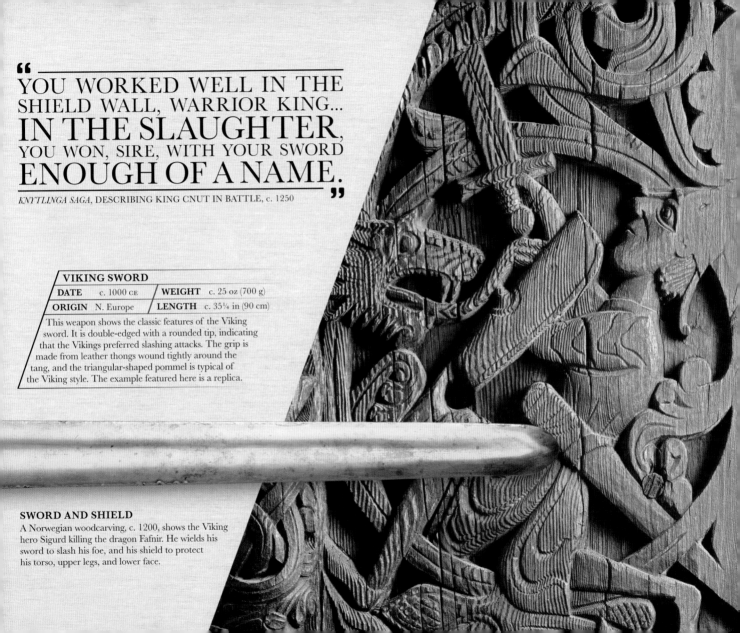

> **"YOU WORKED WELL IN THE SHIELD WALL, WARRIOR KING... IN THE SLAUGHTER, YOU WON, SIRE, WITH YOUR SWORD ENOUGH OF A NAME."**
>
> *KNYTLINGA SAGA*, DESCRIBING KING CNUT IN BATTLE, c. 1250

VIKING SWORD

DATE	c. 1000 CE	**WEIGHT**	c. 25 oz (700 g)
ORIGIN	N. Europe	**LENGTH**	c. 35¼ in (90 cm)

This weapon shows the classic features of the Viking sword. It is double-edged with a rounded tip, indicating that the Vikings preferred slashing attacks. The grip is made from leather thongs wound tightly around the tang, and the triangular-shaped pommel is typical of the Viking style. The example featured here is a replica.

SWORD AND SHIELD

A Norwegian woodcarving, c. 1200, shows the Viking hero Sigurd killing the dragon Fafnir. He wields his sword to slash his foe, and his shield to protect his torso, upper legs, and lower face.

SPEARS AND ARROWS

Before the advent of workable metals, the challenge for ancient warriors was to create sharp, durable spears and arrowheads from natural materials. Mostly, this was achieved through either sharpened and fire-hardened wood, or by knapping (chipping off) pieces of flint or other stone to produce a point or edge. Flint arrowheads in particular reached a high degree of sophistication, before the Stone Age gave way to the Bronze Age during the 3rd–2nd millennium BCE, and the Iron Age a millennium later. The metals produced sharper, harder fighting points, and molding allowed for more uniform designs.

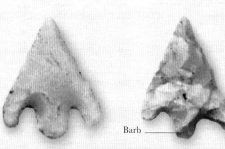

Tang to attach arrowhead to shaft

Barb

FLINT ARROWHEADS

DATE	c. 2700–1800 BCE
ORIGIN	Unknown
LENGTH	2 in (5 cm)

The bow was a significant development in weapon technology, enabling the archer to fire from a distance with power and accuracy. Made of flint, these arrowheads have barbs that would embed themselves deep inside the victim, ensuring that any attempt to remove them would be difficult.

Bow nock to hold bowstring

Pieces of horn glued between wood

Flight made of feathers

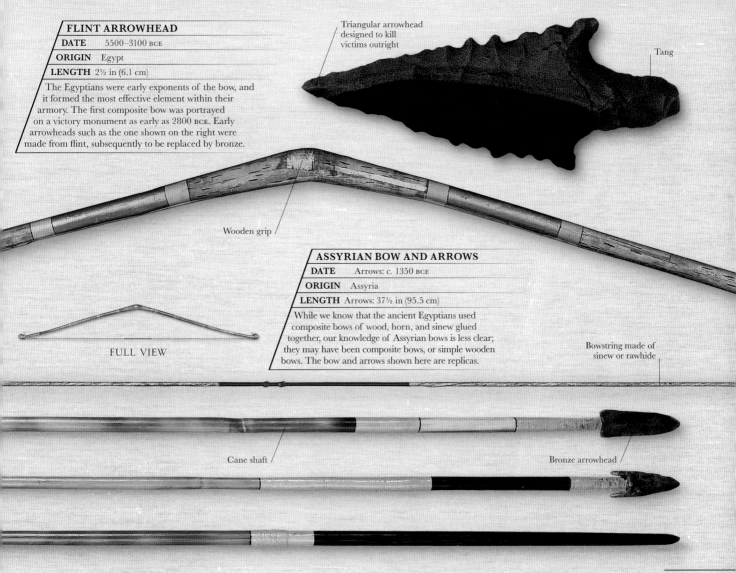

FLINT ARROWHEAD

DATE	5500–3100 BCE
ORIGIN	Egypt
LENGTH	2½ in (6.1 cm)

The Egyptians were early exponents of the bow, and it formed the most effective element within their armory. The first composite bow was portrayed on a victory monument as early as 2800 BCE. Early arrowheads such as the one shown on the right were made from flint, subsequently to be replaced by bronze.

Triangular arrowhead designed to kill victims outright

Tang

Wooden grip

FULL VIEW

ASSYRIAN BOW AND ARROWS

DATE	Arrows: c. 1350 BCE
ORIGIN	Assyria
LENGTH	Arrows: 37½ in (95.5 cm)

While we know that the ancient Egyptians used composite bows of wood, horn, and sinew glued together, our knowledge of Assyrian bows is less clear; they may have been composite bows, or simple wooden bows. The bow and arrows shown here are replicas.

Bowstring made of sinew or rawhide

Cane shaft

Bronze arrowhead

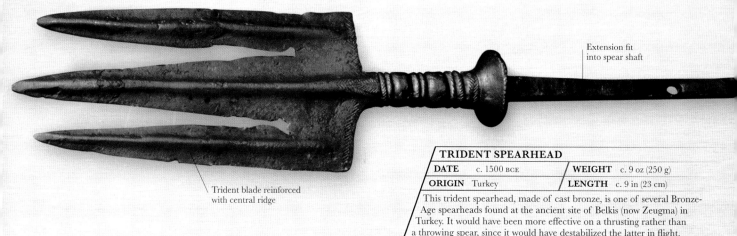

Trident blade reinforced
with central ridge

Extension fit
into spear shaft

TRIDENT SPEARHEAD			
DATE c. 1500 BCE		**WEIGHT** c. 9 oz (250 g)	
ORIGIN Turkey		**LENGTH** c. 9 in (23 cm)	

This trident spearhead, made of cast bronze, is one of several Bronze-Age spearheads found at the ancient site of Belkis (now Zeugma) in Turkey. It would have been more effective on a thrusting rather than a throwing spear, since it would have destabilized the latter in flight.

A BARBED SPEARHEAD
WAS IMPOSSIBLE TO EXTRACT WITHOUT
CAUSING FURTHER INJURY.

Socket for
insertion of shaft

Bronze extension
fit into shaft

Broad head

BRONZE HEAD

DATE	1500–1070 BCE
ORIGIN	Egypt
LENGTH	2¾ in (7 cm)

Used for arming either a thin spear or an arrow,
this bronze head is notable for its pronounced barbs.
Although expensive to produce, bronze arrowheads were
widely used by the Egyptians, who attached them to shafts
made from the long reeds growing along the Nile River.

Pronounced barb

BRONZE SPEARHEAD

DATE	c. 2000 BCE
ORIGIN	Egypt
LENGTH	10 in (25 cm)

This spearhead is typical of those carried by Egyptian infantrymen, whose
main weapon was the spear. Made from bronze, it would have been used
mainly on a thrusting spear. It is covered in fine linen cloth—whose weave can
be seen in this view—perhaps for putting alongside its master in his grave.

Pattern of original
fine Egyptian linen

Leaf-shaped
spear point

Long iron point

Hollow portion of the butt into which the shaft slotted

FULL
VIEW

" THE ENGAGEMENT BEGAN WITH A SHOWER OF ARROWS... WHEN THEY WERE ALL SPENT THEY FOUGHT WITH SWORDS AND SPEARS. "

HERODOTUS, GREEK HISTORIAN, 5TH CENTURY BCE

Spear point

HOPLITE SPEAR BUTT

DATE	4th century BCE
ORIGIN	Macedonia (Greece)
LENGTH	15 in (38 cm)

Made from bronze, this spear butt's main purpose was to act as a counterweight to the head at the other end of the spear. However, if the spearhead broke off in battle the butt could be used as a weapon. A thick bronze ring secured the butt to the spear.

PILUM

DATE	c. 1st century BCE	WEIGHT	c. 6½ lb (3 kg)
ORIGIN	Rome	LENGTH	c. 6 ft (1.8 m)

The *pilum* was a weighted javelin with a long iron spearhead. Designed to pierce enemy shields or armor, the spearhead would bend or break after impact. This not only disabled the enemy's shield, but also prevented him from extracting the *pilum* and throwing it back. The example shown here is a modern-day replica.

LANCEA

DATE	c. 2nd century BCE	WEIGHT	21 oz (600 g)
ORIGIN	Rome	LENGTH	c. 4 ft (1.2 m)

The *lancea* was a light spear that Roman infantry used for both thrusting and throwing. It was much better suited to fighting enemy cavalry than the heavy and unwieldy *pilum* and became the predominant spear in the Roman army during the middle to later years of the Roman Empire.

Long shaft made of ash

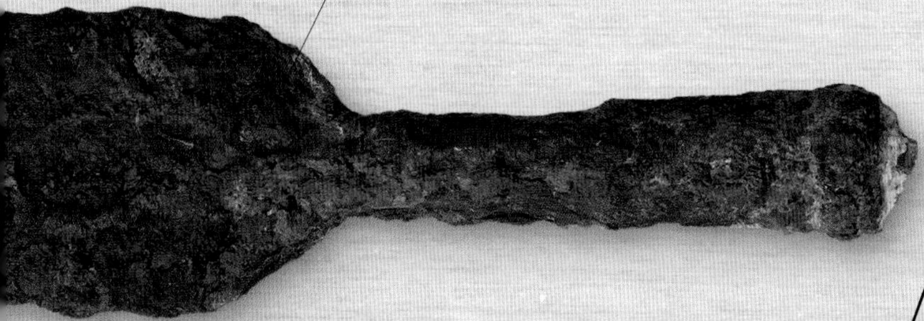

Wide, leaf-shaped spear

GREEK SPEARHEAD

DATE	6th–5th centuries BCE
ORIGIN	Greece
LENGTH	12 in (31 cm)

The spear was the hoplite's principal weapon. He used his short iron sword only when his spear broke during fighting. This spearhead is made of iron and has a broad blade. The missing shaft would have been fashioned from a strong wood such as ash.

Leaf-shaped
head

BRONZE SPEARHEAD

DATE	900–800 BCE
ORIGIN	Unknown
LENGTH	c. 8¼ in (21 cm)

Spears and javelins (throwing spears) played an important role in Celtic battles. Charging at the enemy, the Celtic infantry would hurl javelins from about 90 ft (30 m), breaking up the ranks ahead for single combat. Both the infantry and cavalry used spears as thrusting weapons.

Replica shaft

Socket hammered
tightly to shaft and riveted

SHORT SAXON SPEAR

DATE	400–500 CE
ORIGIN	Northern Europe
LENGTH	Head: 8½ in (21.5 cm)

The spear and javelin were the main weapons of the Saxon and Frankish era. They were carried equally by a lord, his retinue, professional fighters, and troops. As with the Celts, spears were used for hand-to-hand combat, whereas javelins, which tended to be lighter, were thrown before contact with the enemy. The *angon* (Frankish spear) was much like the Roman *pilum* (*pp. 54–55*).

Split socket

MANY ANGLO-SAXON
SPEARS WERE LONGER THAN
THE WARRIOR HIMSELF, GIVING HIM
A KILLING REACH
OUT FROM THE BATTLELINES.

Leaf-shaped
spearhead

LONG SAXON SPEAR

DATE	400–500 CE
ORIGIN	Northern Europe
LENGTH	Head: 19 in (48 cm)

The use of spears is mentioned in an Anglo-Saxon poem about the
battle of Maldon, which took place in Southern England in 991 CE.
It tells how Eorl Byrhtnoth, the Anglo-Saxon leader, kills two men with
javelins, before he is wounded by a Viking spear. Only then does he
draw his sword. Thrusting spears, like the one shown below, were longer
than javelins, with larger heads attached to the shaft with a split socket.

Long head

LOZENGE-SHAPED SPEARHEAD

DATE	600–1000 CE
ORIGIN	Northern Europe
LENGTH	14½ in (36.6 cm)

Throwing spears were important Viking weapons. Their use is recorded in Viking sagas, which include stories of warriors who could throw two spears at once. The Norwegian king Olaf Tryggvasson (r. 995–1000) was said to be able to do this from both hands at the same time.

Steep angle of blade sides produces sharp point

Blade strengthened by rib

Spearhead sharpened on both sides

Long blade inflicted deep injuries

Long, sharp point

Central reinforcing rib

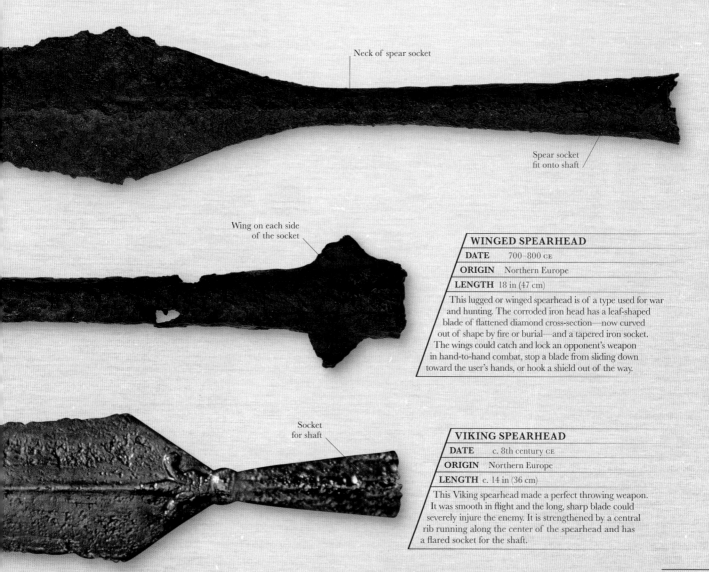

Neck of spear socket

Spear socket
fit onto shaft

Wing on each side
of the socket

WINGED SPEARHEAD

DATE	700–800 CE
ORIGIN	Northern Europe
LENGTH	18 in (47 cm)

This lugged or winged spearhead is of a type used for war
and hunting. The corroded iron head has a leaf-shaped
blade of flattened diamond cross-section—now curved
out of shape by fire or burial—and a tapered iron socket.
The wings could catch and lock an opponent's weapon
in hand-to-hand combat, stop a blade from sliding down
toward the user's hands, or hook a shield out of the way.

Socket
for shaft

VIKING SPEARHEAD

DATE	c. 8th century CE
ORIGIN	Northern Europe
LENGTH	c. 14 in (36 cm)

This Viking spearhead made a perfect throwing weapon.
It was smooth in flight and the long, sharp blade could
severely injure the enemy. It is strengthened by a central
rib running along the center of the spearhead and has
a flared socket for the shaft.

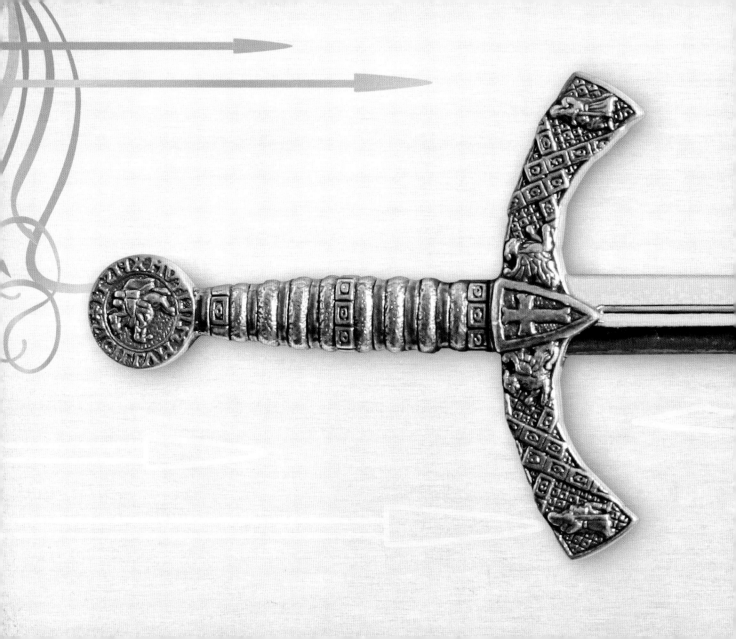

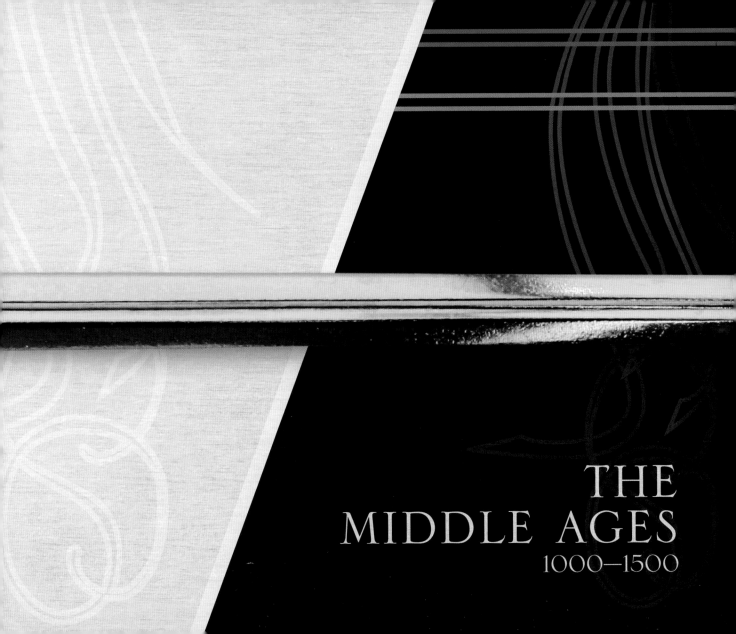

THE
MIDDLE AGES
1000–1500

IN THE HIGH AND LATE MIDDLE AGES, the period roughly defined as c. 1000 to 1500 CE, swords entered a crucial stage in their history. Evolving from the slashing swords of the Vikings into a classic cruciform design (so called because of the development of straight cross-guards that made these swords resemble a cross), European swords entered a period termed as the "knightly phase"—their high cost of production generally made them accessible only to affluent knights. In the Far East, medieval Japan saw the emergence of swords specifically designed for the elite members of the military nobility, known as the samurai. Sword design became increasingly sophisticated and diversified—hilts became more complex, with the addition of more features, and blades were designed in different shapes.

In Europe, swords became longer and more powerful, often designed to be held with a two-handed grip. Typical swords of the early 14th century, for example, had straight, broad, double-edged blades up to 4 ft (1.25 m) long, large pommels, and straight or forward-curving quillons—the extended arms of a cross-guard. In the hands of a skillful knight, such a weapon was capable of causing devastating injuries on unprotected soldiers. Yet, from the end of the 13th century, chain-mail and plate armor pushed sword design in new directions. Slashing weapons were largely useless against armor, so thrusting weapons were developed, featuring blades with a diamond or lozenge cross-section. Such blades were thicker in the middle and therefore more rigid. A well-equipped knight would often carry both a thrusting and a slashing sword into battle. Designs of hilts also developed during this period. Cross-guards steadily became more elaborate, with additional features such as the forefinger hook, which protected the warrior's finger if the sword was gripped by the ricasso for better control. A narrow metal strip called the knuckle guard, which curved over the length of the hilt, protected the warrior's knuckles. These features laid the groundwork for the development of some highly ornate hilts during the Renaissance (14th–17th centuries), especially the hilts of long thrusting swords known as rapiers, which became common in the 16th century.

Outside Europe, sword design followed different paths. The Islamic world, which consisted of the Middle East, North Africa, Central Asia, and India, favored curved, single-edged swords. Such swords were ideal for the cavalry-style warfare of the Muslim armies, and were decorated with scrollwork and religious texts. Farther east, Asian swordsmiths were also producing single-edged swords that displayed some degree of curve. In Japan, prior to the 10th century, the two primary types of blade were the straight single-edged *chokuto* and the double-edged *warabiti-tachi*. From the 10th century, however, Japanese swords, called *katana*, began featuring a graceful curve. By the late medieval period, the samurai had started pairing the long *katana* with a shorter, more curved sword called the *wakazashi*. Two classic sword types also emerged in China during the medieval period—the straight, double-edged *jian* and the deeply curved, single-edged, and one-handed *dao*, as well as its two-handed version, the *dadao*. Although both the *jian* and the *dao* were used up until the 19th century, it was the curved *dao* that predominated, mainly because it suited the style of warfare adopted by the Chinese cavalry. Similarly, India developed the curved *talwar*. Produced from the 14th century, it reached a highly refined form during the 16th century. While all these developments were taking place across the world, certain societies were yet to discover metal and its benefits in sword construction. Weapons used by warriors of the Aztec Empire were still being made from stone and wood, and were no match for the sophisticated European swords they would face in the near future.

Since swords remained expensive items affordable only to affluent officers, staff weapons, or polearms—blades fixed to long wooden shafts—were developed to equip the ordinary foot soldier with powerful killing tools. In Europe, polearms such as the fauchard, glaive, and guisarme enabled the infantry to ward off cavalry attacks, as well as put distance between themselves and the enemy. During the 14th century, the versatile halberd came into use—the weapon featured an ax blade, a long stabbing knife, and a hook to dismount cavalry. Similar types of staff weapon were found across the world, such as the *guan dao* of China and the *saintie* of India. In the right hands, these weapons could easily match the more refined sword in battle.

THE MIDDLE AGES

EUROPEAN SWORDS

In medieval Europe, the sword was the most highly regarded of all weapons. It was not only a magnificent weapon of war—often handed down through the generations—but had also evolved into a symbol of status and prestige; a man became a knight by the dubbing of a sword on his shoulders. Early medieval swords were heavy cutting weapons that were used to hack their way through chain-mail armor. The development of high-quality plate armor led to the introduction of sharply pointed thrusting swords, whose blades became progressively longer.

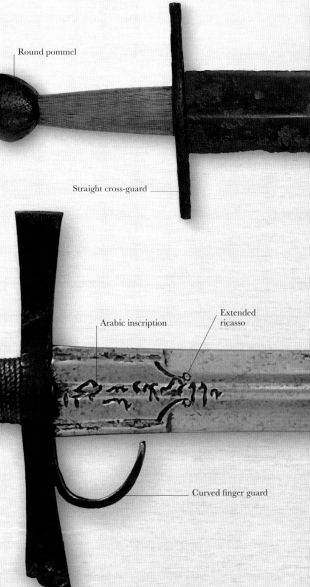

Round pommel

Straight cross-guard

Arabic inscription

Extended ricasso

Curved finger guard

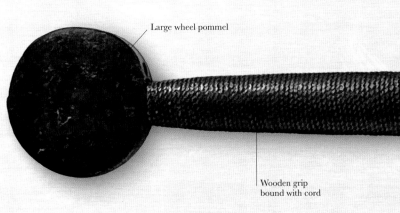

Large wheel pommel

Wooden grip bound with cord

FULL VIEW

Double-edged
cutting blade

CRUSADER SWORD

DATE	12th century	WEIGHT	2¾ lb (1.27 kg)
ORIGIN	Western Europe	LENGTH	38 in (96.5 cm)

This type of sword—with its broad blade, simple cross-guard,
and pommel—became popular during the Crusades and spread
throughout Europe. The heavy cutting blade would have
been devastating against lightly armed opponents.

Long, double-
edged blade

ITALIAN SWORD

DATE	c. 1400	WEIGHT	26 oz (760 g)
ORIGIN	Italy	LENGTH	3½ ft (1.04 m)

This sword, probably Italian in origin, has an Arabic inscription
on its ricasso stating that it was given to the Arsenal of Alexandria
by an Egyptian Sultan in 1432. The long ricasso enabled the
swordsman to hook his forefinger over the cross-guard and grip
the blade, thereby gaining better control.

FULL VIEW

FRENCH SWORD

DATE	14th century	**WEIGHT**	2½ lb (1.16 kg)
ORIGIN	France	**LENGTH**	34 in (85.7 cm)

Reflecting the need to overcome the plate armor that was becoming increasingly common in the 14th century, this powerful sword was used both for delivering heavy cutting blows and for thrusting. The double-edged blade is wide at the hilt and tapers rapidly to a sharp point to penetrate an opponent's armor.

Sharp point for penetrating armor

Disk pommel with edges chamfered (cut off)

Square cross-section tang

Raised shield with incised coat of arms

RIDING SWORD

DATE	c. 1325	**WEIGHT**	25 oz (710 g)
ORIGIN	England	**LENGTH**	32 in (80 cm)

This heavily corroded sword is called a "riding sword," since it was the personal sidearm of a mounted knight. It has a decorated copper-alloy disk pommel and quillons slightly inclining toward the blade, which is double-edged and with a flattened diamond cross-section.

Tapering quillon

FULL VIEW

Shallow fuller

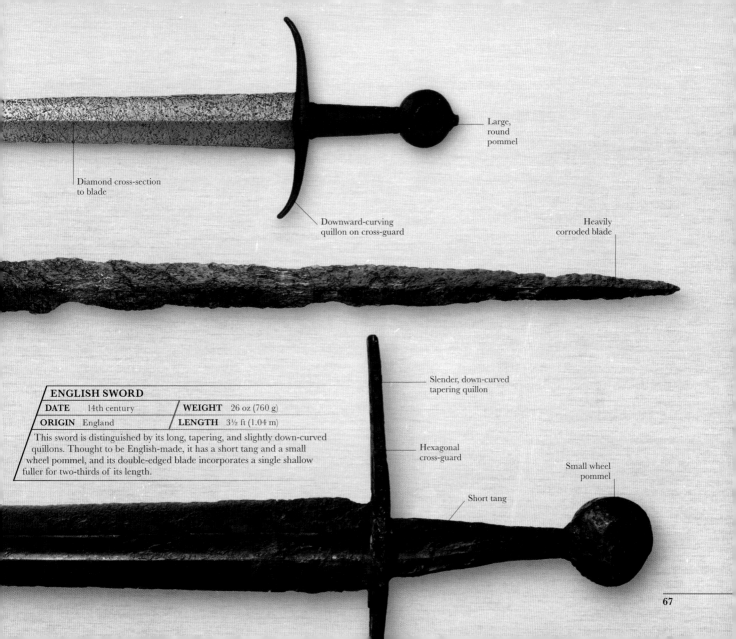

Large,
round
pommel

Diamond cross-section
to blade

Downward-curving
quillon on cross-guard

Heavily
corroded blade

Slender, down-curved
tapering quillon

ENGLISH SWORD

DATE	14th century	**WEIGHT**	26 oz (760 g)
ORIGIN	England	**LENGTH**	3½ ft (1.04 m)

This sword is distinguished by its long, tapering, and slightly down-curved
quillons. Thought to be English-made, it has a short tang and a small
wheel pommel, and its double-edged blade incorporates a single shallow
fuller for two-thirds of its length.

Hexagonal
cross-guard

Short tang

Small wheel
pommel

TOURNAMENT COMBAT

Medieval tournaments were a way for knights to practice and display their skills when not at war. Although warrior games predated the Middle Ages, tournaments seem to have become popular only from the 11th century. There were two main elements to the tournament—the mêlée and the joust.

The mêlée was essentially a free-for-all mock battle between mounted and dismounted knights, who were armed with a wide range of weapons, including falchions, broadswords, bastard swords, great swords, and maces. The objective of the mêlée was to capture or disable competing knights. The competitions could sometimes turn bloody—in 1241, at Neuss in Germany, more than 60 people died in a tournament mêlée. Such extensive loss of life rendered the mêlée unpopular, and by the 14th century jousting became the more prominent tournament game. Jousting involved two mounted, armored knights charging one another with couched lances (a lance clamped under the armpit). The battle took place in special roped-off enclosures within fields, with the knights riding toward each other along each side of a long barrier. The principal objective of the joust was to unseat the opponent with an accurate lance strike to the chest or head—a blow delivered at full gallop. This spectacular event remained popular until the early 17th century.

Grip

Counterweight made of solid oak

Vamplate

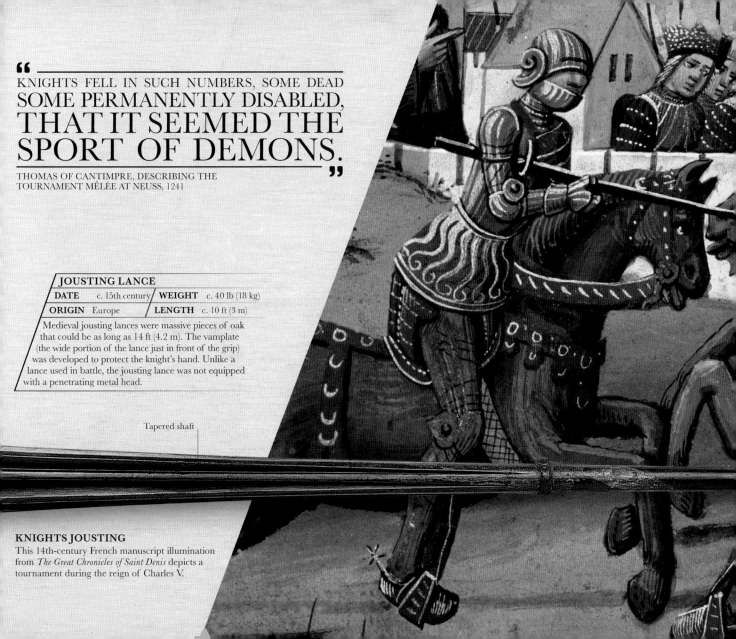

> ## "
> KNIGHTS FELL IN SUCH NUMBERS, SOME DEAD
> ## SOME PERMANENTLY DISABLED,
> # THAT IT SEEMED THE
> # SPORT OF DEMONS.
> "
>
> THOMAS OF CANTIMPRE, DESCRIBING THE
> TOURNAMENT MÊLÉE AT NEUSS, 1241

JOUSTING LANCE

DATE	c. 15th century	WEIGHT	c. 40 lb (18 kg)
ORIGIN	Europe	LENGTH	c. 10 ft (3 m)

Medieval jousting lances were massive pieces of oak that could be as long as 14 ft (4.2 m). The vamplate (the wide portion of the lance just in front of the grip) was developed to protect the knight's hand. Unlike a lance used in battle, the jousting lance was not equipped with a penetrating metal head.

Tapered shaft

KNIGHTS JOUSTING

This 14th-century French manuscript illumination from *The Great Chronicles of Saint Denis* depicts a tournament during the reign of Charles V.

DOUBLE-EDGED SWORD

DATE	1150–1200	WEIGHT	4½ lb (1.95 kg)
ORIGIN	Germany	LENGTH	32 in (82.2 cm)

A knight's rusted medieval broadsword, this sword is characterized by a broad blade and a rounded point. Distinctive features also include a simple cross-guard, short hilt, and large oval pommel. It was used primarily as a heavy cutting sword.

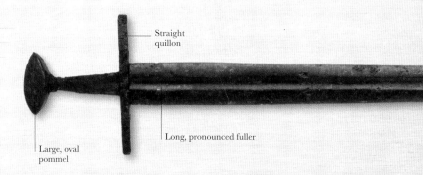

Straight quillon

Large, oval pommel

Long, pronounced fuller

Long, thin fuller

FULL VIEW

HAND-AND-A-HALF SWORD

DATE	Early 15th century	WEIGHT	3¼ lb (1.54 kg)
ORIGIN	England	LENGTH	4 ft (1.19 m)

Also known as a "bastard" sword, this long-bladed weapon was primarily used for thrusting at an opponent. To improve direction and give greater power, it was provided with an extra long handle so that it could be gripped with both hands when necessary.

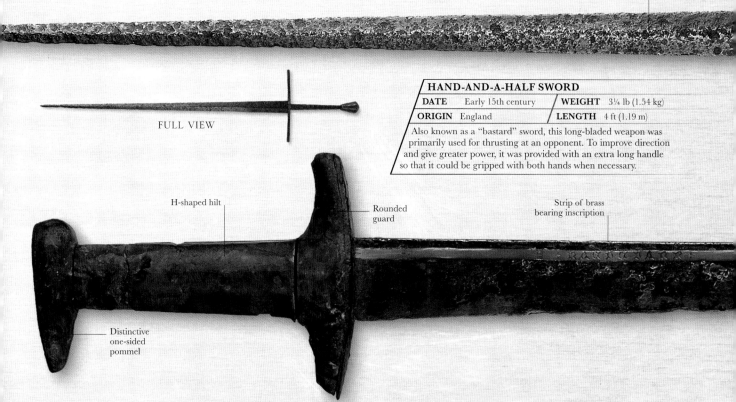

H-shaped hilt

Rounded guard

Strip of brass bearing inscription

Distinctive one-sided pommel

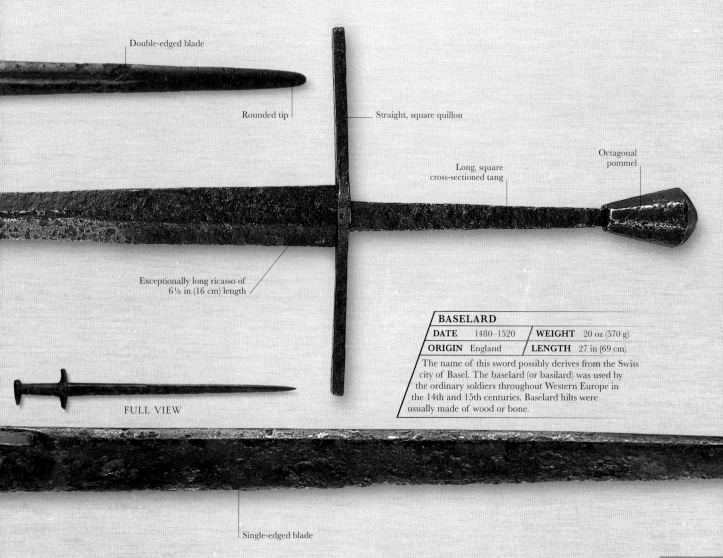

Double-edged blade

Rounded tip

Straight, square quillon

Long, square
cross-sectioned tang

Octagonal
pommel

Exceptionally long ricasso of
6 ½ in (16 cm) length

FULL VIEW

BASELARD

DATE	1480–1520	**WEIGHT**	20 oz (570 g)
ORIGIN	England	**LENGTH**	27 in (69 cm)

The name of this sword possibly derives from the Swiss
city of Basel. The baselard (or basilard) was used by
the ordinary soldiers throughout Western Europe in
the 14th and 15th centuries. Baselard hilts were
usually made of wood or bone.

Single-edged blade

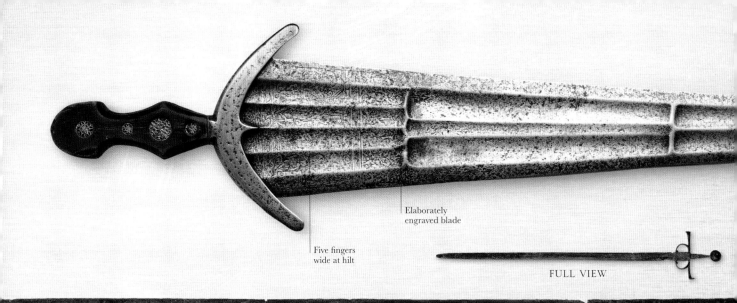

Five fingers
wide at hilt

Elaborately
engraved blade

FULL VIEW

Double-edged blade
of hexagonal
cross-section

Double-edged blade

BRONZE GILDED SWORD

DATE	15th century	WEIGHT	3 lb (1.34 kg)
ORIGIN	Italy	LENGTH	35 in (88.3 cm)

The ornate sword below features bronze gilding on both the hilt
and the pommel. The grip is made of black horn and is carved
to flow into the fish-tailed pommel. The four-sided, double-edged
blade is in remarkably good condition and tapers to a sharp fine point.

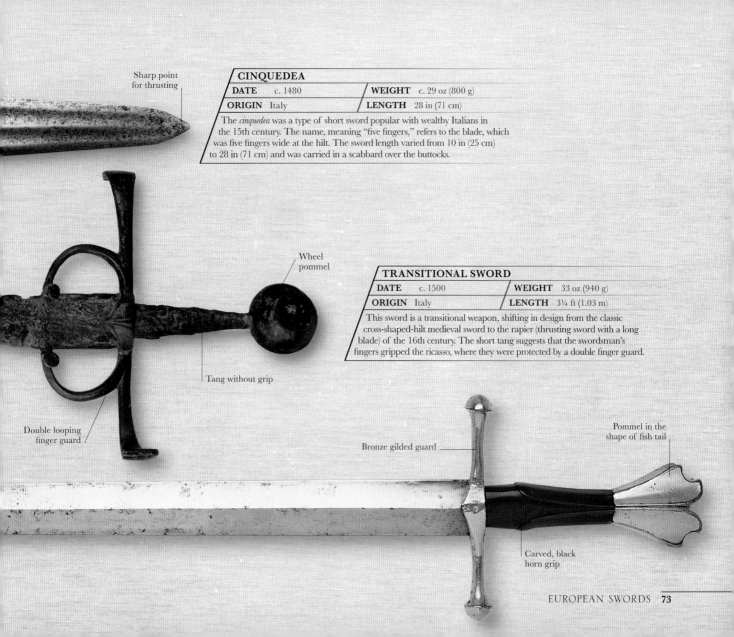

Sharp point
for thrusting

CINQUEDEA

DATE	c. 1480	WEIGHT	c. 29 oz (800 g)
ORIGIN	Italy	LENGTH	28 in (71 cm)

The *cinquedea* was a type of short sword popular with wealthy Italians in
the 15th century. The name, meaning "five fingers," refers to the blade, which
was five fingers wide at the hilt. The sword length varied from 10 in (25 cm)
to 28 in (71 cm) and was carried in a scabbard over the buttocks.

Wheel
pommel

TRANSITIONAL SWORD

DATE	c. 1500	WEIGHT	33 oz (940 g)
ORIGIN	Italy	LENGTH	3¼ ft (1.03 m)

This sword is a transitional weapon, shifting in design from the classic
cross-shaped-hilt medieval sword to the rapier (thrusting sword with a long
blade) of the 16th century. The short tang suggests that the swordsman's
fingers gripped the ricasso, where they were protected by a double finger guard.

Tang without grip

Double looping
finger guard

Pommel in the
shape of fish tail

Bronze gilded guard

Carved, black
horn grip

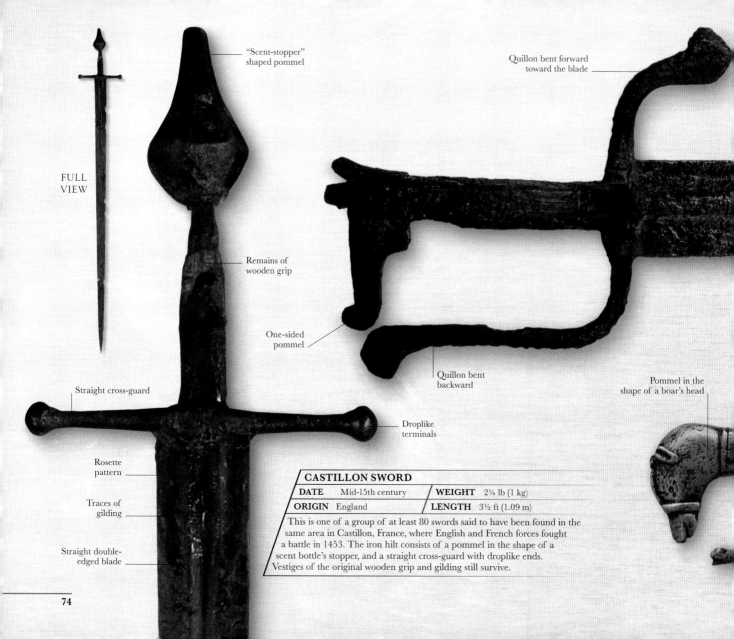

FULL
VIEW

"Scent-stopper"
shaped pommel

Quillon bent forward
toward the blade

Remains of
wooden grip

One-sided
pommel

Quillon bent
backward

Straight cross-guard

Droplike
terminals

Pommel in the
shape of a boar's head

Rosette
pattern

Traces of
gilding

Straight double-
edged blade

CASTILLON SWORD

DATE	Mid-15th century	WEIGHT	2¼ lb (1 kg)
ORIGIN	England	LENGTH	3½ ft (1.09 m)

This is one of a group of at least 80 swords said to have been found in the
same area in Castillon, France, where English and French forces fought
a battle in 1453. The iron hilt consists of a pommel in the shape of a
scent bottle's stopper, and a straight cross-guard with droplike ends.
Vestiges of the original wooden grip and gilding still survive.

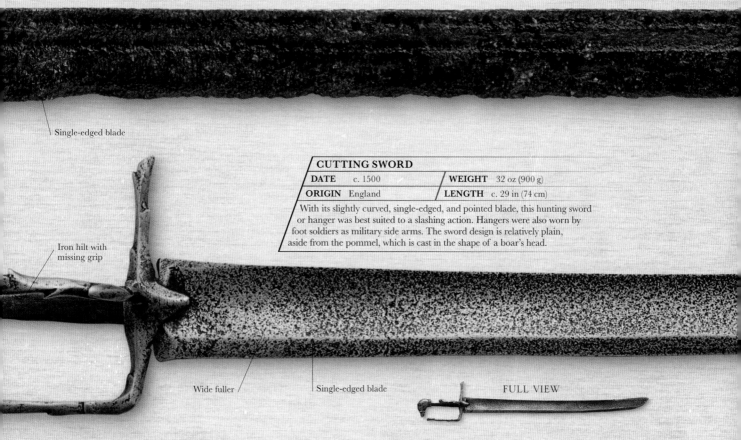

SHORT SWORD

DATE	c. 1500	WEIGHT	28½ oz (790 g)
ORIGIN	England	LENGTH	29½ in (74.5 cm)

Used primarily by foot soldiers, this English-style sword was designed with a single edge and a sharp point. The quillon at the bottom is longer and extends backward toward the pommel, which has a protrusion on the same side, thereby forming a simple knuckle guard.

FULL VIEW

Single-edged blade

CUTTING SWORD

DATE	c. 1500	WEIGHT	32 oz (900 g)
ORIGIN	England	LENGTH	c. 29 in (74 cm)

With its slightly curved, single-edged, and pointed blade, this hunting sword or hanger was best suited to a slashing action. Hangers were also worn by foot soldiers as military side arms. The sword design is relatively plain, aside from the pommel, which is cast in the shape of a boar's head.

Iron hilt with missing grip

Wide fuller

Single-edged blade

FULL VIEW

MEDIEVAL KNIGHT

The knight was the elite fighting man of medieval Europe. Starting off as a mere military servant to a local lord in the 9th or 10th century, he gradually achieved a high social standing among warriors, admired for his skill with the sword and spear.

The shift from a simple soldier to noble warrior during the Middle Ages brought about changes in a knight's armor and weapons. An 11th-century knight typically wore a hauberk (a coat of chain-mail) and a conical helmet. By the 15th century, a knight's armor had evolved into a full suit of expensive plate armor. His weaponry expanded to include war hammers and maces, as well as long, single- or double-edged swwords, such as the greatsword shown here. Although the classic form of combat was charging on horseback, knights were equally adept at fighting on foot. Adapting well to the constantly evolving challenges of the medieval battlefield, knights remained a dominant force until the 16th century.

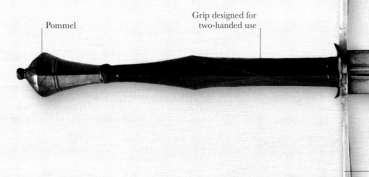

Pommel

Grip designed for
two-handed use

Single-edged
blade

Double fullers

Long, straight quillon on
cross-guard

> ## WHEN BATTLE IS JOINED, NO NOBLE KNIGHT THINKS OF ANYTHING OTHER THAN BREAKING HEADS AND ARMS.
>
> FRENCH BARON BERTRAN DE BORN (c. 1140–1215)

GREATSWORD			
DATE	c. 16th century	**WEIGHT**	c. 5½ lb (2.5 kg)
ORIGIN	Germany	**LENGTH**	c. 4½ ft (1.4 m)

The greatsword was a single-edged weapon that could be swung with both hands to deliver a powerful slashing blow. The blade of this sword was made in Germany, a country famed for the talent of its swordsmiths.

FIERCE COMBAT

This 14th-century illuminated manuscript, depicting German Emperor Henry VII's defeat of Milanese forces in 1311, shows mounted knights attacking each other with broadswords. Medieval knights used greatswords and broadswords during combat. The double-edged broadswords were designed to hack through chain-mail coats.

EUROPEAN DAGGERS

Medieval daggers were used mainly for self-defense, assassinations, and close-combat fighting, where a sword would be too cumbersome, or when a sword had lost or broken in action. Traditionally, daggers were considered a weapon of the lower classes, but during the 14th century, men-at-arms and knights began to carry them, with the weapon normally being worn at the right hip.

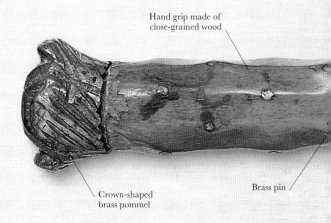

Hand grip made of close-grained wood

Crown-shaped brass pommel

Brass pin

14th CENTURY QUILLON DAGGER

DATE	14th century	WEIGHT	3½ oz (110 g)
ORIGIN	England	LENGTH	12 in (30.8 cm)

This dagger is so named because it resembles a scaled-down version of a sword, with prominent quillons that curve down toward the blade. It has an unusual pommel—mirroring the quillons—that is curled around a rivet. Sword daggers were typically carried by men of high rank, especially when they were not wearing armor.

Scrolling quillons

Tang tapering toward hilt

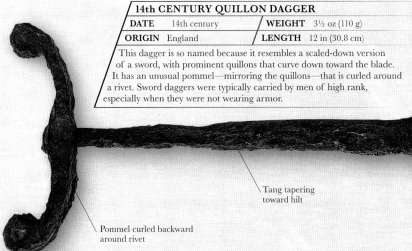

Pommel curled backward around rivet

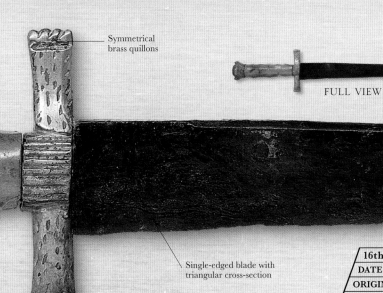

Symmetrical
brass quillons

FULL VIEW

Single-edged blade with
triangular cross-section

16th CENTURY QUILLON DAGGER

DATE	16th century	WEIGHT	9 oz (260 g)
ORIGIN	England	LENGTH	13½ in (34.5 cm)

This English dagger is distinguished by brass quillons, a crown-shaped
brass pommel, and an unusual, scalloped grip highlighted with pins.
The heavy, single-edged blade—triangular in shape, with a spearpoint—
could have been used for both thrusting and cutting.

Double-edged blade with
rectangular cross-section

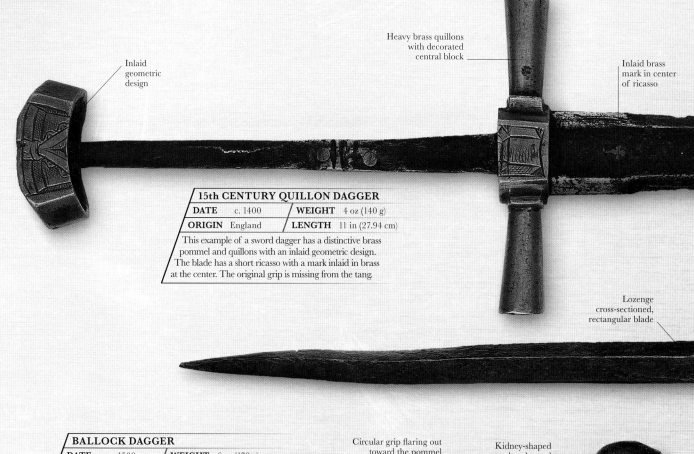

Inlaid geometric design

Heavy brass quillons with decorated central block

Inlaid brass mark in center of ricasso

15th CENTURY QUILLON DAGGER

DATE	c. 1400	**WEIGHT**	4 oz (140 g)
ORIGIN	England	**LENGTH**	11 in (27.94 cm)

This example of a sword dagger has a distinctive brass pommel and quillons with an inlaid geometric design. The blade has a short ricasso with a mark inlaid in brass at the center. The original grip is missing from the tang.

Lozenge cross-sectioned, rectangular blade

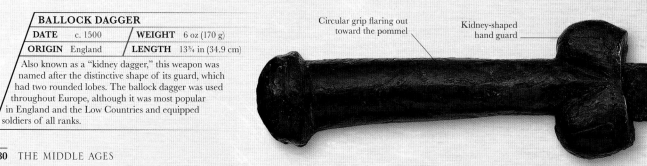

BALLOCK DAGGER

DATE	c. 1500	**WEIGHT**	6 oz (170 g)
ORIGIN	England	**LENGTH**	13¾ in (34.9 cm)

Also known as a "kidney dagger," this weapon was named after the distinctive shape of its guard, which had two rounded lobes. The ballock dagger was used throughout Europe, although it was most popular in England and the Low Countries and equipped soldiers of all ranks.

Circular grip flaring out toward the pommel

Kidney-shaped hand guard

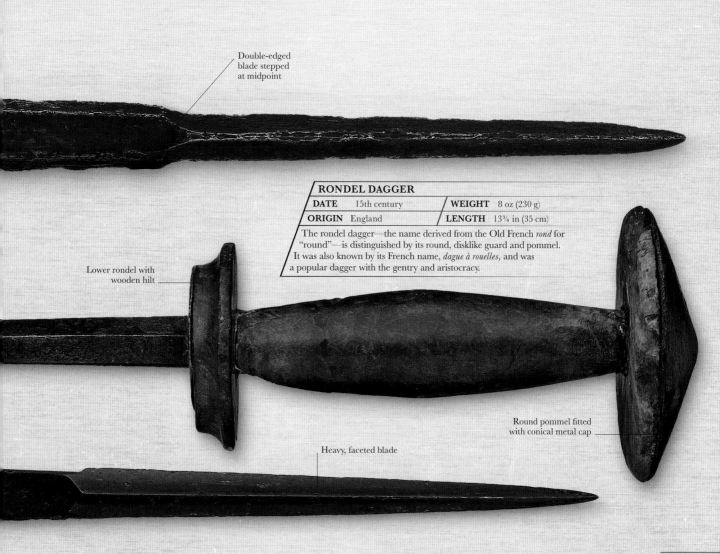

Double-edged
blade stepped
at midpoint

RONDEL DAGGER

DATE	15th century	WEIGHT	8 oz (230 g)
ORIGIN	England	LENGTH	13¾ in (35 cm)

The rondel dagger—the name derived from the Old French *rond* for "round"—is distinguished by its round, disklike guard and pommel. It was also known by its French name, *dague à rouelles*, and was a popular dagger with the gentry and aristocracy.

Lower rondel with
wooden hilt

Round pommel fitted
with conical metal cap

Heavy, faceted blade

BASELARD

DATE	15th century	**WEIGHT**	5 oz (140 g)
ORIGIN	Europe	**LENGTH**	12 in (30.5 cm)

This simple, single-edged short sword would ideally be used against lightly armored opponents. This example has a reconstructed H-shaped hilt—made of bone, with a brass reinforcing strip on the rudimentary cross-guard—combined with the original broad blade that tapers to a sharp point.

Single-edged blade, now heavily corroded

Heavy, straight cross-guard protects hand

Hammerhead pommel

QUILLON DAGGER

DATE	15th century	**WEIGHT**	11 oz (290 g)
ORIGIN	England	**LENGTH**	15¾ in (40 cm)

This dagger is a good example of the more basic and widely used daggers of the late Middle Ages, crudely constructed for the ordinary fighting man. Among its unusual features are its hammerhead pommel and the horizontally S-shaped quillons of the guard.

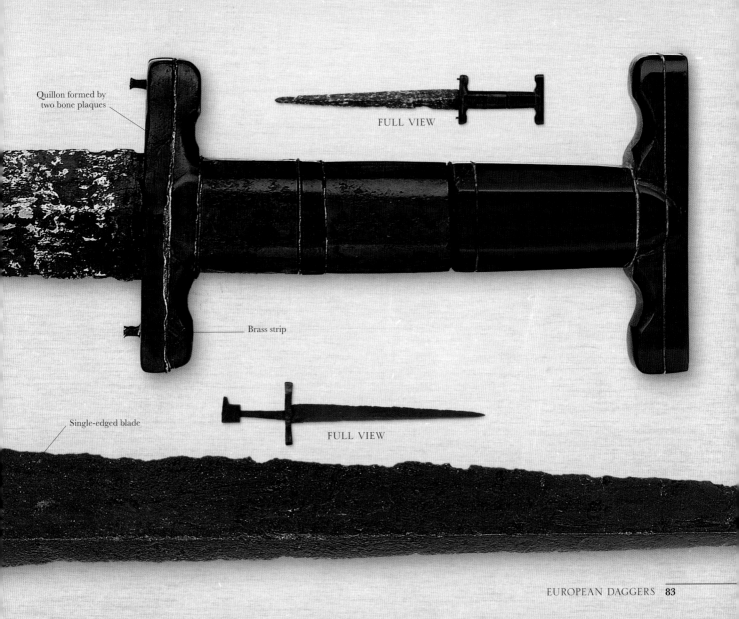

Quillon formed by
two bone plaques

FULL VIEW

Brass strip

Single-edged blade

FULL VIEW

MEDIEVAL FOOT SOLDIER

Knights were impressive warriors, but it was often the humble foot soldier who ensured success in the battles of medieval Europe. Raised from feudal levies or employed as mercenaries, foot soldiers armed themselves with whatever was available. The glaive (*pp. 88–89*) was a popular weapon due to its low cost, but foot soldiers also used knives, daggers, and agricultural tools. Only the wealthier foot soldiers, such as those from noble households, used swords. A sword was often wielded in tandem with a small buckler shield, so called because it was buckled to the soldier's arm and shoulder. The shield parried the enemy's attacks, providing the opening for the sword's thrust or slash.

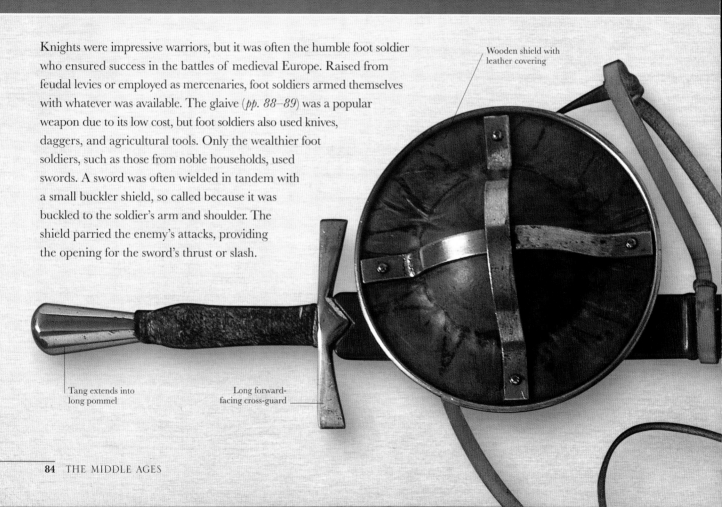

Wooden shield with leather covering

Tang extends into long pommel

Long forward-facing cross-guard

> ## DO NOT ALLOW THE ENEMY
> TO BREAK THROUGH YOUR RANKS... KILL BOTH
> # MAN AND HORSE.

FLEMISH GENERAL WILLIAM OF JÜLICH TO HIS FOOT SOLDIERS, 1302

SINGLE-HANDED SWORD WITH SHIELD	
DATE c. 13th century	**WEIGHT** c. 2¾ lb (1.25 kg)
ORIGIN Britain	**LENGTH** c. 38 in (96.5 cm)

This medieval sword and buckler shield that would have been used by a wealthy foot soldier. The sword (inside the scabbard) follows the cruciform pattern of many medieval swords, with its heavy cross-guard and long, double-edged blade. The buckler shield is made from wood, covered with leather, and reinforced with iron strips. The example shown here is a modern replica.

DANISH FOOT SOLDIERS
A medieval woodcarving depicts an expedition of Danish soldiers. The soldier in the center carries a single-handed sword, slung on his waist belt, while others grip arrows and clubs.

EUROPEAN STAFF WEAPONS

The long, two-handed staff weapons of the Middle Ages were used primarily by infantrymen as a defense against the otherwise invincible armored knight. In 1302, at the battle of Courtrai (in present-day Belgium), a rag-tag army of Flemish peasants and townspeople defeated a force of armored French cavalry using long, axlike weapons, which were forerunners of the halberd. The power generated while thrusting the long shafts of the staff weapons meant that even if armor was not penetrated, the infantry could deliver a severe injury. Cavalry were also armed with pole arms, although these were single-handed weapons like the war hammer and mace. They could be wielded on horseback and were capable of severely injuring even heavily armored soldiers.

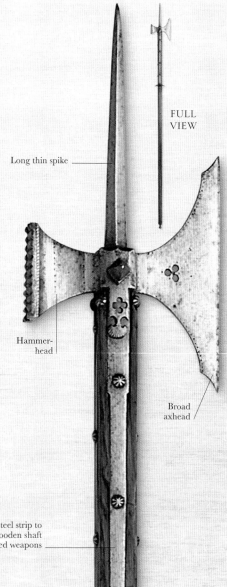

FULL VIEW

Long thin spike

Hammer-head

Broad axhead

POLEAX	
DATE	1470
ORIGIN	France
LENGTH	Head: 12½ in (32 cm)

The poleax was a multipurpose weapon. Its spike was used for thrusting, the ax blade for cutting through armor, and the hammerhead for crushing tissue and bones. This poleax has long langets and a rondel, or disk, which helped to protect the wielder's hands from enemy weapons that slid down the shaft.

Langet, a steel strip to protect wooden shaft from edged weapons

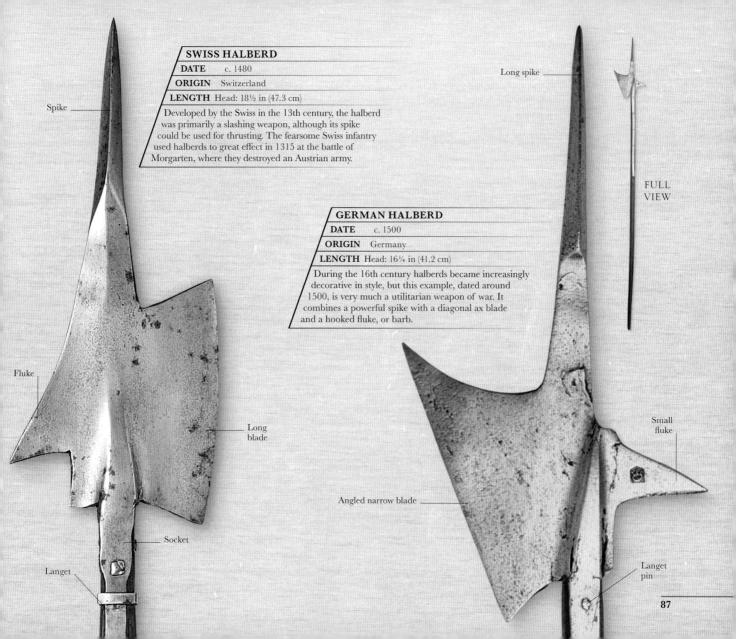

Spike

SWISS HALBERD

DATE	c. 1480
ORIGIN	Switzerland
LENGTH	Head: 18½ in (47.3 cm)

Developed by the Swiss in the 13th century, the halberd was primarily a slashing weapon, although its spike could be used for thrusting. The fearsome Swiss infantry used halberds to great effect in 1315 at the battle of Morgarten, where they destroyed an Austrian army.

Long spike

FULL
VIEW

GERMAN HALBERD

DATE	c. 1500
ORIGIN	Germany
LENGTH	Head: 16¼ in (41.2 cm)

During the 16th century halberds became increasingly decorative in style, but this example, dated around 1500, is very much a utilitarian weapon of war. It combines a powerful spike with a diagonal ax blade and a hooked fluke, or barb.

Fluke

Long
blade

Small
fluke

Angled narrow blade

Socket

Langet

Langet
pin

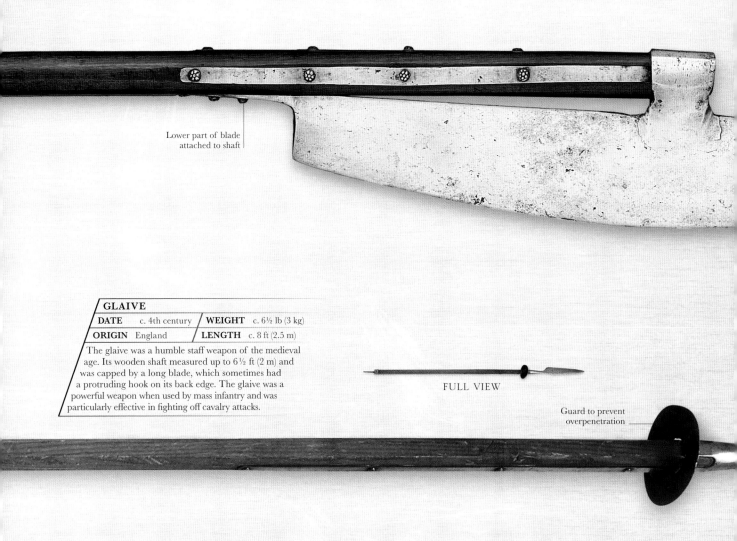

Lower part of blade
attached to shaft

GLAIVE

DATE	c. 4th century	WEIGHT	c. 6½ lb (3 kg)
ORIGIN	England	LENGTH	c. 8 ft (2.5 m)

The glaive was a humble staff weapon of the medieval age. Its wooden shaft measured up to 6 ½ ft (2 m) and was capped by a long blade, which sometimes had a protruding hook on its back edge. The glaive was a powerful weapon when used by mass infantry and was particularly effective in fighting off cavalry attacks.

FULL VIEW

Guard to prevent
overpenetration

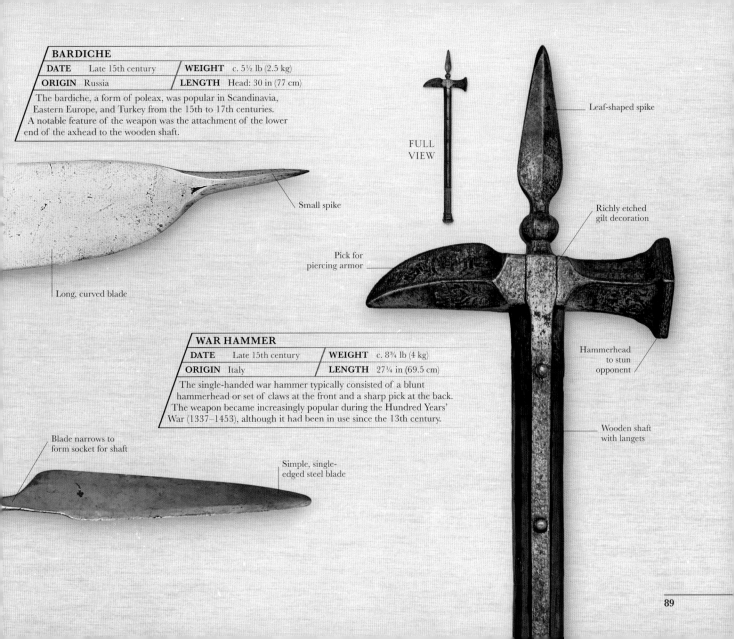

BARDICHE

DATE	Late 15th century	WEIGHT	c. 5½ lb (2.5 kg)
ORIGIN	Russia	LENGTH	Head: 30 in (77 cm)

The bardiche, a form of poleax, was popular in Scandinavia,
Eastern Europe, and Turkey from the 15th to 17th centuries.
A notable feature of the weapon was the attachment of the lower
end of the axhead to the wooden shaft.

Small spike

Long, curved blade

FULL
VIEW

Leaf-shaped spike

Pick for
piercing armor

Richly etched
gilt decoration

Hammerhead
to stun
opponent

WAR HAMMER

DATE	Late 15th century	WEIGHT	c. 8¾ lb (4 kg)
ORIGIN	Italy	LENGTH	27¼ in (69.5 cm)

The single-handed war hammer typically consisted of a blunt
hammerhead or set of claws at the front and a sharp pick at the back.
The weapon became increasingly popular during the Hundred Years'
War (1337–1453), although it had been in use since the 13th century.

Blade narrows to
form socket for shaft

Simple, single-
edged steel blade

Wooden shaft
with langets

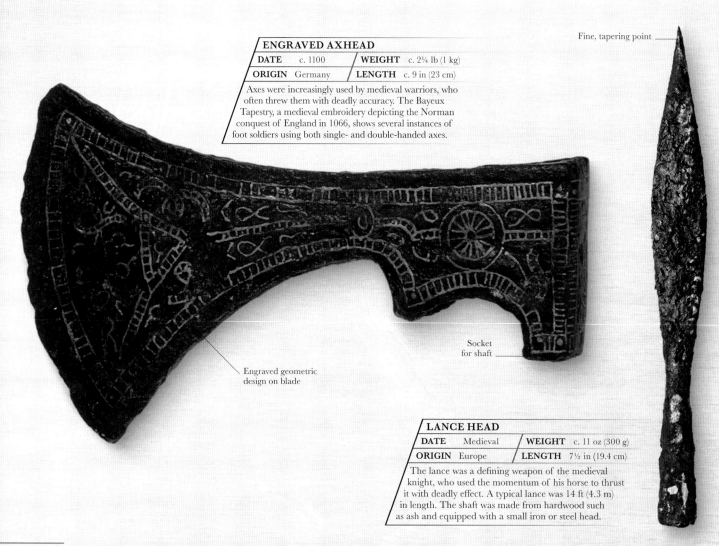

Fine, tapering point

ENGRAVED AXHEAD

DATE	c. 1100	WEIGHT	c. 2¼ lb (1 kg)
ORIGIN	Germany	LENGTH	c. 9 in (23 cm)

Axes were increasingly used by medieval warriors, who often threw them with deadly accuracy. The Bayeux Tapestry, a medieval embroidery depicting the Norman conquest of England in 1066, shows several instances of foot soldiers using both single- and double-handed axes.

Engraved geometric
design on blade

Socket
for shaft

LANCE HEAD

DATE	Medieval	WEIGHT	c. 11 oz (300 g)
ORIGIN	Europe	LENGTH	7½ in (19.4 cm)

The lance was a defining weapon of the medieval knight, who used the momentum of his horse to thrust it with deadly effect. A typical lance was 14 ft (4.3 m) in length. The shaft was made from hardwood such as ash and equipped with a small iron or steel head.

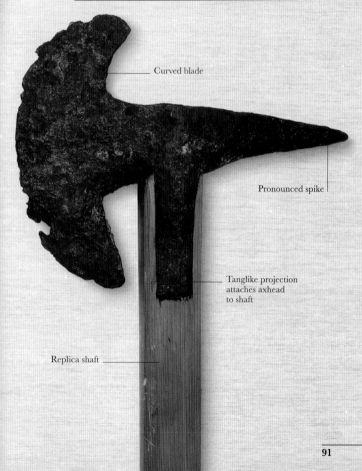

SHORT AX

DATE	14th century
ORIGIN	Europe

Although heavily rusted, the highly curved blade of this
single-handed ax is clearly visible. Unlike other axes,
where the shaft was inserted into the axhead's socket, this
example has a tanglike projection that was forced over the
shaft. Another distinctive feature is the spike at the back.

Curved blade

Circular socket

Pronounced spike

Replica shaft

Tanglike projection
attaches axhead
to shaft

LONG-HANDLED AX

DATE	13th century
ORIGIN	Europe

In the 11th century axes were used only by the
English Saxons and Scandinavian warriors, but
during the next two centuries, the weapon became
common throughout continental Europe. This
long-handled ax was used with both hands.

Replica shaft

MEDIEVAL FIGHT BOOKS

Frequent wars in 14th-century Europe led to a growing interest in acquiring fighting skills. As a result, techniques of armed fighting began to be steadily recorded in fight books—practical combat guides for professional soldiers, or men-at-arms. By using illustrations as well as text, such books offered step-by-step instructions on fighting techniques. For example, to master an arming sword (below), a swordsman could refer to a fight book for instructions on how to parry, stab, slash, and fight against armored and polearm-equipped opponents. Volumes ranged from short pamphlets to major works that included all styles of fighting. The most impressive volumes came from Italy and Germany, such as *Fior di Battaglia* ("flower of battle") by Fiore dei Liberi and a series of *fechtbuchs* ("fight books") by Hans Talhoffer, a German fencing master.

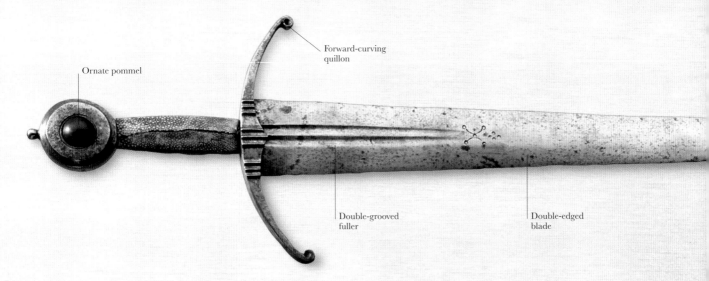

Ornate pommel

Forward-curving quillon

Double-grooved fuller

Double-edged blade

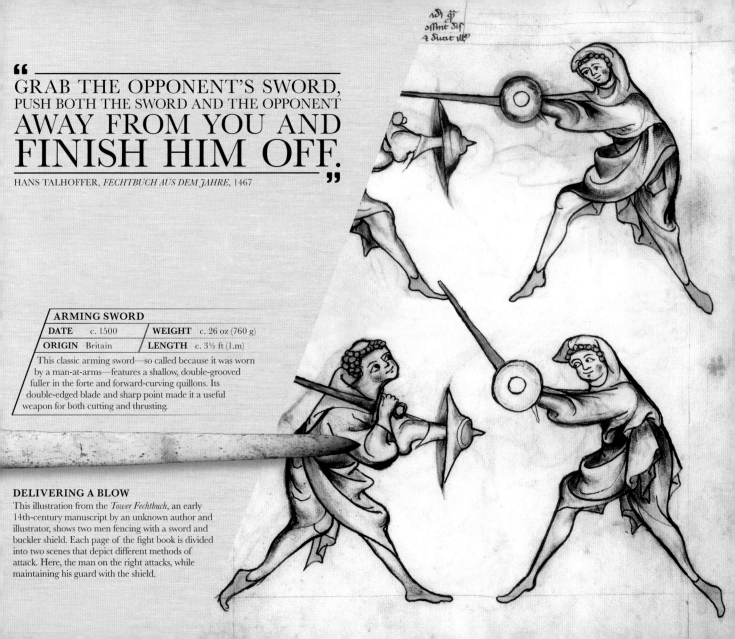

ARMING SWORD

DATE	c. 1500	WEIGHT	c. 26 oz (760 g)
ORIGIN	Britain	LENGTH	c. 3½ ft (1.m)

This classic arming sword—so called because it was worn by a man-at-arms—features a shallow, double-grooved fuller in the forte and forward-curving quillons. Its double-edged blade and sharp point made it a useful weapon for both cutting and thrusting.

DELIVERING A BLOW

This illustration from the *Tower Fechtbuch*, an early 14th-century manuscript by an unknown author and illustrator, shows two men fencing with a sword and buckler shield. Each page of the fight book is divided into two scenes that depict different methods of attack. Here, the man on the right attacks, while maintaining his guard with the shield.

AZTEC BLADES

Warfare in the Aztec Empire, which covered much of what is now Mexico, was driven by the need for a regular supply of prisoners for human sacrifice. Although the Aztecs had bows, slings, and throwing spears, they preferred to use close-quarters cutting weapons to disable an enemy, often by a blow to the legs. For their blades, the Aztecs made extensive use of obsidian (a volcanic glass) and flint, both of which could be honed to razorlike sharpness, although the blades could be easily damaged. Ultimately, the Aztecs' Stone-Age weaponry proved no match for the steel and gunpowder of the Spanish invaders who conquered the region in the 16th century.

FLINT KNIVES	
DATE	c. 1500
ORIGIN	Aztec Empire
LENGTH	12 in (30 cm)

Practical and easy to make by flaking (*pp. 8–9*), flint knives like these two examples had many purposes in Aztec society. However, they were most frequently used by priests for carrying out human sacrifice, in preference to obsidian knives, because obsidian, although sharper than flint, is extremely brittle.

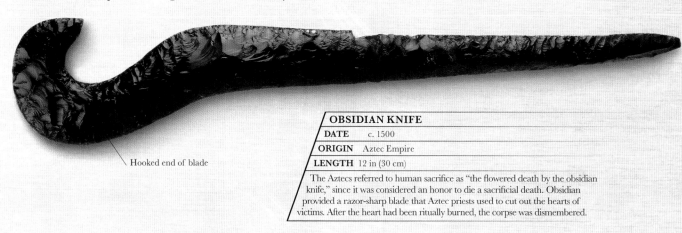

Hooked end of blade

OBSIDIAN KNIFE	
DATE	c. 1500
ORIGIN	Aztec Empire
LENGTH	12 in (30 cm)

The Aztecs referred to human sacrifice as "the flowered death by the obsidian knife," since it was considered an honor to die a sacrificial death. Obsidian provided a razor-sharp blade that Aztec priests used to cut out the hearts of victims. After the heart had been ritually burned, the corpse was dismembered.

Serrated edge

DECORATED FLINT KNIFE

DATE	c. 1500
ORIGIN	Aztec Empire
LENGTH	12 in (30 cm)

This decorated flint knife was found in the Great Temple, which stood in the center of the Aztec capital, Tenochtitlan. More than 20,000 victims were sacrificed at the dedication of the temple in 1487. Knives were sometimes decorated to resemble the face of the god to whom sacrifice was offered.

Eye made of shell and obsidian or hematite

Teeth shaped from shell

Head and shaft are
made of wood

Obsidian tooth set in
groove along edge of club

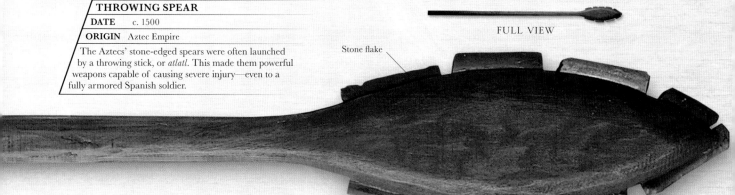

THROWING SPEAR

DATE c. 1500

ORIGIN Aztec Empire

The Aztecs' stone-edged spears were often launched
by a throwing stick, or *atlatl*. This made them powerful
weapons capable of causing severe injury—even to a
fully armored Spanish soldier.

FULL VIEW

Stone flake

MAQUAHUITL (CLUB)

DATE	c. 1500
ORIGIN	Aztec Empire
LENGTH	30 in (75 cm)

The main close-quarters weapon was a wooden club with sharp obsidian teeth wedged into its head. Known as a *maquahuitl*, it was wielded like a sword, delivering a razorlike cut that could sever a horse's head.

ORNATE CHALCEDONY KNIFE

DATE	c. 1500
ORIGIN	Aztec Empire
LENGTH	12½ in (31.7 cm)

The handle of this sacrificial knife represents an eagle warrior, one of the prestigious orders of Aztec fighting men, and is decorated with colorful mosaic of stones and shell. The blade is made of chalcedony, a type of quartz.

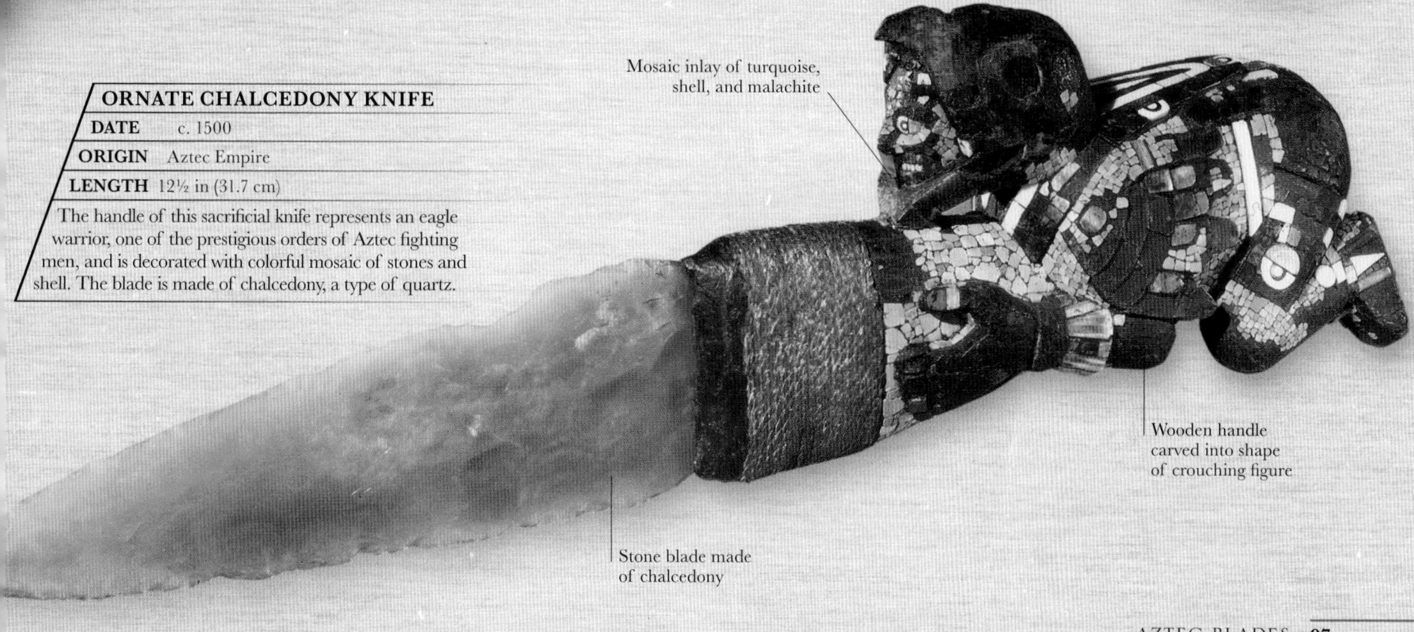

Mosaic inlay of turquoise, shell, and malachite

Wooden handle carved into shape of crouching figure

Stone blade made of chalcedony

JAPANESE AND CHINESE BLADES

The swords used by Japanese samurai warriors were among the finest cutting weapons ever made. Japanese swordsmiths used a complex process of smelting, forging, and hammering to create curved blades that were immensely hard, but not brittle. The steel of the sharp cutting edge was specially treated by a process known as quenching, in which the swordsmith wrapped the blade with clay but left the cutting edge exposed. The blade was then heated and dipped in a water bath; the rapid cooling ensured full hardness to the cutting edge. The relatively softer, flat *mune*, or back of the blade, was used to block blows, since the samurai carried no shield. Chinese swords, which were sometimes straight rather than curved, had little of the almost mystical prestige of their Japanese equivalents.

Brown silk binding

Leather-wrapped, two-handed hilt

Gilt iron decoration

CHINESE SWORD IN SCABBARD

DATE	c. 1570	WEIGHT	3 lb (1.30 kg)
ORIGIN	China	LENGTH	35½ in (90.3 cm)

This straight Chinese sword, decorated with Buddhist emblems, was made for presentation to a Tibetan monastery, hence its elaborate details. The scabbard is made of wood, but covered with gilt iron decoration.

KATANA

DATE	1501	WEIGHT	23 oz (660 g)
ORIGIN	Japan	LENGTH	36¾ in (93.6 cm)

The samurai's *katana*, or long sword, was worn with
the cutting edge uppermost, so that it could deliver
a sweeping cut in a single movement. This *katana* is
signed by swordsmith Kunitoshi.

Mune

ANTI-CAVALRY SWORD

DATE	c. 16th century	WEIGHT	c. 3⅓ lb (1.5 kg)
ORIGIN	China	LENGTH	c. 5 ft (1.5 m)

From the 8th century CE onward, the Chinese developed several varieties
of the anti-cavalry sword. These consisted of a long, single-edged blade—
generally around 4 ft (1.2 m) long—attached to a two-handed grip. These
weapons were intended for use against the legs of enemy horses, as well as
against the rider himself.

Long, slightly curved
cutting blade

Monster motif
decoration on
hand guard

Tsuba
(hand guard)

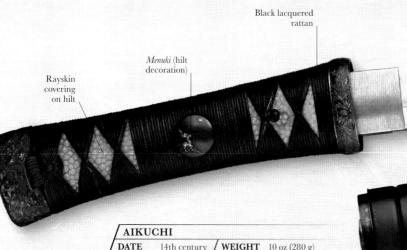

Black lacquered
rattan

Menuki (hilt
decoration)

Rayskin
covering
on hilt

AIKUCHI

DATE	14th century	**WEIGHT**	10 oz (280 g)
ORIGIN	Japan	**LENGTH**	c. 21½ in (55 cm)

The *aikuchi* was one of the many types of Japanese
dagger, distinguished by having no hand guard
(*tsuba*). It was often carried by aging samurai in semi-
retirement. This *aikuchi*, shown with its scabbard, is
a 19th-century reproduction of a medieval weapon.

Sageo (cord) for fastening
scabbard to belt

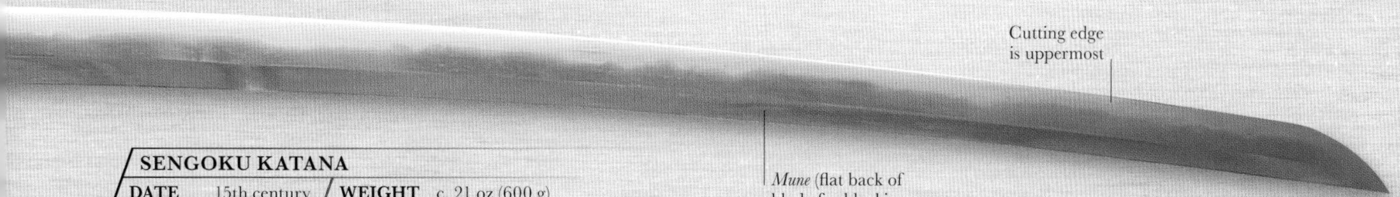

Cutting edge
is uppermost

Mune (flat back of
blade for blocking
enemy blows)

SENGOKU KATANA

DATE	15th century	WEIGHT	c. 21 oz (600 g)
ORIGIN	Japan	LENGTH	42 in (106.5 cm)

Attributed to the Shizu group of swordsmiths, this
katana blade dates from the Sengoku period. The
sword could be used with one hand, although a
two-handed grip was needed for full power.

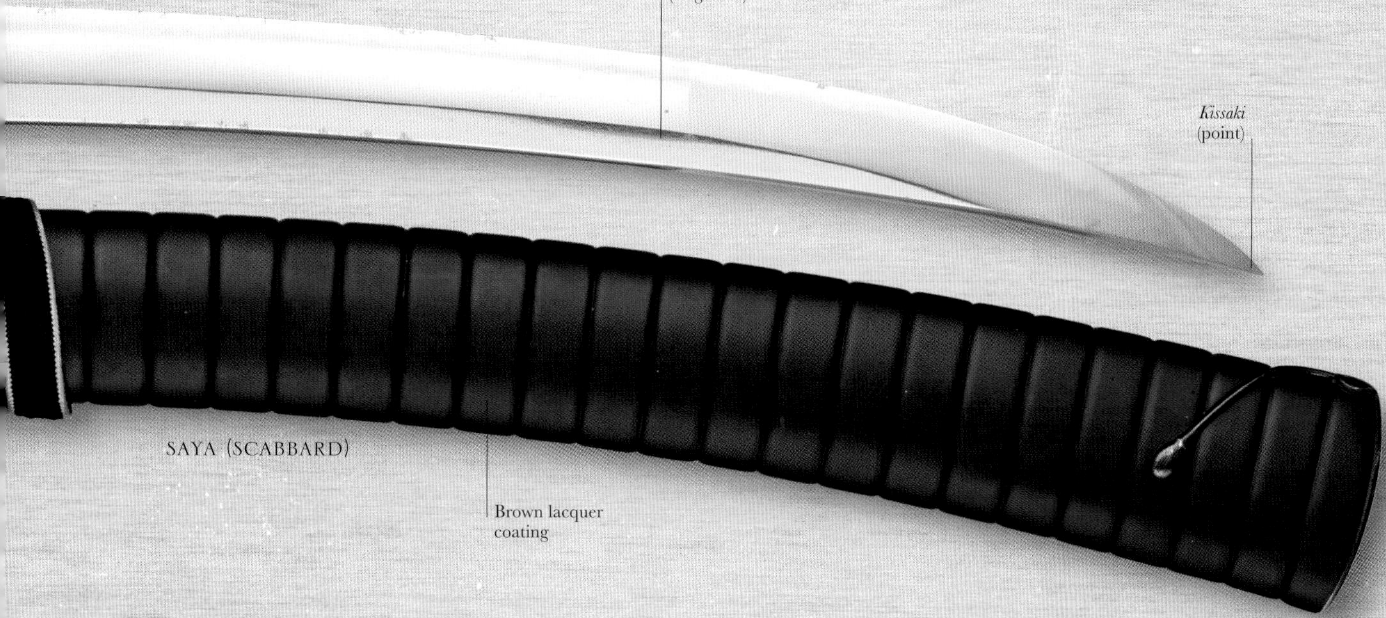

High *shinogi*
(ridge line)

Kissaki
(point)

SAYA (SCABBARD)

Brown lacquer
coating

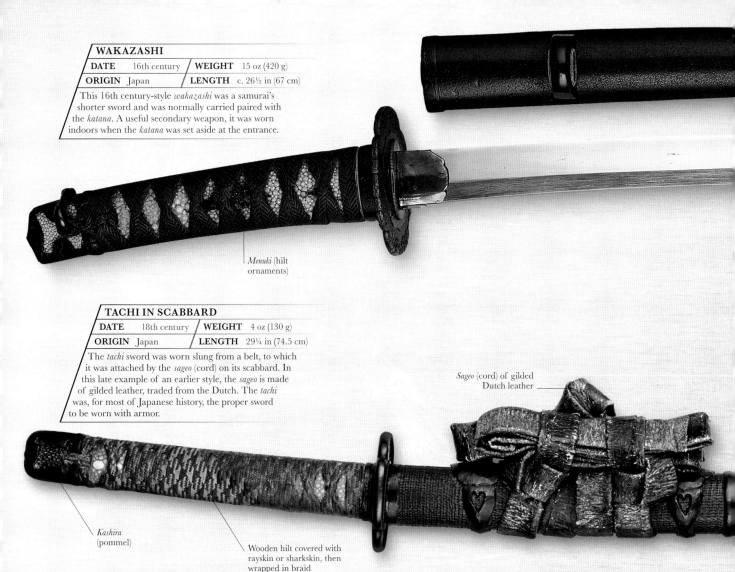

WAKAZASHI

DATE	16th century	WEIGHT	15 oz (420 g)
ORIGIN	Japan	LENGTH	c. 26½ in (67 cm)

This 16th century-style *wakazashi* was a samurai's shorter sword and was normally carried paired with the *katana*. A useful secondary weapon, it was worn indoors when the *katana* was set aside at the entrance.

Menuki (hilt ornaments)

TACHI IN SCABBARD

DATE	18th century	WEIGHT	4 oz (130 g)
ORIGIN	Japan	LENGTH	29¼ in (74.5 cm)

The *tachi* sword was worn slung from a belt, to which it was attached by the *sageo* (cord) on its scabbard. In this late example of an earlier style, the *sageo* is made of gilded leather, traded from the Dutch. The *tachi* was, for most of Japanese history, the proper sword to be worn with armor.

Sageo (cord) of gilded Dutch leather

Kashira (pommel)

Wooden hilt covered with rayskin or sharkskin, then wrapped in braid

SCABBARD

Hamon (temper pattern)
on blade edge

THE ADVANTAGE OF THE SAMURAI SWORD
WAS THAT IT COULD BE DRAWN QUICKLY AND
DELIVER A KILLING BLOW
AS IT WAS DRAWN.

Kojire (scabbard end)

Lacquered
wooden
scabbard

SHAOLIN MONK

The Shaolin monks' spiritual center lies at the Shaolin temple at Song Shan, Henan Province, China. Legend has it that the fighting skills of the Shaolin monks stretch back to the 6th century CE. The Indian Buddhist monk Bodhidharma, who became temple master in 512 CE, is believed to have taught the monks techniques to improve their skills in self-defense, much needed in bandit-ridden China. Legend or not, what is certain is that, by the late medieval period, the Shaolin monks were accomplished practitioners of martial arts, skilled with a variety of bladed weapons as well as in unarmed combat. A collection of 18 original Shaolin weapons is used to this day by the Shaolin monks, including the *guan dao* shown here, the *san jian liang ren dao* (three-pointed halberd), and the crescent-shaped *zi-wou* knife.

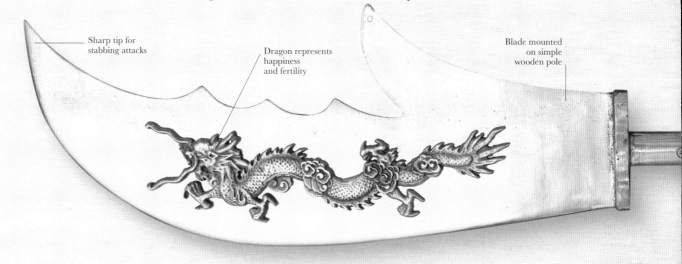

Sharp tip for stabbing attacks

Dragon represents happiness and fertility

Blade mounted on simple wooden pole

THE SHAOLIN BROADSWORD IS KNOWN AS "THE MARSHALL" AND THE STRAIGHT SWORD IS "THE GENTLEMAN."

GUAN DAO			
DATE	10th century	**WEIGHT**	c. 11 lb (5 kg)
ORIGIN	China	**LENGTH**	c. 6 ft (1.8 m)

The *guan dao*, also known as a *yan yue dao* ("reclining Moon blade"), is a form of halberd. Some medieval versions weighed more than 44 lb (20 kg), although most were purely training weapons. The example here is a replica.

KUNG FU FIGHTING

A modern warrior monk of the Shaolin Temple displays his *kung fu* skills on the Song Shan Mountain near the temple. He wields the *guan dao*, which requires tremendous strength in the arms and shoulders, as well as a good sense of balance.

BI SHOU

DATE	c. 1400	**WEIGHT**	c. 7 oz (200 g) each
ORIGIN China		**LENGTH**	c. 7 in (17.8 cm)

Known as *bi shou*, these daggers were often carried in pairs. They could easily be hidden inside a pair of boots or a jacket and were either thrown or used for stabbing. The tassel stabilized the dagger in flight, improving its accuracy, but slowed it down, limiting its penetration. These examples are modern replicas.

FULL VIEW

CHINESE DAO

DATE	1572–1620	**WEIGHT**	3 lb (1.35 kg)
ORIGIN China		**LENGTH**	3¼ ft (1 m)

This single-edged, curved *dao* is similar to the Indian *talwar* and *shamshir* (*pp. 180–81*) and the European saber (*pp. 130–31*). The blade, with its long, deep curve, is known in Chinese as *liuyedao* (willow-leaf knife). The fullers on the back of the sword strengthened and lightened the blade, the latter effect essential on such a large weapon.

Ring-shaped pommel

Curved quillon on hand guard

Long handle enables one- or two-handed grip

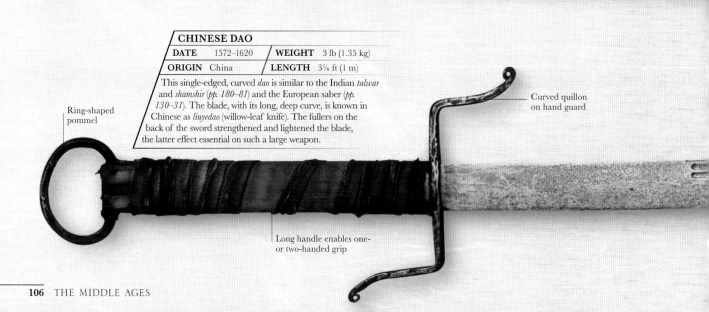

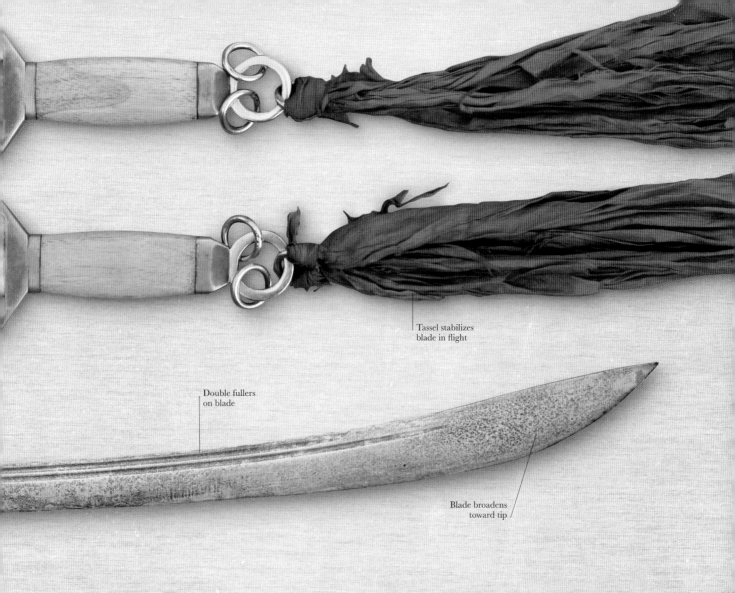

Tassel stabilizes
blade in flight

Double fullers
on blade

Blade broadens
toward tip

ASIAN STAFF WEAPONS

Medieval Asian armies deployed a wide range of staff weapons, including maces (clubs with metal heads), long-handled battle-axes, and weapons with blades or pointed heads. Some of these were little more than developments of agricultural implements or simple clubs; nevertheless, they were highly effective in face-to-face combat. Although gradually rendered obsolete by gunpowder, many such staff weapons remained in use in some Asian armies into the 18th and even 19th centuries.

A WARRIOR WIELDING A SOLID IRON MACE REQUIRED GREAT UPPER-BODY STRENGTH AND A WIDE-LEGGED STANCE FOR BALANCE.

FULL VIEW

Iron shaft reeded with raised ribs

Hole for peg to fix tang to shaft

FULL VIEW

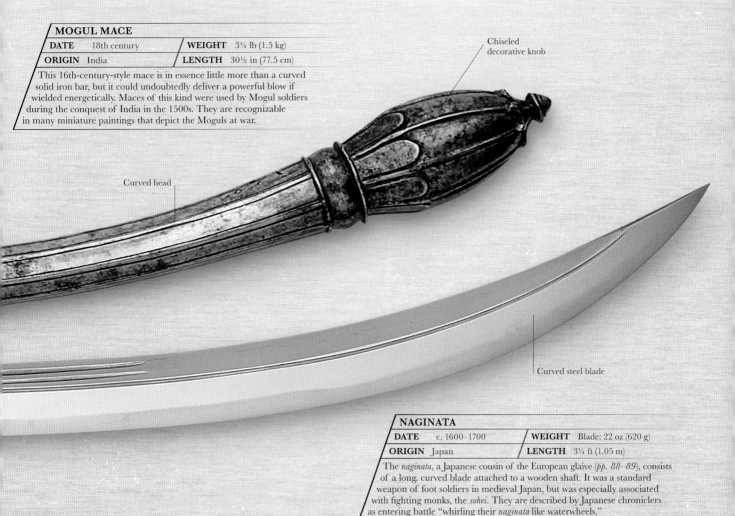

MOGUL MACE

DATE	18th century	WEIGHT	3¼ lb (1.5 kg)
ORIGIN	India	LENGTH	30½ in (77.5 cm)

This 16th-century-style mace is in essence little more than a curved solid iron bar, but it could undoubtedly deliver a powerful blow if wielded energetically. Maces of this kind were used by Mogul soldiers during the conquest of India in the 1500s. They are recognizable in many miniature paintings that depict the Moguls at war.

Chiseled decorative knob

Curved head

Curved steel blade

NAGINATA

DATE	c. 1600–1700	WEIGHT	Blade: 22 oz (620 g)
ORIGIN	Japan	LENGTH	3¼ ft (1.05 m)

The *naginata*, a Japanese cousin of the European glaive (*pp. 88–89*), consists of a long, curved blade attached to a wooden shaft. It was a standard weapon of foot soldiers in medieval Japan, but was especially associated with fighting monks, the *sohei*. They are described by Japanese chroniclers as entering battle "whirling their *naginata* like waterwheels."

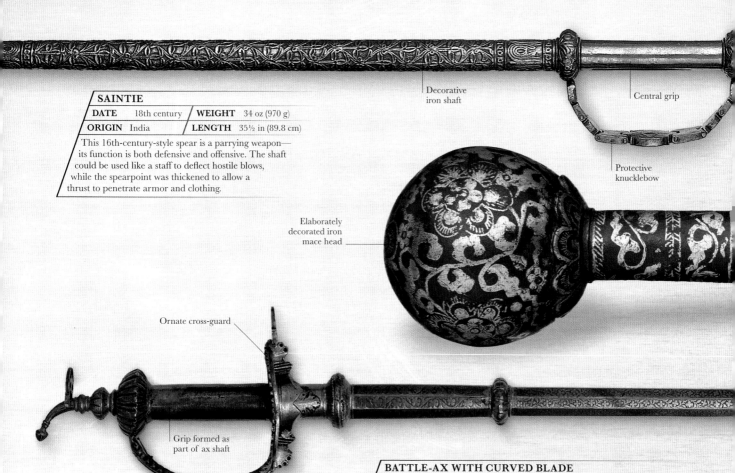

SAINTIE

DATE	18th century	**WEIGHT**	34 oz (970 g)
ORIGIN	India	**LENGTH**	35½ in (89.8 cm)

This 16th-century-style spear is a parrying weapon—
its function is both defensive and offensive. The shaft
could be used like a staff to deflect hostile blows,
while the spearpoint was thickened to allow a
thrust to penetrate armor and clothing.

Decorative
iron shaft

Central grip

Protective
knucklebow

Elaborately
decorated iron
mace head

Ornate cross-guard

Grip formed as
part of ax shaft

Single-strand
knuckle guard

BATTLE-AX WITH CURVED BLADE

DATE	17th century	**WEIGHT**	2¼ lb (1 kg)
ORIGIN	India	**LENGTH**	17½ in (44 cm)

In Asia, as in medieval Europe, the battle-ax became a weapon of choice
for aristocratic cavalrymen to use when fighting dismounted. No helmet
or armor could offer sure protection against its powerful blow. The spikes
radiating around the axhead could do damage as well as the blade.

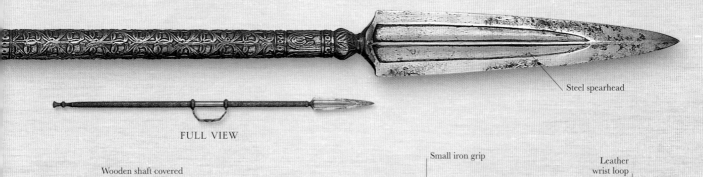

Steel spearhead

FULL VIEW

Wooden shaft covered
with polished rayskin

Small iron grip

Leather
wrist loop

Spikes around
axhead

Metal shaft

Ornate curved blade

DECORATED IRON MACE

DATE	14th century	WEIGHT	2½ lb (1.17 kg)
ORIGIN	China/Mongolia	LENGTH	15½ in (40 cm)

This splendid mace dates from the period of Chinese history in which
the rule of the Mongol invaders was overthrown and the native Ming
dynasty took power. The elaborate decoration on the mace head, shaft,
and handle suggests that it was made for a warrior of high status, possibly
a member of the Mongol elite fighting on horseback.

ARROWS AND BOLTS

During the Middle Ages, the design of arrowheads was refined, with improved penetration and injury capabilities in warfare and hunting. Penetration through armor came from the bodkin point, a small arrowhead with a square cross-section, while barbed arrows were designed to deliver severe internal injuries. From the 12th century, the crossbow and the longbow became popular in Europe. The crossbow, which was invented in China, fired short, powerful bolts. It was highly accurate and effective against armored knights and in siege warfare. But it had a slower rate of fire than the longbow, an improved version of the ordinary bow.

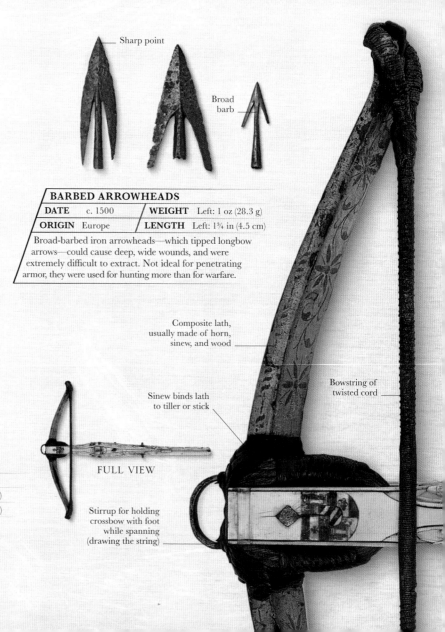

Sharp point

Broad barb

BARBED ARROWHEADS

DATE	c. 1500	WEIGHT	Left: 1 oz (28.3 g)
ORIGIN	Europe	LENGTH	Left: 1¾ in (4.5 cm)

Broad-barbed iron arrowheads—which tipped longbow arrows—could cause deep, wide wounds, and were extremely difficult to extract. Not ideal for penetrating armor, they were used for hunting more than for warfare.

Composite lath, usually made of horn, sinew, and wood

Bowstring of twisted cord

Sinew binds lath to tiller or stick

FULL VIEW

HUNTING CROSSBOW

DATE	c. 1460	WEIGHT	9¾ lb (4.4 kg)
ORIGIN	Europe	LENGTH	28¼ in (72 cm)

The crossbow was an excellent weapon for hunting because the hunter could carry the bow predrawn and loaded with a bolt, ready to shoot. It was also powerful enough to penetrate deep into an animal's body.

Stirrup for holding crossbow with foot while spanning (drawing the string)

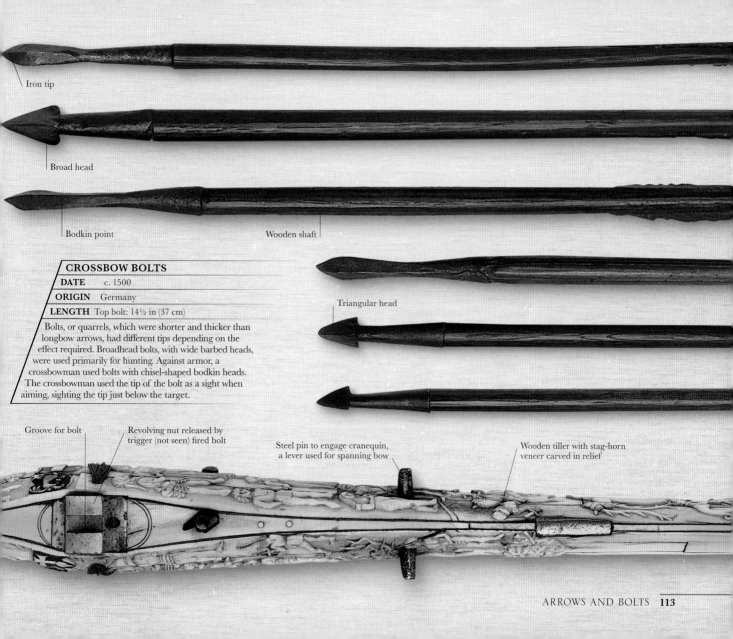

Iron tip

Broad head

Bodkin point

Wooden shaft

CROSSBOW BOLTS

DATE   c. 1500

ORIGIN   Germany

LENGTH   Top bolt: 14½ in (37 cm)

Bolts, or quarrels, which were shorter and thicker than longbow arrows, had different tips depending on the effect required. Broadhead bolts, with wide barbed heads, were used primarily for hunting. Against armor, a crossbowman used bolts with chisel-shaped bodkin heads. The crossbowman used the tip of the bolt as a sight when aiming, sighting the tip just below the target.

Triangular head

Groove for bolt

Revolving nut released by trigger (not seen) fired bolt

Steel pin to engage cranequin, a lever used for spanning bow

Wooden tiller with stag-horn veneer carved in relief

BLADE VS. BOW

With improvements in bows and arrows, swordsmen had to develop new tactics to counter the growing reach of archers using longbows and crossbows. For example, during the Hundred Years' War between England and France (1337–1453), English or Welsh longbow archers could fire 12 arrows a minute at ranges of up to 650 ft (200 m). They could even penetrate plate armor with the right type of arrowhead. For the sword-armed cavalry facing them, the obvious tactical solution was to cross open ground quickly, to minimize the risk of exposure to enemy arrows. Archers wore little armor, since they were not expected to engage in close-quarters combat. So if a knight could get close to an archer, his sword skills could be very effective. The long bastard sword shown below would be ideal against a mixed force of archers, infantry, and knights. Gripped one-handed, it could be used against lightly armored archers from horseback, while a two-handed grip gave extra power for thrusting attacks against heavily armored opponents. Ultimately, however, projectile weapons signaled the long-term decline of sword-armed cavalry.

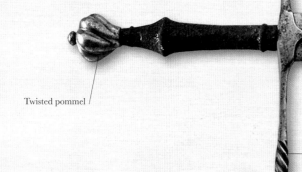

Twisted pommel

Broad fuller to reduce weight and increase flexible strength

Straight cross-guard

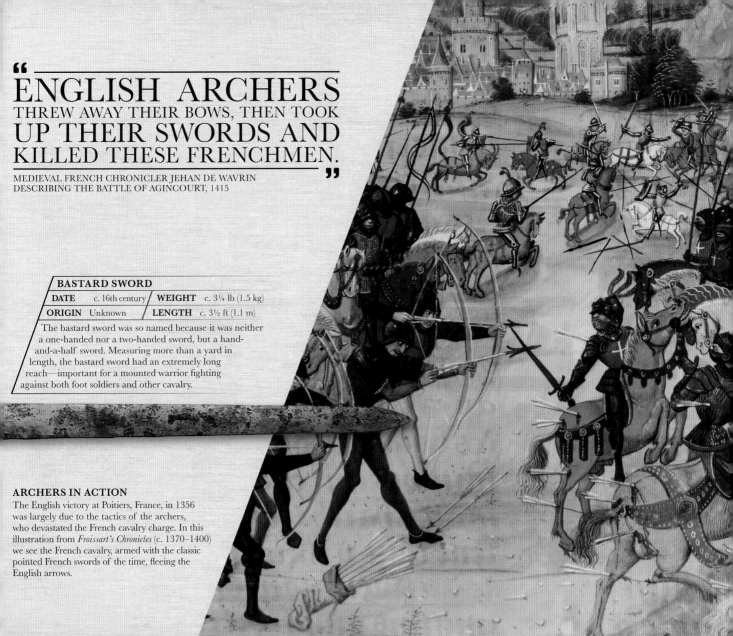

"ENGLISH ARCHERS
THREW AWAY THEIR BOWS, THEN TOOK
UP THEIR SWORDS AND
KILLED THESE FRENCHMEN."

MEDIEVAL FRENCH CHRONICLER JEHAN DE WAVRIN
DESCRIBING THE BATTLE OF AGINCOURT, 1415

BASTARD SWORD			
DATE	c. 16th century	**WEIGHT**	c. 3¼ lb (1.5 kg)
ORIGIN	Unknown	**LENGTH**	c. 3½ ft (1.1 m)

The bastard sword was so named because it was neither
a one-handed nor a two-handed sword, but a hand-
and-a-half sword. Measuring more than a yard in
length, the bastard sword had an extremely long
reach—important for a mounted warrior fighting
against both foot soldiers and other cavalry.

ARCHERS IN ACTION
The English victory at Poitiers, France, in 1356
was largely due to the tactics of the archers,
who devastated the French cavalry charge. In this
illustration from *Froissart's Chronicles* (c. 1370–1400)
we see the French cavalry, armed with the classic
pointed French swords of the time, fleeing the
English arrows.

THE AGE OF
SWORDSMANSHIP
1500—1775

THE HISTORY OF SWORDMAKING reached its peak in the period between 1500 and 1775. Despite the rising popularity and importance of firearms, introduced into warfare during the 14th century, the sword continued to be the ultimate weapon of the military elite. It also became a striking element of civilian fashion in many parts of the world. The period also saw both swords and daggers evolve into a bewildering variety of types. However, by the end of the 18th century, their popularity and use had started to decline, and swords would never again have such influence in warfare or culture.

The diversification in sword types and design from the 16th to the 18th centuries was particularly pronounced in Europe. The long, narrow, and sharp-pointed rapier became one of the defining swords of this period, with its elaborate hilt designs and straight, thrusting blades. Rapiers were worn by both officers and gentlemen, though the blades of rapiers worn by the latter tended to be more slender and lighter than the military equivalents. During the 17th century, the smallsword emerged as the fashion accessory of choice. It was a lighter form of the rapier, and was characterized by a plainer hilt with a U-shaped knuckle guard and simple shell guard to protect the wielder's hand. The smallsword was a perfect thrusting sword, and soon became the preferred weapon for duels. However, rapiers and smallswords were not the only two blades on offer during this period. In Eastern Europe, proximity to the Islamic Middle East led to the introduction of the curved swords called sabers, which soon became popular. During the 17th and 18th centuries, sabers also found their way into the cavalry weaponry of Western armies. Originally produced for hunting, the robust hanger swords—so called because of the way they were hung from the belt—were also becoming part of standard military weaponry in several armies during the 18th century. Swords were also manufactured specifically for the act of execution. These featured a two-handed grip and a broad, long blade with a rounded or even a square tip—there was no need for thrusting when beheading a prisoner.

The diversity of swords during this period is also reflected in a complicated range of hilt designs. Designs ranged from a hanger sword with simple S-shaped quillons, to swords with basket hilts that encased the user's hand in a protective cage of metalwork. The designs of rapiers were particularly flamboyant, with various shells, cups, and plates acting as a hand guard. The quillons were sometimes twisted to form multistrand knuckle guards.

Experimentation and diversity were not confined to Europe. In Africa, for example, bladed weaponry ranged from high-quality swords inspired by European designs to a mass of tribal ceremonial and combat weapons with no equivalents elsewhere. Many knives had broad, organic shapes, or featured multiple points. There are more than 100 different types of African throwing knife alone. South and Southeast Asian blades also show distinctive national or regional forms, such as the undulating Malayan *kris* dagger. In India and the Middle East, the highly curved *shamshir*, a heavy slashing sword, became a popular weapon in the 16th and 17th centuries. The *shamshir* and other Islamic swords were often decorated with gold or silver inlay-work, scrollwork, and religious text. Japan continued its fine tradition of samurai sword production, albeit under the restrictive rule of the Tokugawa Shogunate (1603–1868), also called the Edo period, which limited sword ownership. Across the world, swordsmiths took great pride in their craft and, on the wave of rising affluence brought about by international and colonial trade, produced some of the finest blades in history.

During this period, a critical development had started to take place. The 1642 memoirs of French army marshal Jacques de Puységur refer to soldiers using bayonets. Bayonets were blades of varying lengths that could be attached to the muzzle of a gun, effectively converting the gun into a polearm. Early bayonets were of a plug variety—they fit straight into the gun's muzzle, which prevented the gun from being fired. Soon, socket bayonets followed—these had a ring to slot them around the muzzle, allowing the gun to be fired even with the bayonet attached. By the end of the 18th century, when the use of firearms and artillery had become widespread, the foot soldier could wield a gun and a blade in a single weapon.

THE AGE OF SWORDSMANSHIP

TWO-HANDED SWORDS

During the Middle Ages most infantry swords were relatively light and easy to wield, but by the late 15th century a distinctive group of larger and heavier weapons grew in popularity, particularly in Germany. These two-handed swords were known as *doppelhänder* (double-hander) or *beidenhände* (both-hander) and were specialized weapons. The Landsknecht mercenaries (*pp. 166–67*) who used them were called *doppelsöldner* and received double pay, but they earned it. They were expected to hack their way into enemy pike units (*pp. 176–77*). The double-handed swords were also used for ceremonial duties and executions.

Spherical pommel

Cross-guard

Wooden grip

Wheel-shaped pommel

Long, broad, double-edged blade

SCOTTISH CLAYMORE

DATE	c. 1620	WEIGHT	5½ lb (2.5 kg)
ORIGIN	Scotland	LENGTH	c. 5 ft (1.5 m)

This two-handed sword is the true Scottish claymore, the great double-edged broadsword used by Scottish Highlanders from the 15th to the early 17th century. The word "claymore" comes from the Gaelic *claidheamohmor*, meaning "great sword."

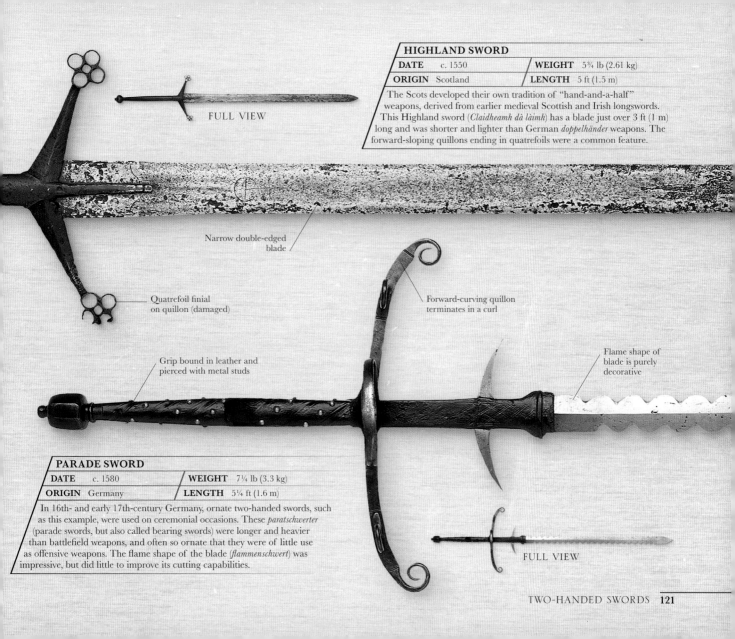

HIGHLAND SWORD

DATE	c. 1550	WEIGHT	5¾ lb (2.61 kg)
ORIGIN	Scotland	LENGTH	5 ft (1.5 m)

The Scots developed their own tradition of "hand-and-a-half" weapons, derived from earlier medieval Scottish and Irish longswords. This Highland sword (*Claidheamh dà làimh*) has a blade just over 3 ft (1 m) long and was shorter and lighter than German *doppelhänder* weapons. The forward-sloping quillons ending in quatrefoils were a common feature.

FULL VIEW

Narrow double-edged blade

Quatrefoil finial on quillon (damaged)

Forward-curving quillon terminates in a curl

Flame shape of blade is purely decorative

Grip bound in leather and pierced with metal studs

PARADE SWORD

DATE	c. 1580	WEIGHT	7¼ lb (3.3 kg)
ORIGIN	Germany	LENGTH	5¼ ft (1.6 m)

In 16th- and early 17th-century Germany, ornate two-handed swords, such as this example, were used on ceremonial occasions. These *paratschwerter* (parade swords, but also called bearing swords) were longer and heavier than battlefield weapons, and often so ornate that they were of little use as offensive weapons. The flame shape of the blade (*flammenschwert*) was impressive, but did little to improve its cutting capabilities.

FULL VIEW

FOR EXECUTION BY SWORD THE VICTIM KNELT IN FRONT OF THE SWORDSMAN, WHO DELIVERED A TWO-HANDED STRIKE TO THE NECK. REMOVING THE HEAD WITH A SINGLE BLOW WAS THE MARK OF AN EXPERT EXECUTIONER.

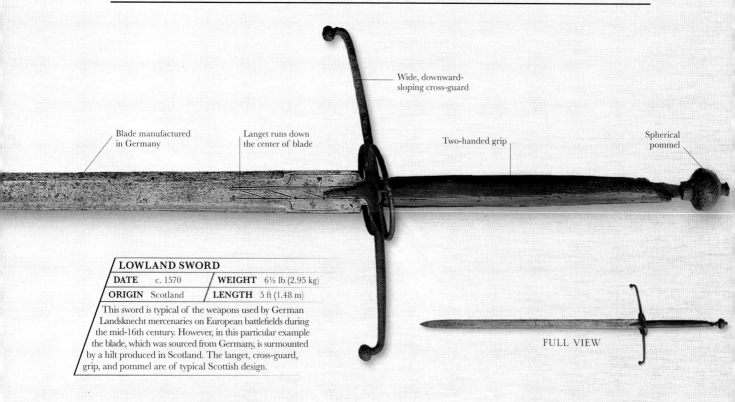

Wide, downward-sloping cross-guard

Blade manufactured in Germany

Langet runs down the center of blade

Two-handed grip

Spherical pommel

FULL VIEW

LOWLAND SWORD

DATE	c. 1570	WEIGHT	6½ lb (2.95 kg)
ORIGIN	Scotland	LENGTH	5 ft (1.48 m)

This sword is typical of the weapons used by German Landsknecht mercenaries on European battlefields during the mid-16th century. However, in this particular example the blade, which was sourced from Germany, is surmounted by a hilt produced in Scotland. The langet, cross-guard, grip, and pommel are of typical Scottish design.

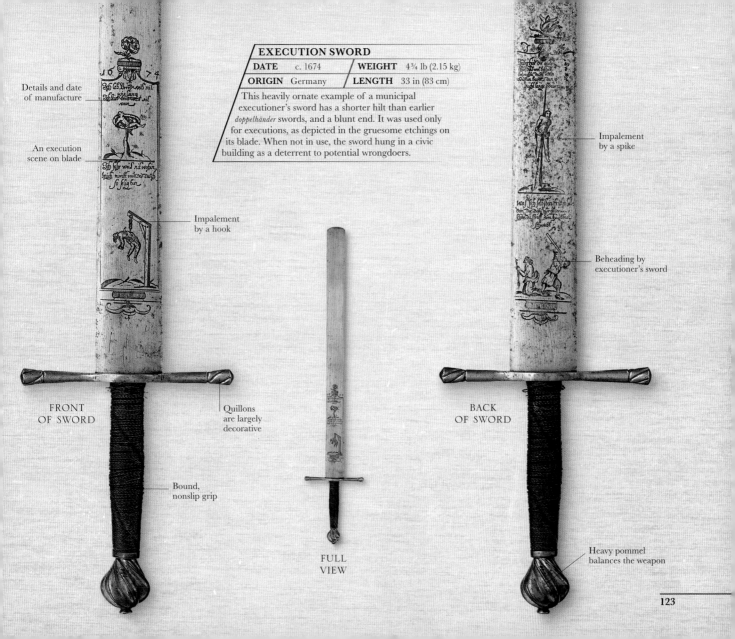

Details and date of manufacture

An execution scene on blade

Impalement by a hook

FRONT OF SWORD

Quillons are largely decorative

Bound, nonslip grip

EXECUTION SWORD

DATE	c. 1674	WEIGHT	4¾ lb (2.15 kg)
ORIGIN	Germany	LENGTH	33 in (83 cm)

This heavily ornate example of a municipal executioner's sword has a shorter hilt than earlier *doppelhänder* swords, and a blunt end. It was used only for executions, as depicted in the gruesome etchings on its blade. When not in use, the sword hung in a civic building as a deterrent to potential wrongdoers.

Impalement by a spike

Beheading by executioner's sword

BACK OF SWORD

FULL VIEW

Heavy pommel balances the weapon

EUROPEAN INFANTRY AND CAVALRY SWORDS

The military revolution that followed the Renaissance meant that firepower was becoming increasingly important, but *arme blanche* (cold steel) still remained a battle-winning weapon, particularly for cavalry (horse-mounted soldiers). From the 16th century onward, most infantry (foot soldier) swords tended to be used as thrusting weapons. But the cavalry still needed to slash downward at infantry, so they favored larger, double-edged swords that could be used equally well against mounted and dismounted opponents. However, standardized military sword patterns now emphasized style as much as practicality. They were more elegant but probably no less deadly.

Quillon affords extra protection to swordsman's hand

Simple brass-plated steel ring guard

FULL VIEW

CAVALRY SWORD			
DATE	c. 1630	**WEIGHT**	3 lb (1.33 kg)
ORIGIN	Sweden	**LENGTH**	3½ ft (1.08 m)

Cavalrymen during the 16th and 17th centuries relied on variants of the broadsword, such as this finely engraved Swedish weapon. A brass-plated ring guard protected the swordsman's hand, while the simply shaped pommel is reminiscent of late medieval weapons. The straight blade could be used with equal efficiency as a cutting or thrusting weapon.

Intricate engraving suggests weapon belonged to an officer

INFANTRY SWORD

DATE	c. 1500	WEIGHT	32 oz (910 g)
ORIGIN	Switzerland	LENGTH	35¼ in (90 cm)

Compared to the basket-hilted sword, this weapon offered little protection to the swordsman. However, its grip allowed it to be wielded by both hands, a feature more useful to a foot soldier than a cavalry officer.

Curves on quillon could trap an opponent's blade

FULL VIEW

Simple wooden grip allows single- or double-handed hold

Religious icons often decorated the blades of Renaissance weapons

FULL VIEW

Three fullers on blade

BASKET-HILTED SWORD

DATE	Hilt: c. 1540	WEIGHT	3 lb (1.36 kg)
ORIGIN	England	LENGTH	3¼ ft (1.04 m)

This broadsword (a sword with wide, double-edged blade) consists of an early 17th-century German blade, which is attached to an English basket hilt. The basket hilt dates from over a century before the blade was cast.

Silver-encrusted hilt

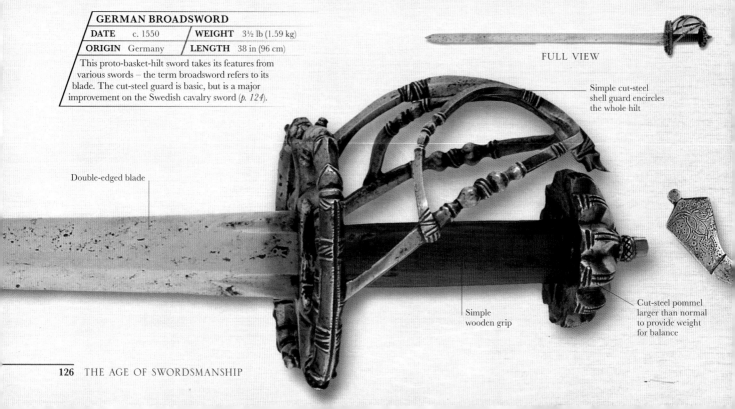

Single fuller imparts
greater strength to blade

GERMAN BROADSWORD

DATE	c. 1550	**WEIGHT**	3½ lb (1.59 kg)
ORIGIN	Germany	**LENGTH**	38 in (96 cm)

This proto-basket-hilt sword takes its features from
various swords – the term broadsword refers to its
blade. The cut-steel guard is basic, but is a major
improvement on the Swedish cavalry sword (*p. 124*).

FULL VIEW

Simple cut-steel
shell guard encircles
the whole hilt

Double-edged blade

Simple
wooden grip

Cut-steel pommel
larger than normal
to provide weight
for balance

Maker's
mark

Ornate
scrollwork
on guard

Solid steel plate
often perforated with
heart-shaped designs

FULL
VIEW

Blade lacks
fuller

S-shaped
quillon typical
of this era

CAVALRY SWORD

DATE	1750	WEIGHT	3 lb (1.36 kg)
ORIGIN	England	LENGTH	3¼ ft (1 m)

By the mid-18th century cavalry swords had developed
into two types: light, curved blades for light cavalry,
and longer, heavier, straight blades for heavy cavalry.
This example is typical of those used by European
heavy cavalry for over a century. The single fuller
(groove along the back of the blade) indicated that
the blade was single-edged.

DÜSACK

DATE	c. 1570	WEIGHT	3¼ lb (1.5 kg)
ORIGIN	Germany	LENGTH	3¼ ft (1.02 m)

The *düsack* or *dussak* was primarily a south German and
Austrian weapon of war. Its curved blade, based on the
design of a saber (a curved-bladed sword, typically used
by cavalry) made it a useful cutting weapon, while its
enclosed guard offered good protection to the swordsman.
Early 17th-century woodcuts suggest that the *düsack* was
also used as a dueling weapon in southern Germany.

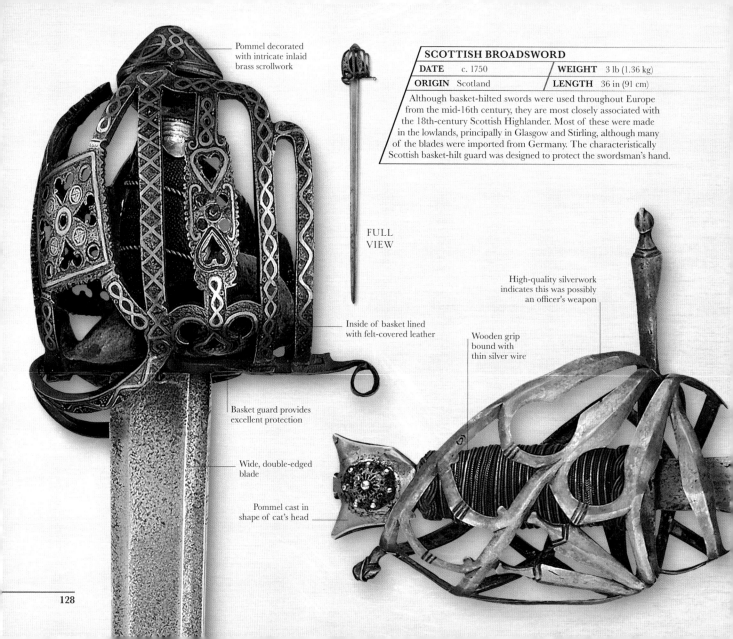

Pommel decorated with intricate inlaid brass scrollwork

SCOTTISH BROADSWORD

DATE	c. 1750	WEIGHT	3 lb (1.36 kg)
ORIGIN	Scotland	LENGTH	36 in (91 cm)

Although basket-hilted swords were used throughout Europe from the mid-16th century, they are most closely associated with the 18th-century Scottish Highlander. Most of these were made in the lowlands, principally in Glasgow and Stirling, although many of the blades were imported from Germany. The characteristically Scottish basket-hilt guard was designed to protect the swordsman's hand.

FULL VIEW

Inside of basket lined with felt-covered leather

High-quality silverwork indicates this was possibly an officer's weapon

Wooden grip bound with thin silver wire

Basket guard provides excellent protection

Wide, double-edged blade

Pommel cast in shape of cat's head

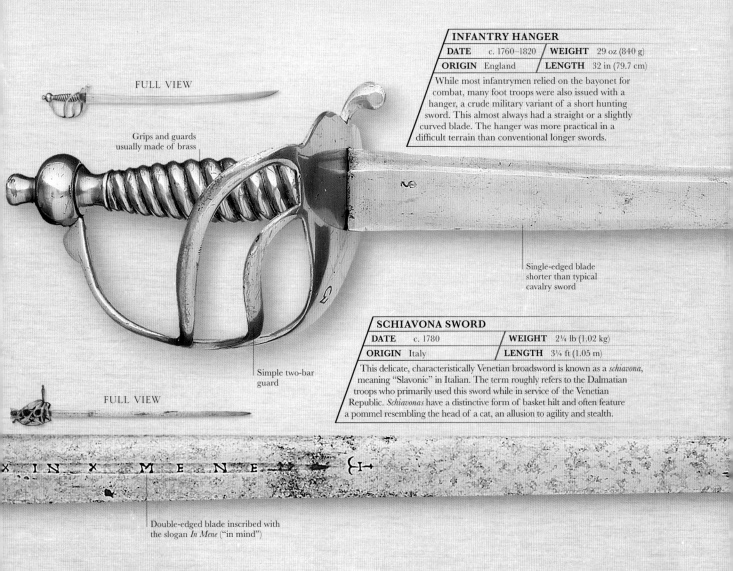

FULL VIEW

INFANTRY HANGER

DATE	c. 1760–1820	**WEIGHT**	29 oz (840 g)
ORIGIN	England	**LENGTH**	32 in (79.7 cm)

While most infantrymen relied on the bayonet for combat, many foot troops were also issued with a hanger, a crude military variant of a short hunting sword. This almost always had a straight or a slightly curved blade. The hanger was more practical in a difficult terrain than conventional longer swords.

Grips and guards
usually made of brass

Single-edged blade
shorter than typical
cavalry sword

Simple two-bar
guard

SCHIAVONA SWORD

DATE	c. 1780	**WEIGHT**	2¼ lb (1.02 kg)
ORIGIN	Italy	**LENGTH**	3¼ ft (1.05 m)

This delicate, characteristically Venetian broadsword is known as a *schiavona*, meaning "Slavonic" in Italian. The term roughly refers to the Dalmatian troops who primarily used this sword while in service of the Venetian Republic. *Schiavonas* have a distinctive form of basket hilt and often feature a pommel resembling the head of a cat, an allusion to agility and stealth.

FULL VIEW

X IN X MENE

Double-edged blade inscribed with
the slogan *In Mene* ("in mind")

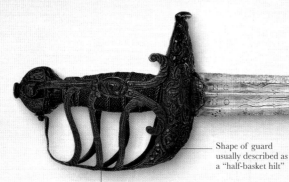

Steel hilt decorated
with simple cast
scrollwork

Shape of guard
usually described as
a "half-basket hilt"

CAVALRY SWORD

DATE	c. 1775	WEIGHT	30 oz (850 g)
ORIGIN	England	LENGTH	33 in (83.8 cm)

This sword is typical of the single-edged swords carried by heavy cavalry
for much of the 18th century. While cavalrymen still used swords to deliver
swinging cuts, it was considered more practical for heavy cavalry to thrust at
the enemy, that is, use the point of the sword instead of the edge. This weapon
was dual purpose, without being particularly well suited for either type of
swordplay. After 1780, most British Army swords were designed to set patterns.

Decoration on hilt
shows sword belonged
to an officer

Style of guard in
contemporary
rococo design

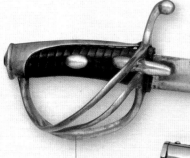

Three-barred
guard

Suspension ring to attach
scabbard to belt loop or straps

MORTUARY SWORD

DATE	1640–60	WEIGHT	32 oz (910 g)
ORIGIN	England/Germany	LENGTH	36 in (91 cm)

The name of this sword has two possible derivations. It could either be named because of the hilt's resemblance to the human rib cage, or derived from a 19th-century term related to the supposed likeness of portrait heads on the hilt to the executed King Charles I. These swords were widely used by cavalrymen during the English Civil War that preceded the execution of the king in 1649. Although the blade was made in Germany, the hilt of this weapon is of a uniquely English design.

Double-edged blade with two fullers to reduce weight

FRENCH SABER

DATE	1802	WEIGHT	c. 2½ lb (1.2 kg)
ORIGIN	France	LENGTH	c. 29 in (73.6 cm)

French light cavalry liked to thrust with the point of the blade as well as deliver swinging cuts. As a result, their sabers had narrower blades than their British counterparts. This is an XI model, introduced in 1802–03. The steel scabbard is tougher than earlier brass and leather examples.

Polished steel

SCABBARD

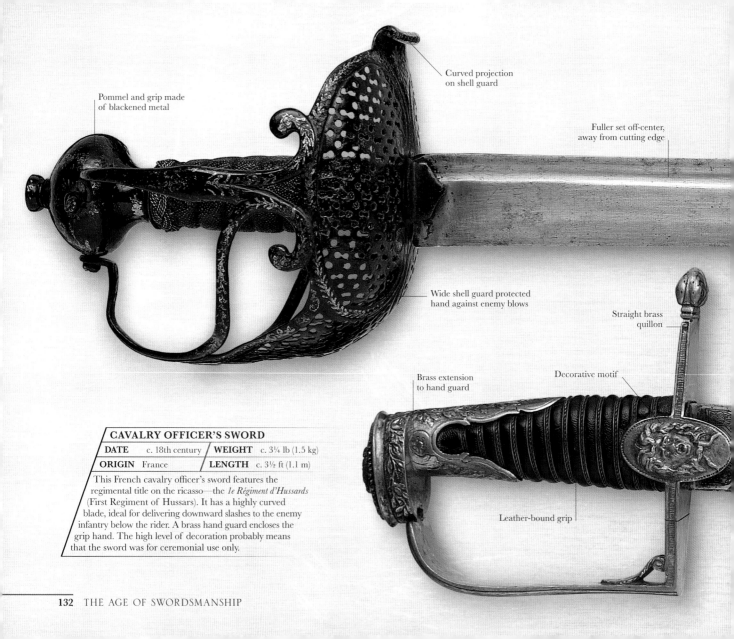

Curved projection
on shell guard

Pommel and grip made
of blackened metal

Fuller set off-center,
away from cutting edge

Wide shell guard protected
hand against enemy blows

Straight brass
quillon

Decorative motif

Brass extension
to hand guard

Leather-bound grip

CAVALRY OFFICER'S SWORD			
DATE	c. 18th century	**WEIGHT**	c. 3¼ lb (1.5 kg)
ORIGIN	France	**LENGTH**	c. 3½ ft (1.1 m)

This French cavalry officer's sword features the
regimental title on the ricasso—the *1e Régiment d'Hussards*
(First Regiment of Hussars). It has a highly curved
blade, ideal for delivering downward slashes to the enemy
infantry below the rider. A brass hand guard encloses the
grip hand. The high level of decoration probably means
that the sword was for ceremonial use only.

FULL VIEW

OLIVER CROMWELL'S SWORD			
DATE	17th century	**WEIGHT**	c. 3 lb (1.4 kg)
ORIGIN	Britain	**LENGTH**	c. 3½ ft (1.1 m)

This sword is reputed to have been carried by Oliver Cromwell, the famous English soldier and statesman, at the battle of Drogheda in 1649. It features an elaborate "mortuary style" hilt. It has a wire-wound sharkskin grip, which would have provided a solid grip for sweaty hands during actual combat.

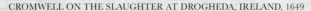

" I FORBADE THEM TO SPARE ANY THAT WERE IN ARMS... THEY PUT TO THE SWORD ABOUT 2,000 MEN "

CROMWELL ON THE SLAUGHTER AT DROGHEDA, IRELAND, 1649

Regimental inscription on ricasso

FULL VIEW

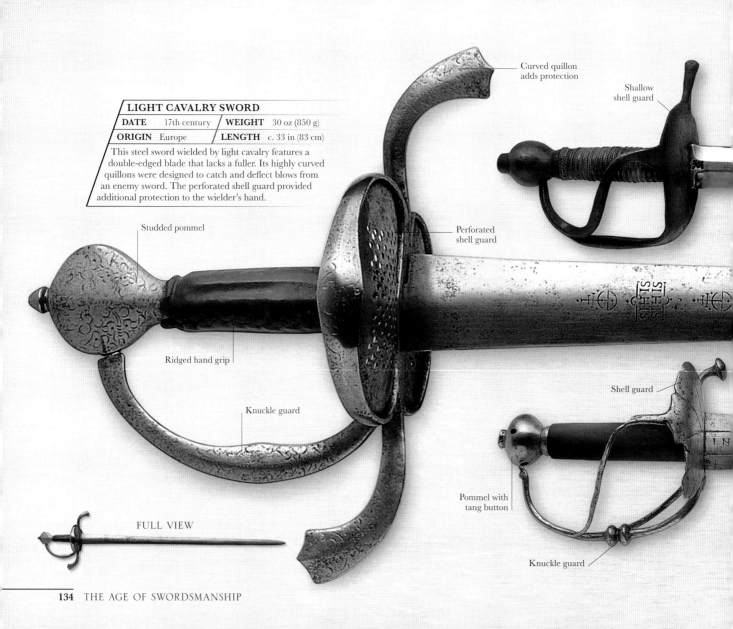

LIGHT CAVALRY SWORD

DATE	17th century	WEIGHT	30 oz (850 g)
ORIGIN	Europe	LENGTH	c. 33 in (83 cm)

This steel sword wielded by light cavalry features a
double-edged blade that lacks a fuller. Its highly curved
quillons were designed to catch and deflect blows from
an enemy sword. The perforated shell guard provided
additional protection to the wielder's hand.

Curved quillon
adds protection

Shallow
shell guard

Studded pommel

Perforated
shell guard

Ridged hand grip

Knuckle guard

Shell guard

Pommel with
tang button

Knuckle guard

FULL VIEW

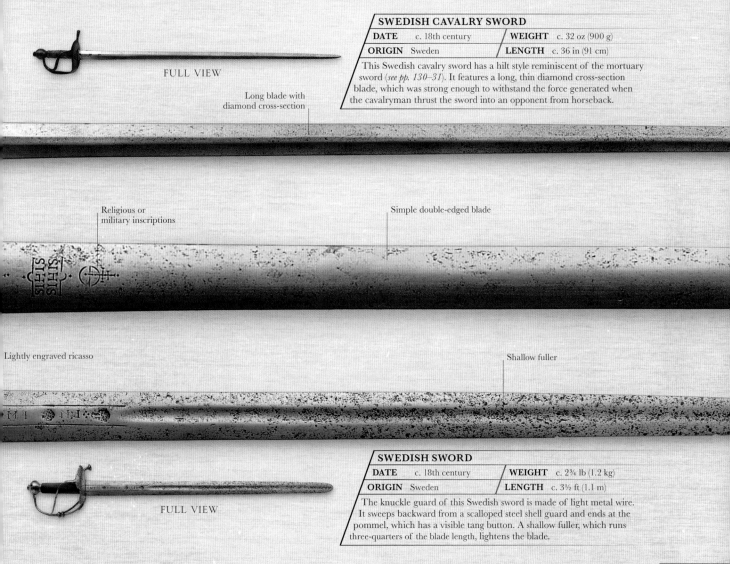

FULL VIEW

SWEDISH CAVALRY SWORD

DATE	c. 18th century	**WEIGHT**	c. 32 oz (900 g)
ORIGIN	Sweden	**LENGTH**	c. 36 in (91 cm)

This Swedish cavalry sword has a hilt style reminiscent of the mortuary sword (*see pp. 130–31*). It features a long, thin diamond cross-section blade, which was strong enough to withstand the force generated when the cavalryman thrust the sword into an opponent from horseback.

Long blade with
diamond cross-section

Religious or
military inscriptions

Simple double-edged blade

Lightly engraved ricasso

Shallow fuller

FULL VIEW

SWEDISH SWORD

DATE	c. 18th century	**WEIGHT**	c. 2¾ lb (1.2 kg)
ORIGIN	Sweden	**LENGTH**	c. 3½ ft (1.1 m)

The knuckle guard of this Swedish sword is made of light metal wire. It sweeps backward from a scalloped steel shell guard and ends at the pommel, which has a visible tang button. A shallow fuller, which runs three-quarters of the blade length, lightens the blade.

DUELING

Dueling—the settling of a dispute or matter of honor through individual combat—has ancient origins. The Vikings were known to engage in *holmanga*, duels in which two fighters slashed at one another until blood was drawn or money offered in settlement. In Europe, dueling thrived from the Middle Ages until the late 19th century, although from the 17th century it was increasingly prohibited by law in many countries. Rapiers, such as the swept-hilt version shown below, and smallswords (*pp. 142–45*) were common dueling weapons, sometimes provided in paired sets to duelists by their assistants, who would check the weapons to ensure neither party had an unfair advantage over the other.

The rules of a duel were fairly simple. After one party had issued a formal challenge, the date, time, and venue would be agreed to. The fight was usually amateur, since not everyone was a swordsman. It would be stopped, by agreement, at either first blood drawn, serious injury, or death. *Codes duelo* (dueling codes) were written to lay down a strict etiquette for these events.

Pommel could be used as improvised striking weapon

Intricate swept-hilt guard

Rigid blade of diamond cross-section

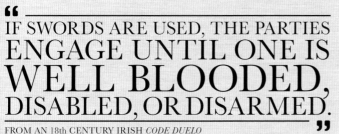

SWEPT-HILT RAPIER

DATE	1600–60	WEIGHT	2¾ lb (1.27 kg)
ORIGIN	Europe	LENGTH	4¼ ft (1.3 m)

This classic infantry weapon of the 17th century was designed purely as a thrusting weapon. Swordplay using the point of the sword was considered the art of a gentleman—in addition to being a military weapon, the rapier was the duelist's weapon of choice, until it was replaced by the pistol in the late 17th century.

PARISIAN DUEL

This illustration by French artist Maurice Leloir (1851–1940) shows two men fighting a duel using rapiers. Since not all citizens were trained in swordplay, some accounts of duels mention little more than two people stabbing each another until one died.

EUROPEAN RAPIERS

In the 16th century the rapier became the status symbol of a swordsman, showing that he was a man of substance and knew how to use his sword. The term is derived from the 15th-century Spanish term *espada ropera*, or "sword of the robes," meaning the weapon of a gentleman. By 1500, the rapier was used throughout Europe, and it would remain the premier gentleman's sword until the late 17th century. Although it was certainly used on the battlefield, it was more readily associated with court, dueling, and fashion— hence the tendency toward delicate, intricate designs.

PAPPENHEIM-HILT RAPIER			
DATE	1630	**WEIGHT**	2¾ lb (1.25 kg)
ORIGIN	Germany	**LENGTH**	4½ in (1.4 m)

This style of rapier was popularized by Count Pappenheim, an imperial general of the Thirty Years' War (1618–48), a war that involved most of the countries of Europe at some point. Designed for military use, the Pappenheim-hilt rapier was soon copied throughout Europe, since its two pierced shell guards provided good protection for the swordsman.

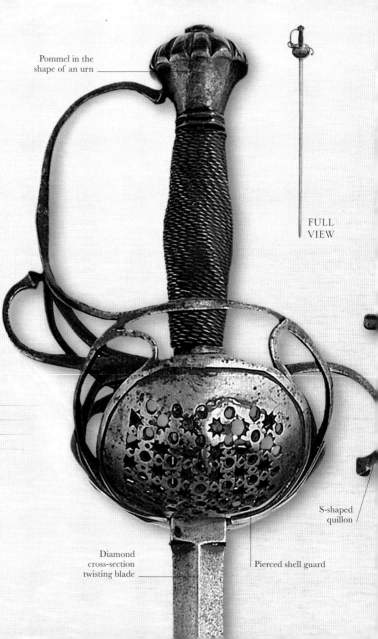

Pommel in the shape of an urn

FULL VIEW

S-shaped quillon

Diamond cross-section twisting blade

Pierced shell guard

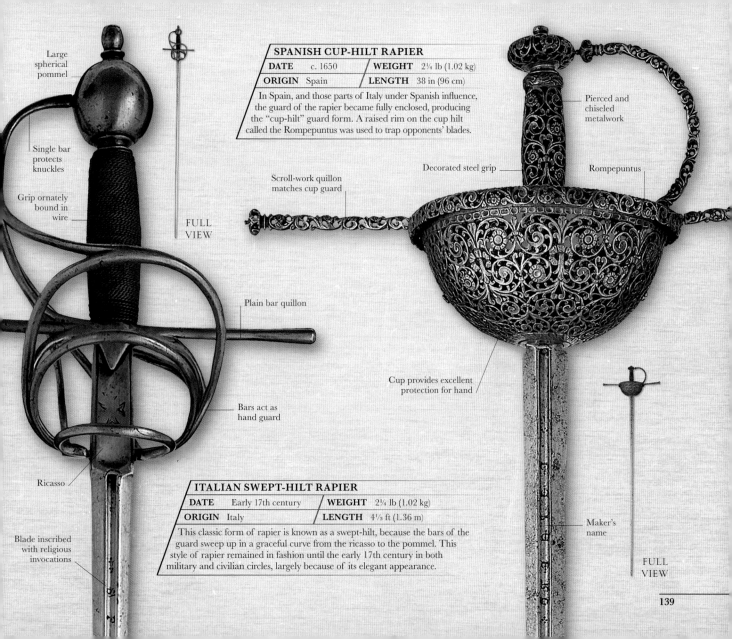

Large
spherical
pommel

Single bar
protects
knuckles

Grip ornately
bound in
wire

FULL
VIEW

Ricasso

Blade inscribed
with religious
invocations

SPANISH CUP-HILT RAPIER

DATE	c. 1650	WEIGHT	2¼ lb (1.02 kg)
ORIGIN	Spain	LENGTH	38 in (96 cm)

In Spain, and those parts of Italy under Spanish influence,
the guard of the rapier became fully enclosed, producing
the "cup-hilt" guard form. A raised rim on the cup hilt
called the Rompepuntus was used to trap opponents' blades.

Scroll-work quillon
matches cup guard

Decorated steel grip

Pierced and
chiseled
metalwork

Rompepuntus

Plain bar quillon

Cup provides excellent
protection for hand

Bars act as
hand guard

ITALIAN SWEPT-HILT RAPIER

DATE	Early 17th century	WEIGHT	2¼ lb (1.02 kg)
ORIGIN	Italy	LENGTH	4⅓ ft (1.36 m)

This classic form of rapier is known as a swept-hilt, because the bars of the
guard sweep up in a graceful curve from the ricasso to the pommel. This
style of rapier remained in fashion until the early 17th century in both
military and civilian circles, largely because of its elegant appearance.

Maker's
name

FULL
VIEW

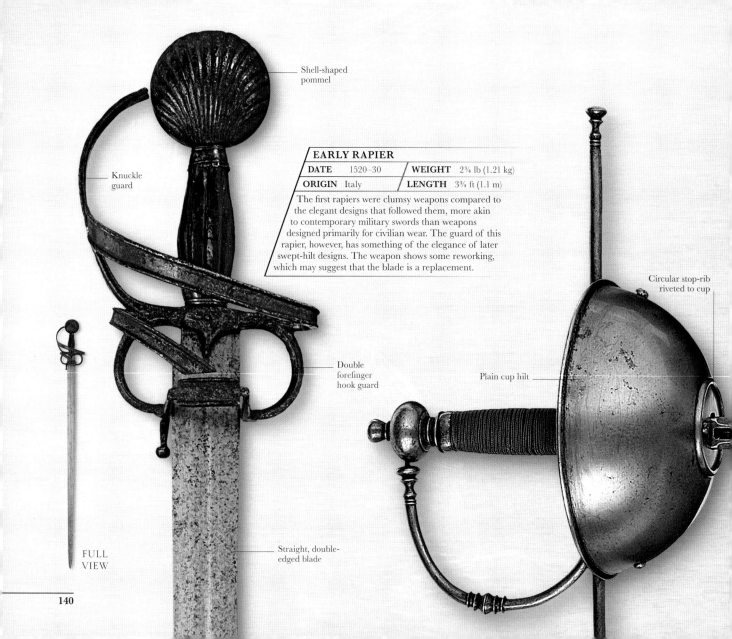

Shell-shaped
pommel

Knuckle
guard

EARLY RAPIER

DATE	1520–30	WEIGHT	2¾ lb (1.21 kg)
ORIGIN	Italy	LENGTH	3¾ ft (1.1 m)

The first rapiers were clumsy weapons compared to
the elegant designs that followed them, more akin
to contemporary military swords than weapons
designed primarily for civilian wear. The guard of this
rapier, however, has something of the elegance of later
swept-hilt designs. The weapon shows some reworking,
which may suggest that the blade is a replacement.

Double
forefinger
hook guard

Circular stop-rib
riveted to cup

Plain cup hilt

Straight, double-
edged blade

FULL
VIEW

Hilt designed to
provide added
protection

Thickened blade

FULL VIEW

ENGLISH SWEPT-HILT RAPIER

DATE	1590	WEIGHT	3 lb (1.39 kg)
ORIGIN	England	LENGTH	50½ in (128 cm)

Another variant of a swept-hilt rapier design, this
weapon might be less elegant than its counterparts,
but its small, perforated shell guards offered better
protection. In this example the grip is bound in woven
wire, which suggests this rapier was made as a dress
sword rather than for military use.

Swept hilt of
chiseled iron

Simple ricasso

Shallow diamond
cross-section blade

ITALIAN CUP-HILT RAPIER

DATE	c. 1680	WEIGHT	32 oz (900 g)
ORIGIN	Italy	LENGTH	4 ft (1.2 m)

Unlike other rapiers, this weapon, belonging to a later period, was
designed as a fencing piece rather than as a weapon, and hence denoted
gentlemanly status. It has an extremely narrow diamond cross-section
blade, and a simple, unadorned cup hilt.

FULL VIEW

EUROPEAN SMALLSWORDS

A development of the rapier, the smallsword came into general use in Western Europe toward the end of the 17th century. It was a civilian weapon—an essential item of dress for any gentleman that also acted as a dueling sword. Intended solely for thrusting, the smallsword typically had a stiff triangular blade, without sharpened edges, which in the hands of a skillful swordsman was a deadly fencing weapon. Although simple in overall design—the handguard consisting of a small cup, and finger and knuckle guards—many smallswords were magnificently decorated, reflecting the status of their owners.

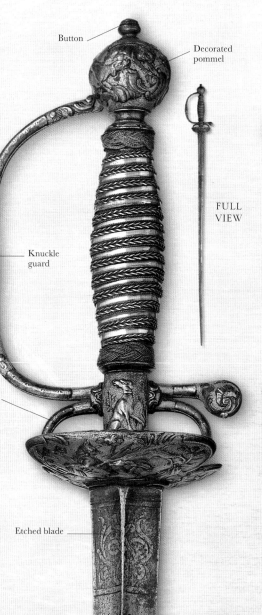

Button

Decorated pommel

FULL VIEW

Knuckle guard

Acorn button

Finger-guard branches

Etched blade

ETCHED SWORD

DATE	c. 1720	WEIGHT	14 oz (400 g)
ORIGIN	France	LENGTH	34¾ in (88.5 cm)

This fine sword is decorated with hunting scenes of hounds and game etched in relief against a matte gold background. The steel hilt has a spherical pommel and button, and the grip is bound with silver ribbon and plated silver wire.

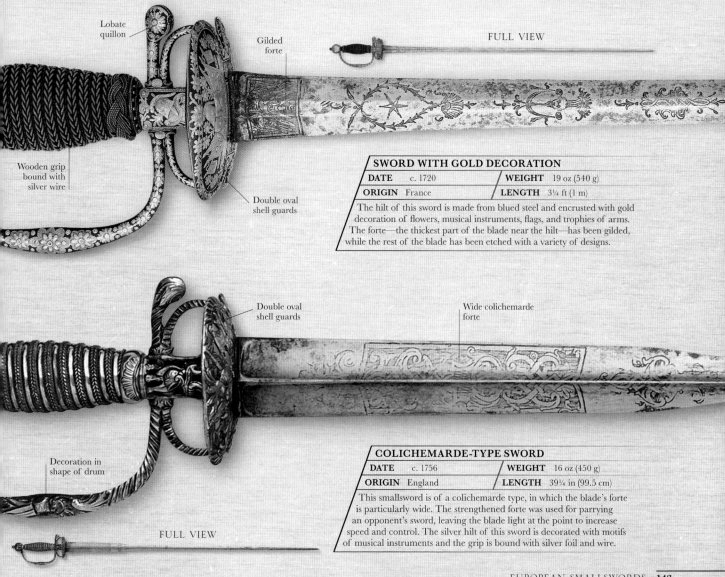

Lobate
quillon

Gilded
forte

FULL VIEW

Wooden grip
bound with
silver wire

Double oval
shell guards

SWORD WITH GOLD DECORATION

DATE	c. 1720	WEIGHT	19 oz (540 g)
ORIGIN	France	LENGTH	3¼ ft (1 m)

The hilt of this sword is made from blued steel and encrusted with gold
decoration of flowers, musical instruments, flags, and trophies of arms.
The forte—the thickest part of the blade near the hilt—has been gilded,
while the rest of the blade has been etched with a variety of designs.

Double oval
shell guards

Wide colichemarde
forte

Decoration in
shape of drum

FULL VIEW

COLICHEMARDE-TYPE SWORD

DATE	c. 1756	WEIGHT	16 oz (450 g)
ORIGIN	England	LENGTH	39¼ in (99.5 cm)

This smallsword is of a colichemarde type, in which the blade's forte
is particularly wide. The strengthened forte was used for parrying
an opponent's sword, leaving the blade light at the point to increase
speed and control. The silver hilt of this sword is decorated with motifs
of musical instruments and the grip is bound with silver foil and wire.

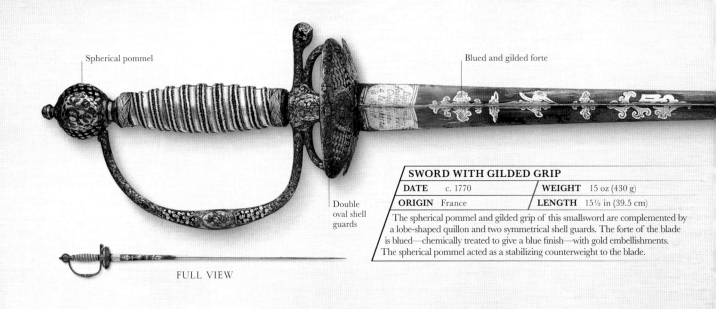

Spherical pommel

Blued and gilded forte

Double oval shell guards

FULL VIEW

SWORD WITH GILDED GRIP

| **DATE** c. 1770 | **WEIGHT** 15 oz (430 g) |
| **ORIGIN** France | **LENGTH** 15½ in (39.5 cm) |

The spherical pommel and gilded grip of this smallsword are complemented by a lobe-shaped quillon and two symmetrical shell guards. The forte of the blade is blued—chemically treated to give a blue finish—with gold embellishments. The spherical pommel acted as a stabilizing counterweight to the blade.

SWORD WITH WIRE KNUCKLE GUARD

| **DATE** c. 1825 | **WEIGHT** 16 oz (450 g) |
| **ORIGIN** England | **LENGTH** 39 in (99 cm) |

This sword's distinguishing features are the urn-shaped pommel, a knuckle guard of cut-steel beads strung on wire, and a dished oval guard decorated with pierced triangles in three rows. The blade is blued for much of its length with gold decoration.

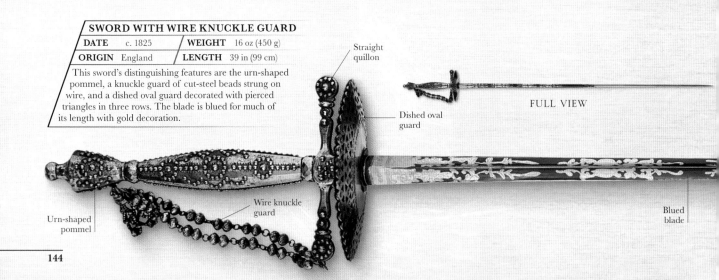

Straight quillon

FULL VIEW

Dished oval guard

Urn-shaped pommel

Wire knuckle guard

Blued blade

Urn-shaped
pommel

Wooden case with
velvet lining

Steel scabbard

FULL VIEW

CASE SWORD

DATE c. 1825	**WEIGHT** 16 oz (450 g)
ORIGIN England	**LENGTH** 39 in (99 cm)

Boxed within a sword case, this British smallsword has an urn-shaped
pommel, a faceted steel grip, and a knuckle guard of cut-steel beads
on wire. Below the straight quillons is a dished oval guard. The blade
is encased in a steel scabbard.

EUROPEAN HUNTING SWORDS

During the 16th century, specialized hunting swords came into widespread use among Europe's aristocracy. The swords were short in length and often had a slightly curved, single-edged blade, typically of very robust design to cope with the rigors of hunting. For the most part, hunting swords were used to finish off an animal wounded by a spear or shot. In the case of boar swords, however, they might act as the primary weapon, the boar being killed from horseback by a single powerful thrust. Hunting swords were often elaborately decorated and frequently featured engraved scenes of the chase. During the 18th century, the hanger hunting sword, with its short, curved, single-edged blade, acted as a model for the ordinary soldier's fighting sword.

Gilt pommel in shape of lion's head

Curved quillon terminating in lion's head

Cross-guard with acanthus leaf decoration

Shell guard with lion motif

Medici coat of arms

Single-edged blade

ITALIAN HUNTING HANGER			
DATE	c. 1550	**WEIGHT**	3½ lb (1.68 kg)
ORIGIN	Italy	**LENGTH**	24 in (61 cm)

This magnificently decorated hanger may have belonged to Cosimo de Medici (1519–74). It was probably used in the hunting of large game such as wolves or bears. The sword is decorated with the Medici coat of arms and has extensive gilt work on the cross-guard and pommel.

Mushroom-shaped pommel cap

Modern, velvet-covered grip

FULL VIEW

THE HUNTING SWORD
MEANT THE HUNTER DIDN'T HAVE TO
LOAD A FLINTLOCK GUN TO FINISH OFF
WOUNDED PREY.

Iron guard in shape of ribbons

Decorated quillon

ENGLISH HUNTING HANGER			
DATE	c. 1640	**WEIGHT**	30 oz (860 g)
ORIGIN	England	**LENGTH**	29½ in (75 cm)

This is an ornate hunting sword of the hanger type.
Its blackened iron hilt is decorated with encrusted
patterns in silver. The shell guard is formed as if of
three interlaced ribbon ends, and the decoration
at the pommel echoes this design.

Single-edged German blade

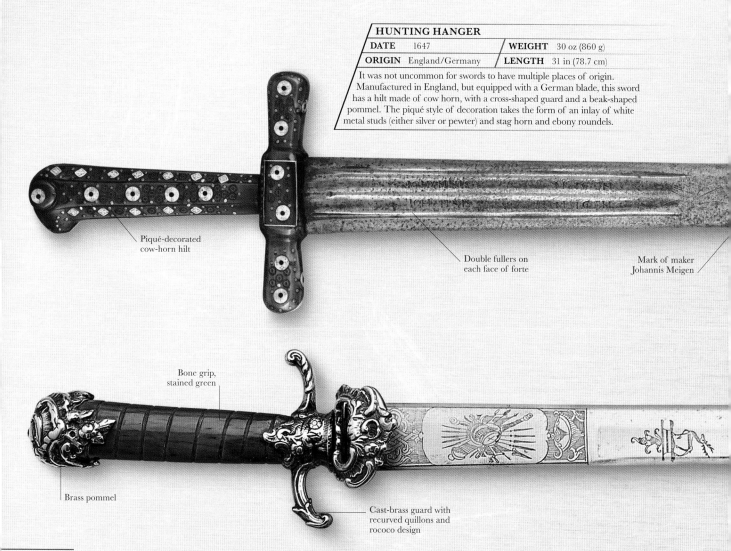

HUNTING HANGER

DATE	1647	WEIGHT	30 oz (860 g)
ORIGIN	England/Germany	LENGTH	31 in (78.7 cm)

It was not uncommon for swords to have multiple places of origin. Manufactured in England, but equipped with a German blade, this sword has a hilt made of cow horn, with a cross-shaped guard and a beak-shaped pommel. The piqué style of decoration takes the form of an inlay of white metal studs (either silver or pewter) and stag horn and ebony roundels.

Piqué-decorated
cow-horn hilt

Double fullers on
each face of forte

Mark of maker
Johannis Meigen

Bone grip,
stained green

Brass pommel

Cast-brass guard with
recurved quillons and
rococo design

IN 1600, SIR JOHN RAMSEY PLUNGED HIS HANGER INTO AN ASSASSIN WHO WAS ATTEMPTING TO KILL KING JAMES VI.

Double-edged blade
with hatchet point
(curved diagonal front edge)

STRAIGHT HANGER

DATE	c. 1780	**WEIGHT**	30 oz (860 g)
ORIGIN	France	**LENGTH**	29½ in (75 cm)

This short hunting sword from the late 18th century is
of a more decorative than functional design. The brass
guard and pommel are complemented by a straight,
finely engraved, single-edged blade.

Single-edged,
pointed blade

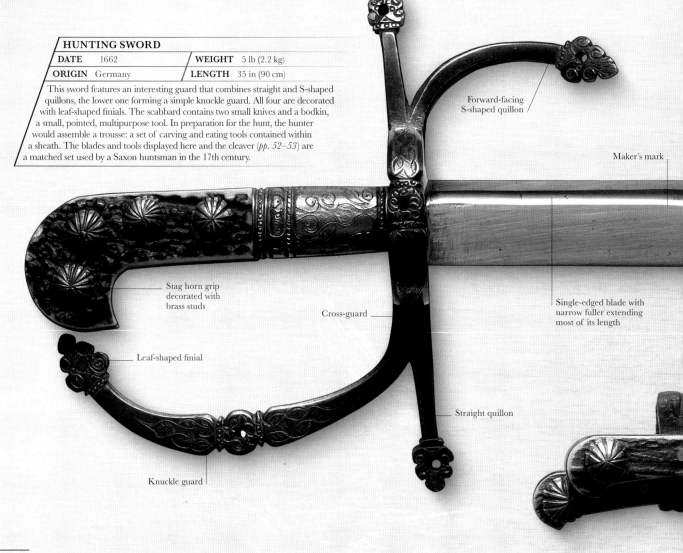

HUNTING SWORD

DATE	1662	WEIGHT	5 lb (2.2 kg)
ORIGIN	Germany	LENGTH	35 in (90 cm)

This sword features an interesting guard that combines straight and S-shaped quillons, the lower one forming a simple knuckle guard. All four are decorated with leaf-shaped finials. The scabbard contains two small knives and a bodkin, a small, pointed, multipurpose tool. In preparation for the hunt, the hunter would assemble a trousse: a set of carving and eating tools contained within a sheath. The blades and tools displayed here and the cleaver (*pp. 52–53*) are a matched set used by a Saxon huntsman in the 17th century.

Forward-facing
S-shaped quillon

Maker's mark

Stag horn grip
decorated with
brass studs

Cross-guard

Single-edged blade with
narrow fuller extending
most of its length

Leaf-shaped finial

Straight quillon

Knuckle guard

FULL VIEW

Pouch for knives
and bodkin

File for sharpening knives

Sharp tip for
making holes

BODKIN

SCABBARD

HUNTING CLEAVER

DATE	c. 1662	WEIGHT	2½ lb (1 kg)
ORIGIN	Germany	LENGTH	18 in (46 cm)

Once the hunting sword (*p. 150*) delivered the *coup de grace* to the wounded animal, the cleaver was used to dismember the carcass. This sharp, heavy blade would have little trouble in cutting through animal joints, including those of larger beasts such as boar and deer.

Guard

Maker's mark

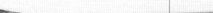

Sharp blade for trimming meat

CARVING KNIFE

Initials refer to the owner John George II, Elector of Saxony

Five meat-trimming utensils in side pocket

Heavy single-edged blade

SCABBARD

COSSACK WARRIOR

The Cossacks were a people of Eurasian or Slavic descent who established themselves in Ukraine and southern Russia sometime around the 14th century. They produced talented mounted soldiers, who fought in various state armies as raiders, scouts, and light cavalry.

The Cossacks were known for their skill with a blade. Their traditional sword, the *shashka*, was a single-edged saber-like weapon with a curved pommel, but no hand guard. It was ideal for slashing attacks while mounted on a horse, since the absence of a hand guard enabled the Cossack to make a cut using the full length of the blade. In addition to the *shashka*, the Cossacks also used a similarly designed short sword called a *kindjal*, which was used when fighting on foot or in close combat. Both of these slashing swords had very sharp points and could be used for thrusting, too. The Cossacks also used long lances, and although they quickly mastered muskets and rifles, Cossacks were known for their saber charges, which were recorded as late as World War I.

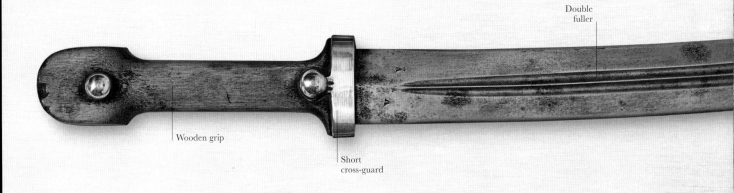

Double fuller

Wooden grip

Short cross-guard

> ## COSSACKS ARE THE BEST
> LIGHT TROOPS AMONG ALL THAT EXIST.
> ## IF I HAD THEM IN MY ARMY,
> ## I WOULD GO THROUGH
> ## ALL THE WORLD WITH THEM.

NAPOLEON I, FRENCH EMPEROR (r. 1804–14), ON THE COSSACKS
DURING THE NAPOLEONIC WARS (1799–1815)

KINDJAL

DATE	c. 18th century	**WEIGHT**	c. 24½ oz (700 g)
ORIGIN	Russia	**LENGTH**	c. 17 in (43 cm)

This curved short sword originated in the Caucasus, from
where it was adopted by the Cossacks, along with the
shashka. The wooden grip of the *kindjal* shown here is held
in place by brass rivets and the blade has a double fuller.
Sometimes triple fullers are also seen on both these swords.

RIDING HIGH

In this still from the 1965 film *Dr. Zhivago*, a mounted
Cossack warrior holds his sword aloft. The sword is
most likely a *shashka*, often used on horseback.
A warrior would use the shorter *kindjal* once he
was dismounted.

EUROPEAN DAGGERS

The dagger's prime role as a weapon of self-defense continued into the 16th and 17th centuries, and some new variants evolved, including the left-hand dagger, also known as the *maingauche* (French for left hand). This dagger was held in the left hand, to complement a sword or rapier held in the right. Typically with forward-facing quillons, the left-hand dagger parried thrusts and cuts from the opponent's blade, and also acted as an offensive weapon in its own right. The bayonet, another modification of the dagger, continues to be used to this day.

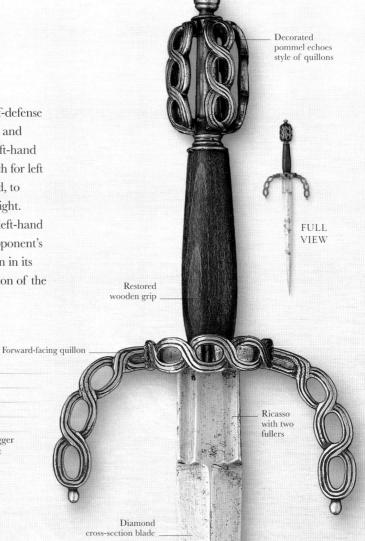

Decorated pommel echoes style of quillons

FULL VIEW

Restored wooden grip

Forward-facing quillon

QUILLON DAGGER

DATE	c. 1600
ORIGIN	Western Europe
LENGTH	16½ in (42 cm)

The forward-facing quillons of this left-hand dagger were intended to trap an opponent's blade so that it could be deflected safely. The ricasso here has two fullers to lighten what would otherwise be a weighty part of the blade.

Ricasso with two fullers

Diamond cross-section blade

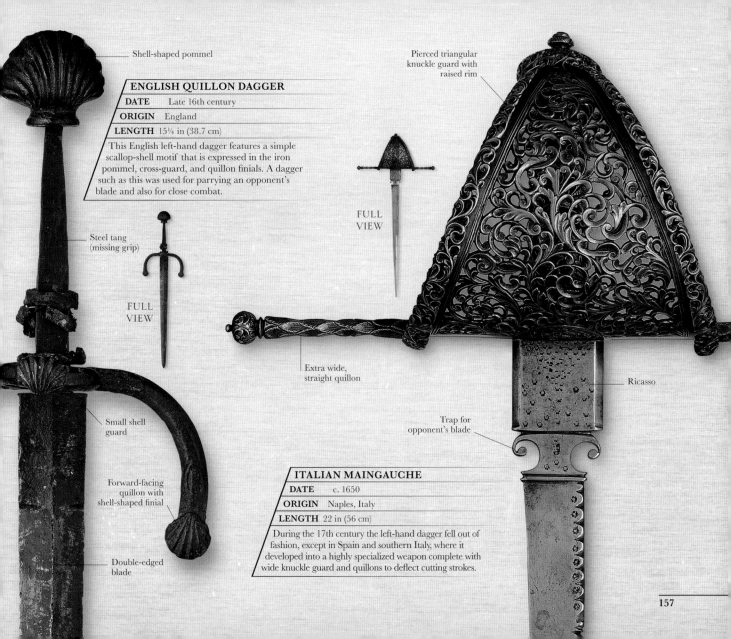

Shell-shaped pommel

Pierced triangular knuckle guard with raised rim

ENGLISH QUILLON DAGGER

DATE	Late 16th century
ORIGIN	England
LENGTH	15¼ in (38.7 cm)

This English left-hand dagger features a simple scallop-shell motif that is expressed in the iron pommel, cross-guard, and quillon finials. A dagger such as this was used for parrying an opponent's blade and also for close combat.

FULL VIEW

Steel tang (missing grip)

FULL VIEW

Small shell guard

Extra wide, straight quillon

Ricasso

Trap for opponent's blade

Forward-facing quillon with shell-shaped finial

ITALIAN MAINGAUCHE

DATE	c. 1650
ORIGIN	Naples, Italy
LENGTH	22 in (56 cm)

During the 17th century the left-hand dagger fell out of fashion, except in Spain and southern Italy, where it developed into a highly specialized weapon complete with wide knuckle guard and quillons to deflect cutting strokes.

Double-edged blade

Blade has three
etched foliate panels

Double-edged blade
with medial ridge

SCABBARD

Small scabbard for
extra knife (missing)

" IT WAS A SERVICEABLE DUDGEON
EITHER FOR FIGHTING OR FOR DRUDGING. "

SAMUEL BUTLER (1612–1680), POET AND SATIRIST, IN THE MOCK-EPIC POEM *HUDIBRAS*, 1662–64

Diamond-section,
double-edged blade

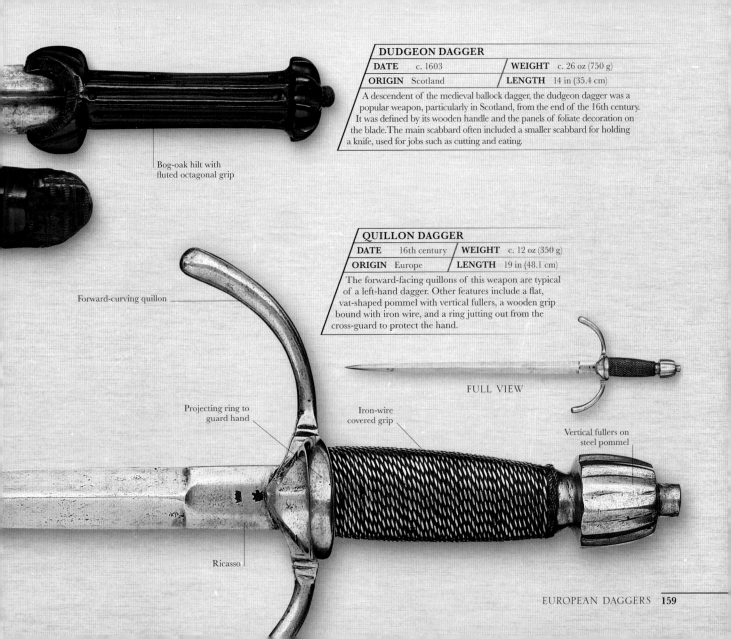

DUDGEON DAGGER

DATE	c. 1603	WEIGHT	c. 26 oz (750 g)
ORIGIN	Scotland	LENGTH	14 in (35.4 cm)

A descendent of the medieval ballock dagger, the dudgeon dagger was a popular weapon, particularly in Scotland, from the end of the 16th century. It was defined by its wooden handle and the panels of foliate decoration on the blade. The main scabbard often included a smaller scabbard for holding a knife, used for jobs such as cutting and eating.

Bog-oak hilt with fluted octagonal grip

QUILLON DAGGER

DATE	16th century	WEIGHT	c. 12 oz (350 g)
ORIGIN	Europe	LENGTH	19 in (48.1 cm)

The forward-facing quillons of this weapon are typical of a left-hand dagger. Other features include a flat, vat-shaped pommel with vertical fullers, a wooden grip bound with iron wire, and a ring jutting out from the cross-guard to protect the hand.

Forward-curving quillon

FULL VIEW

Projecting ring to guard hand

Iron-wire covered grip

Vertical fullers on steel pommel

Ricasso

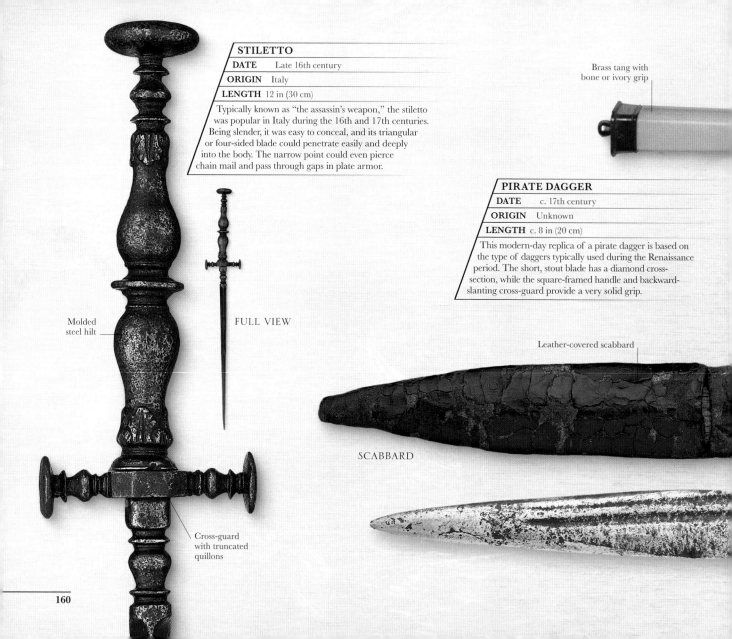

STILETTO

DATE	Late 16th century
ORIGIN	Italy
LENGTH	12 in (30 cm)

Typically known as "the assassin's weapon," the stiletto was popular in Italy during the 16th and 17th centuries. Being slender, it was easy to conceal, and its triangular or four-sided blade could penetrate easily and deeply into the body. The narrow point could even pierce chain mail and pass through gaps in plate armor.

Brass tang with bone or ivory grip

Molded steel hilt

FULL VIEW

Cross-guard with truncated quillons

PIRATE DAGGER

DATE	c. 17th century
ORIGIN	Unknown
LENGTH	c. 8 in (20 cm)

This modern-day replica of a pirate dagger is based on the type of daggers typically used during the Renaissance period. The short, stout blade has a diamond cross-section, while the square-framed handle and backward-slanting cross-guard provide a very solid grip.

Leather-covered scabbard

SCABBARD

Backward-curving
cross-guard

Diamond-section blade

SCABBARD

HIGHLAND DIRK

DATE	Early 18th century
ORIGIN	Scotland
LENGTH	12–18 in (30–45 cm)

In the 16th and 17th centuries, Scottish highlanders armed themselves with long, unadorned daggers called dirks. Like the dudgeon, the dirk evolved from the medieval ballock dagger (*pp. 80-81*). Toward the end of the 18th century the dirk became increasingly ceremonial in form. It was often decorated with silver pommel caps and ferrules (metal rings to secure the wrapping on the grip).

Wooden hilt with strap-
interlace work on grip

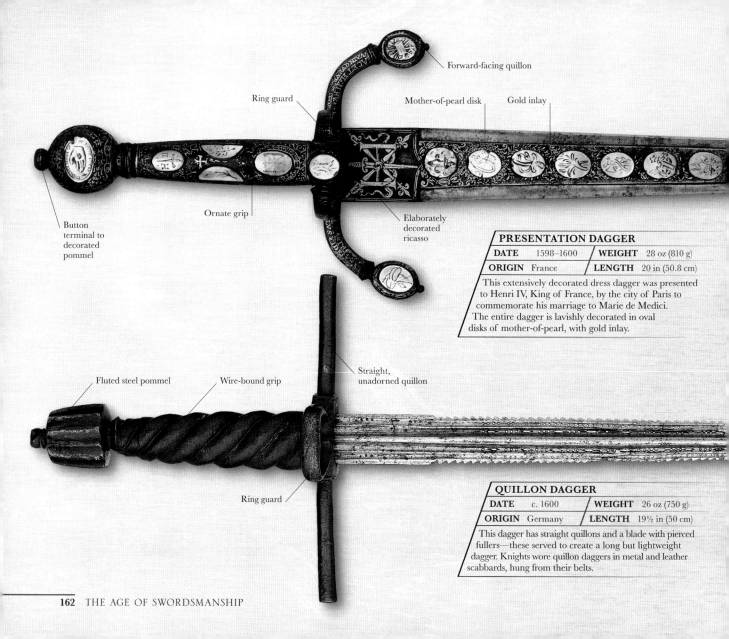

Forward-facing quillon

Ring guard

Mother-of-pearl disk   Gold inlay

Button
terminal to
decorated
pommel

Ornate grip

Elaborately
decorated
ricasso

PRESENTATION DAGGER

| DATE | 1598–1600 | WEIGHT | 28 oz (810 g) |
| ORIGIN | France | LENGTH | 20 in (50.8 cm) |

This extensively decorated dress dagger was presented
to Henri IV, King of France, by the city of Paris to
commemorate his marriage to Marie de Medici.
The entire dagger is lavishly decorated in oval
disks of mother-of-pearl, with gold inlay.

Fluted steel pommel   Wire-bound grip

Straight,
unadorned quillon

Ring guard

QUILLON DAGGER

| DATE | c. 1600 | WEIGHT | 26 oz (750 g) |
| ORIGIN | Germany | LENGTH | 19½ in (50 cm) |

This dagger has straight quillons and a blade with pierced
fullers—these served to create a long but lightweight
dagger. Knights wore quillon daggers in metal and leather
scabbards, hung from their belts.

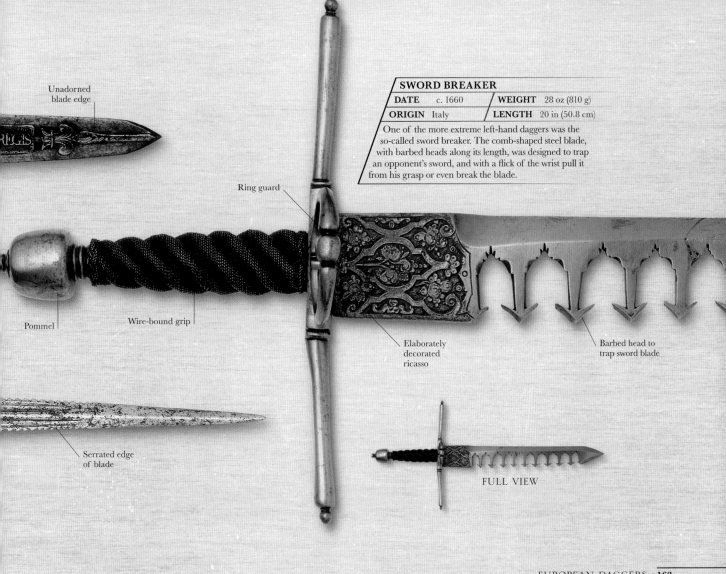

Unadorned
blade edge

SWORD BREAKER

| **DATE** | c. 1660 | **WEIGHT** | 28 oz (810 g) |
| **ORIGIN** | Italy | **LENGTH** | 20 in (50.8 cm) |

One of the more extreme left-hand daggers was the
so-called sword breaker. The comb-shaped steel blade,
with barbed heads along its length, was designed to trap
an opponent's sword, and with a flick of the wrist pull it
from his grasp or even break the blade.

Ring guard

Pommel

Wire-bound grip

Elaborately
decorated
ricasso

Barbed head to
trap sword blade

Serrated edge
of blade

FULL VIEW

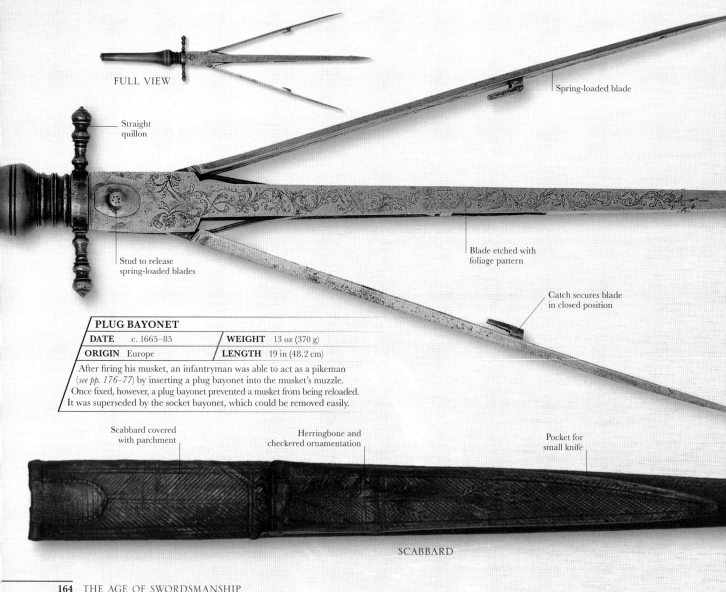

FULL VIEW

Straight
quillon

Spring-loaded blade

Stud to release
spring-loaded blades

Blade etched with
foliage pattern

Catch secures blade
in closed position

PLUG BAYONET

DATE	c. 1665–85	**WEIGHT**	13 oz (370 g)
ORIGIN	Europe	**LENGTH**	19 in (48.2 cm)

After firing his musket, an infantryman was able to act as a pikeman
(*see pp. 176–77*) by inserting a plug bayonet into the musket's muzzle.
Once fixed, however, a plug bayonet prevented a musket from being reloaded.
It was superseded by the socket bayonet, which could be removed easily.

Scabbard covered
with parchment

Herringbone and
checkered ornamentation

Pocket for
small knife

SCABBARD

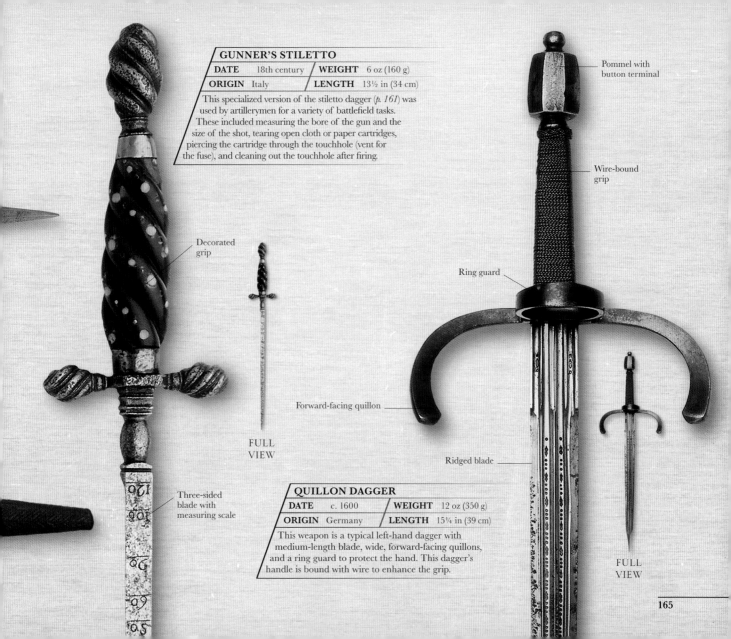

GUNNER'S STILETTO

DATE	18th century	WEIGHT	6 oz (160 g)
ORIGIN	Italy	LENGTH	13½ in (34 cm)

This specialized version of the stiletto dagger (*p. 161*) was used by artillerymen for a variety of battlefield tasks. These included measuring the bore of the gun and the size of the shot, tearing open cloth or paper cartridges, piercing the cartridge through the touchhole (vent for the fuse), and cleaning out the touchhole after firing.

Decorated grip

FULL VIEW

Three-sided blade with measuring scale

Pommel with button terminal

Wire-bound grip

Ring guard

Forward-facing quillon

Ridged blade

QUILLON DAGGER

DATE	c. 1600	WEIGHT	12 oz (350 g)
ORIGIN	Germany	LENGTH	15¼ in (39 cm)

This weapon is a typical left-hand dagger with medium-length blade, wide, forward-facing quillons, and a ring guard to protect the hand. This dagger's handle is bound with wire to enhance the grip.

FULL VIEW

LANDSKNECHT

The Landsknecht ("land servants") were German-speaking infantry formed under the authority of German Emperor Maximilian I in 1486, in response to threats from French and Burgundian mercenaries and Swiss pikemen.

Essentially swords for hire, the Landsknecht were lured into service from central and northern Europe by decent pay, opportunities to plunder, and a life of adventure. With their militarily unorthodox style of dress, the Landsknecht mercenaries cut a dash on the battlefield during the 15th and 16th centuries. Yet their flamboyant clothing masked the violent and unpredictable nature of these men. Most Landsknecht were armed with pikes (*pp. 176–77*), which were cheap to purchase, but *doppelsöldner* ("double-pay men") were specialists in using the *Zweihander* ("two-handed") broadsword to smash their way into enemy ranks. Landsknecht soldiers were loyal up to the point they were paid—Landsknecht bands sacked Rome in 1527 over unpaid wages.

Long double-handed grip to help balance weight

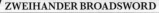

ZWEIHANDER BROADSWORD

DATE	c. 1550	WEIGHT	7 lb (3.18 kg)
ORIGIN	Germany	LENGTH	4½ ft (1.4 m)

This two-handed broadsword was designed as a battlefield weapon and is of a type used by the Landsknecht. The sword has a blunt tip because it was intended to be used to hack through enemy units rather than to pierce its victims.

Parrying lugs deflect enemy's sword strikes

Straight cross-guard

> ## "WE TOOK ROME BY STORM, PUT OVER 6000 MEN TO THE SWORD, AND BURNED DOWN A GREAT PART OF THE CITY."
>
> PAUL DOLSTEIN, LANDSKNECHT, ON THE SACK OF ROME, 1527

Blade sharpened on one edge

FLAMBOYANT WARRIOR

This stained glass panel depicts a standard bearer dressed in the typically florid style of the Landsknecht, including colored hose and a hat crowned with feathers. He carries a two-handed broadsword with forward-curving quillons.

EUROPEAN ONE-HANDED STAFF WEAPONS

Single-handed staff weapons were developed for use by horsemen. These were simple but brutal weapons whose primary role was to fracture plate armor or inflict internal injuries to an opponent. The pick or spike of a war hammer was useful for penetrating gaps in enemy armor, while the flanges, or projections, on mace heads could be sharpened into bladelike edges. A crushing blow from a staff weapon would have dented the joints of an opponent's armor, limiting his ability to move and fight. Despite their clublike nature, many staff weapons were carried by men of high birth and, as a result, were finely crafted and elaborately decorated.

THE PICK OF A BATTLE HAMMER COULD BECOME STUCK FAST IN THE BODY OF ITS VICTIM.

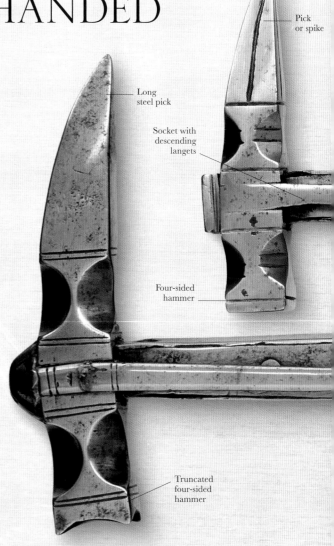

Pick or spike

Long steel pick

Socket with descending langets

Four-sided hammer

Truncated four-sided hammer

FULL VIEW

HORSEMAN'S HAMMER

DATE	16th century	WEIGHT	11¾ lb (5.4 kg)
ORIGIN	Germany	LENGTH	21½ in (54.6 cm)

This four-sided hammer is counterbalanced by a longer pick that is also four-sided. The square-shaped socket extends into four langets that run down the sides of the wooden shaft. This war hammer would have been part of the armament of a cavalryman.

HORSEMAN'S HAMMER

DATE	16th century	WEIGHT	Head: 29 oz (820 g)
ORIGIN	Europe	LENGTH	Head: 8½ in (21.5 cm)

Popular with cavalrymen for smashing plate armor, war hammers were also used by those fighting on foot in tournaments. During the 16th century, the size of the pick was increased, while the hammer was made smaller. This suggested a more central role for the pick in combat.

FULL VIEW

MACE WITH FLANGED HEAD

DATE	16th century	WEIGHT	3½ lb (1.56 kg)
ORIGIN	Europe	LENGTH	24¾ in (62.9 cm)

From the late 15th century, most maces were made of steel, with a number of flanges on the mace head—seven was a common number. Each flange was attached to a central tubular core by brazing, in which different metal parts were joined together by fusing a layer of brass between the adjoining surfaces.

Steel finial

Flange brazed to central core

MACE WITH CONICAL FINIAL

DATE	16th century	WEIGHT	3½ lb (1.56 kg)
ORIGIN	Europe	LENGTH	23 in (60 cm)

Made of steel, this mace has a conical finial fitted above seven flanges, each of which is drawn to a concave-sided point. The shaft is decorated with scrolling vine foliage in shallow relief. The flanged mace was the most common type of mace in use during the 16th century.

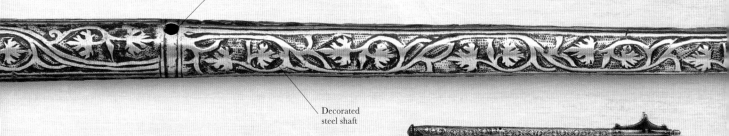

Wrist-loop hole

Decorated steel shaft

FULL VIEW

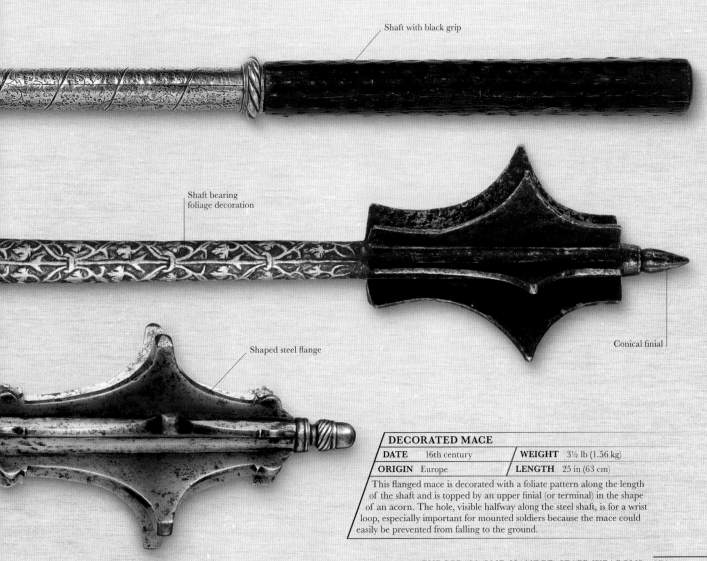

Shaft with black grip

Shaft bearing
foliage decoration

Conical finial

Shaped steel flange

DECORATED MACE

DATE	16th century	**WEIGHT**	3½ lb (1.56 kg)
ORIGIN	Europe	**LENGTH**	25 in (63 cm)

This flanged mace is decorated with a foliate pattern along the length of the shaft and is topped by an upper finial (or terminal) in the shape of an acorn. The hole, visible halfway along the steel shaft, is for a wrist loop, especially important for mounted soldiers because the mace could easily be prevented from falling to the ground.

EUROPEAN TWO-HANDED STAFF WEAPONS

Staff weapons, especially when combined with bows, had proved highly effective against cavalry during the Middle Ages. They gave the infantryman the ability to keep the enemy horse and rider at a distance. Few horses had the spirit to surmount a bristling wall of blades, while the length of the staff weapons enabled the infantryman to strike the mounted soldier up in the saddle. In the 16th century they continued to be the foot soldier's most effective weapon. Swiss mercenaries popularized the halberd (*p. 87*), which, in the hands of a strong man, was capable of smashing through plate armor. So was the poleax, the weapon favored by armored knights when fighting on foot. By the early 17th century, these weapons were steadily replaced by the pike (*pp. 176–77*).

Steel spike

FULL VIEW

Hammer or fluke

Axhead

Langet protecting wooden shaft

POLEAX

DATE   16th century

ORIGIN   Germany

LENGTH   Axhead: 11 in (28 cm)

Popular in the 15th and 16th centuries with knights fighting on foot, the poleax consisted of an axhead balanced by a hammer or fluke that was topped by a steel spike. All three were useful elements in penetrating plate armor. The weapon's name derives from "poll," the old English name for head.

Edged blade

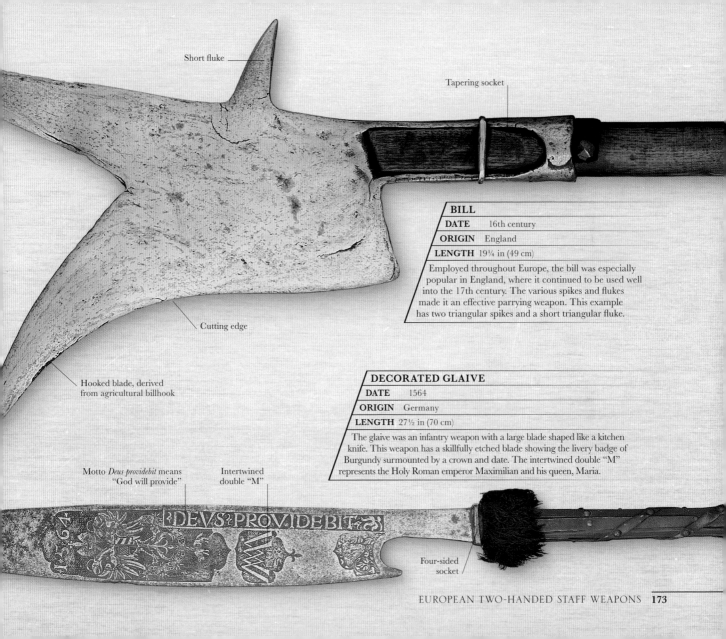

Short fluke

Tapering socket

BILL

DATE	16th century
ORIGIN	England
LENGTH	19¼ in (49 cm)

Employed throughout Europe, the bill was especially popular in England, where it continued to be used well into the 17th century. The various spikes and flukes made it an effective parrying weapon. This example has two triangular spikes and a short triangular fluke.

Cutting edge

Hooked blade, derived from agricultural billhook

DECORATED GLAIVE

DATE	1564
ORIGIN	Germany
LENGTH	27½ in (70 cm)

The glaive was an infantry weapon with a large blade shaped like a kitchen knife. This weapon has a skillfully etched blade showing the livery badge of Burgundy surmounted by a crown and date. The intertwined double "M" represents the Holy Roman emperor Maximilian and his queen, Maria.

Motto *Deus providebit* means "God will provide"

Intertwined double "M"

DEVS·PROVIDEBIT

Four-sided socket

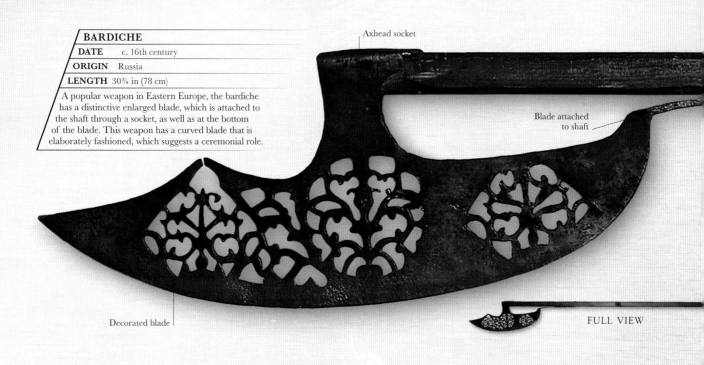

BARDICHE

DATE	c. 16th century
ORIGIN	Russia
LENGTH	30¾ in (78 cm)

A popular weapon in Eastern Europe, the bardiche has a distinctive enlarged blade, which is attached to the shaft through a socket, as well as at the bottom of the blade. This weapon has a curved blade that is elaborately fashioned, which suggests a ceremonial role.

Axhead socket

Blade attached to shaft

Decorated blade

FULL VIEW

One of four langets

THE BRUTAL HOOKED FLUKE
OF THE HALBERD WAS SUNK INTO A CAVALRYMAN'S ARMOR
AND USED TO DRAG HIM TO THE GROUND.

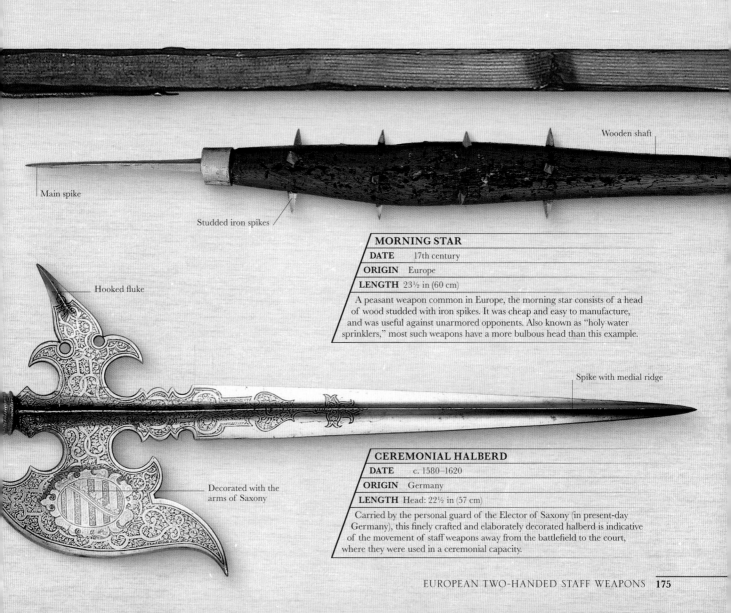

Wooden shaft

Main spike

Studded iron spikes

MORNING STAR

DATE	17th century
ORIGIN	Europe
LENGTH	23½ in (60 cm)

A peasant weapon common in Europe, the morning star consists of a head of wood studded with iron spikes. It was cheap and easy to manufacture, and was useful against unarmored opponents. Also known as "holy water sprinklers," most such weapons have a more bulbous head than this example.

Hooked fluke

Spike with medial ridge

Decorated with the arms of Saxony

CEREMONIAL HALBERD

DATE	c. 1580–1620
ORIGIN	Germany
LENGTH	Head: 22½ in (57 cm)

Carried by the personal guard of the Elector of Saxony (in present-day Germany), this finely crafted and elaborately decorated halberd is indicative of the movement of staff weapons away from the battlefield to the court, where they were used in a ceremonial capacity.

PIKEMAN

Pikemen had a profound effect on warfare in Europe from the 14th to the 18th century. The pike weapon reached up to 18 ft (5 m) in length—much longer than a traditional spear—and was capped by a hefty spearhead. When used on its own, the pike was a cumbersome, heavy weapon, but used in massed ranks, it revolutionized warfare. Pike-armed infantry, known as pikemen, were usually formed into squares—solid blocks of up to 100 men each, arranged in a 10-by-10 rank configuration. These blocks bristled with pikes. When attacking enemy ranks,

the pikemen would advance, at first with the pikes held high, then with the spearheads lowered, creating a layered wall of blades for the final offensive thrust. If they were surrounded by enemy cavalry, pikemen presented their pikes in a 360-degree pattern to keep the mounted troops at bay. Swiss and German pikeman were, for a time, almost invincible in battle, but with the rise of the use of firearms and the advent of the bayonet, the pike as an infantry weapon had almost become obsolete by the end of the 17th century.

Simple
wooden shaft

PIKE			
DATE	c. 15th century	**WEIGHT**	c. 11 lb (5 kg)
ORIGIN	Europe	**LENGTH**	c. 18 ft (5 m)

This pike shows the essential simplicity of the weapon. The spearhead is of a double-edged, leaf-style design, and is riveted onto the long wooden shaft. If the pole broke or became too weak, the spearhead was easily detached and could then be attached to another pole.

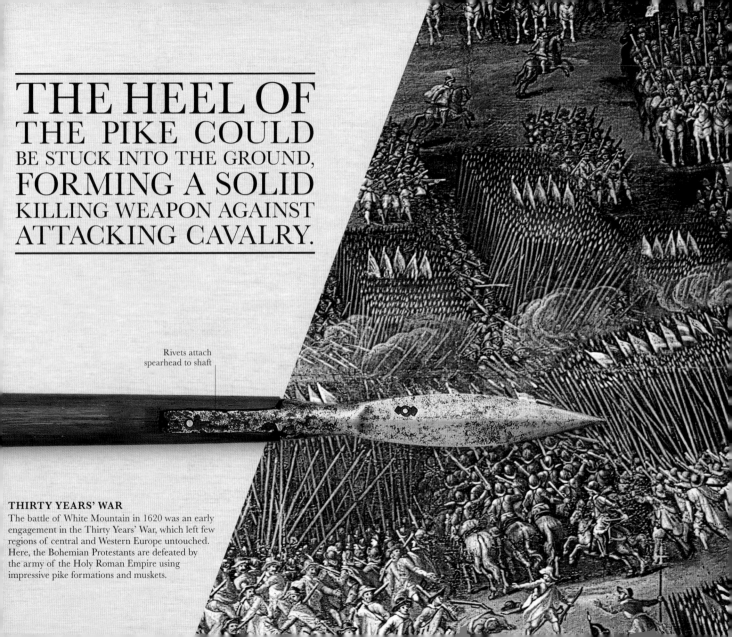

THE HEEL OF
THE PIKE COULD
BE STUCK INTO THE GROUND,
FORMING A SOLID
KILLING WEAPON AGAINST
ATTACKING CAVALRY.

Rivets attach
spearhead to shaft

THIRTY YEARS' WAR
The battle of White Mountain in 1620 was an early
engagement in the Thirty Years' War, which left few
regions of central and Western Europe untouched.
Here, the Bohemian Protestants are defeated by
the army of the Holy Roman Empire using
impressive pike formations and muskets.

INDIAN AND SRI LANKAN SWORDS

The establishment of the Mogul empire in India in the 16th century brought with it the fine curved swords found throughout India, Sri Lanka, and the Islamic world. These *talwars* and *shamshirs* were superb cutting instruments that achieved near perfection in form and function. Although many Hindu princes adopted the *talwar*, the traditional straight-bladed Hindu *khanda* continued to be made. By the 18th century, many sword blades were imported from Europe, where they were being manufactured in Indian designs.

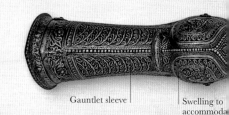

Gauntlet sleeve

Swelling to accommodate grip

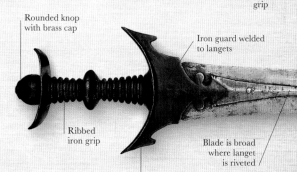

Rounded knop with brass cap

Iron guard welded to langets

Ribbed iron grip

Spiked flares

Blade is broad where langet is riveted

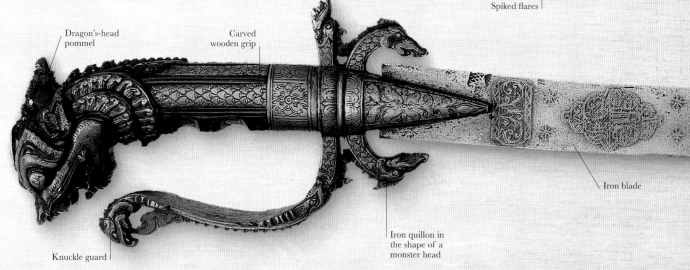

Dragon's-head pommel

Carved wooden grip

Iron blade

Knuckle guard

Iron quillon in the shape of a monster head

Solingen maker's mark

GAUNTLET SWORD

DATE	17th century	WEIGHT	c. 29 oz (800 g)
ORIGIN	Germany/India	LENGTH	c. 3½ ft (1.12 m)

This 17th-century Indian gauntlet sword was a fearsome thrusting weapon. The gauntlet sleeve provided excellent protection to the hand and the wrist. The blade was made in Solingen, a sword-producing center in Germany. Good-quality European blades were often used in Asia, and vice versa.

Double-edged blade

MALABAR COAST SWORD

DATE	18th century	WEIGHT	23 oz (650 g)
ORIGIN	Malabar, India	LENGTH	33 in (83 cm)

This straight, double-edged sword from southern India has a ribbed iron grip and a curved guard and pommel plate. Spiked flares on the sides of the guard prevented the sword from being grabbed from the swordsman's hand. Langets were riveted to the blade to strengthen its attachment to the hilt.

Brass-wire inlay decoration

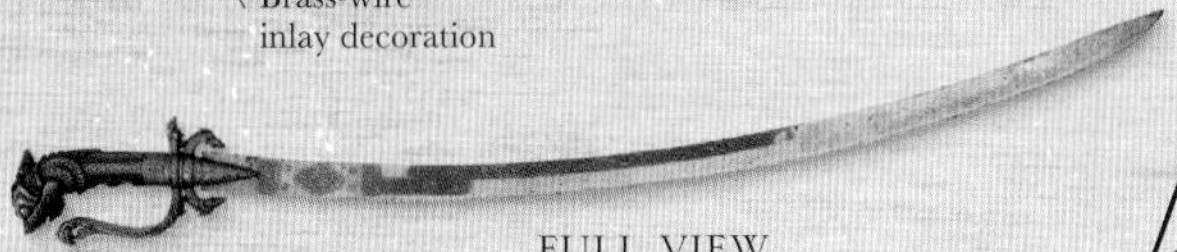

KASTANE

DATE	Hilt: 17th century	WEIGHT	20 oz (550 g)
ORIGIN	Sri Lanka	LENGTH	36 in (92 cm)

The *kastane*, the characteristic sword of Sri Lanka, had a short, curved blade, usually imported, and a hilt carved with fantastical decorations. Its value as a work of craftsmanship equaled its effectiveness as a weapon. The example shown here dates from the time of the Portuguese occupation of Sri Lanka.

FULL VIEW

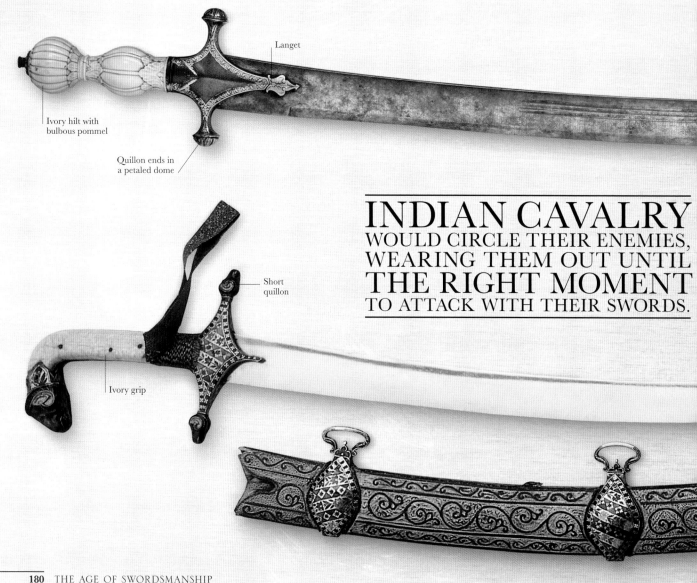

Langet

Ivory hilt with
bulbous pommel

Quillon ends in
a petaled dome

Short
quillon

Ivory grip

INDIAN CAVALRY
WOULD CIRCLE THEIR ENEMIES,
WEARING THEM OUT UNTIL
THE RIGHT MOMENT
TO ATTACK WITH THEIR SWORDS.

Curved
steel blade

Deeply curved,
tapering blade

TALWAR

DATE	Early 17th century	WEIGHT	2¼ lb (1.04 kg)
ORIGIN	Mogul India	LENGTH	37¾ in (95.7 cm)

The *talwar*, of Persian origin, was the quintessential sword of
Mogul India. Many were works of outstanding craftsmanship.
The curve of this *talwar* is more shallow than those of swords
produced later in the Mogul period.

SHAMSHIR

DATE	Early 19th century	WEIGHT	30 oz (860 g)
ORIGIN	Lucknow, India	LENGTH	37 in (93 cm)

The *shamshir* is the sword known to Europeans as the scimitar.
It came to India in the 16th century from Persia. This example
follows the typical Persian design, with its deeply curved, single-edged,
tapering blade. In combat, it was superbly suited to slashing, but
less effective for thrusting.

SCABBARD

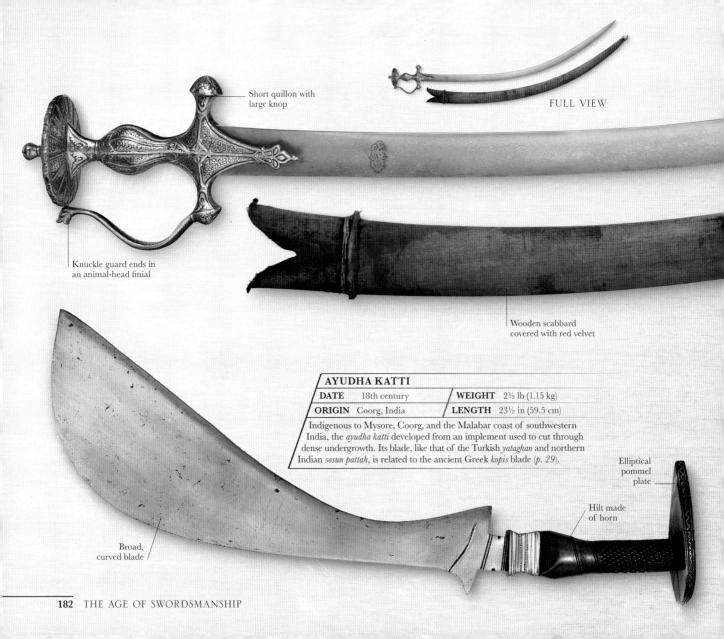

Short quillon with
large knop

FULL VIEW

Knuckle guard ends in
an animal-head finial

Wooden scabbard
covered with red velvet

AYUDHA KATTI

DATE	18th century	**WEIGHT**	2½ lb (1.15 kg)
ORIGIN	Coorg, India	**LENGTH**	23½ in (59.5 cm)

Indigenous to Mysore, Coorg, and the Malabar coast of southwestern
India, the *ayudha katti* developed from an implement used to cut through
dense undergrowth. Its blade, like that of the Turkish *yataghan* and northern
Indian *sosun pattah*, is related to the ancient Greek *kopis* blade (*p. 29*).

Elliptical
pommel
plate

Hilt made
of horn

Broad,
curved blade

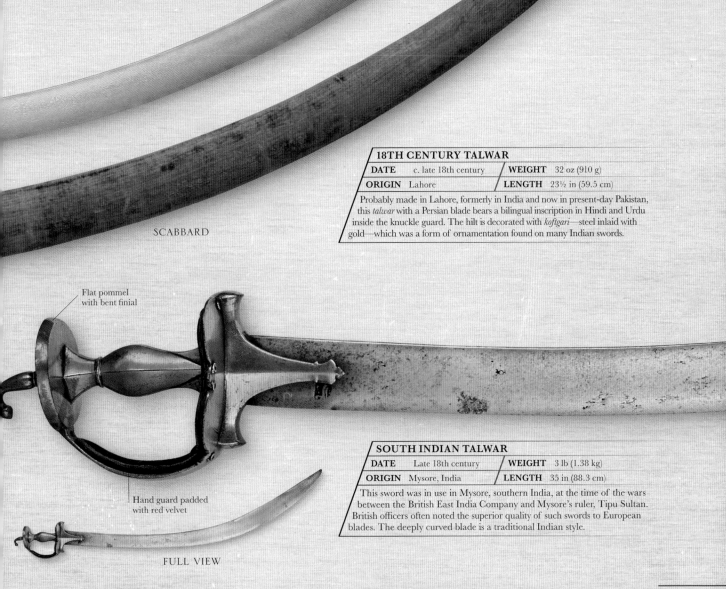

SCABBARD

18TH CENTURY TALWAR

DATE	c. late 18th century	WEIGHT	32 oz (910 g)
ORIGIN	Lahore	LENGTH	23½ in (59.5 cm)

Probably made in Lahore, formerly in India and now in present-day Pakistan, this *talwar* with a Persian blade bears a bilingual inscription in Hindi and Urdu inside the knuckle guard. The hilt is decorated with *koftgari*—steel inlaid with gold—which was a form of ornamentation found on many Indian swords.

Flat pommel
with bent finial

Hand guard padded
with red velvet

SOUTH INDIAN TALWAR

DATE	Late 18th century	WEIGHT	3 lb (1.38 kg)
ORIGIN	Mysore, India	LENGTH	35 in (88.3 cm)

This sword was in use in Mysore, southern India, at the time of the wars between the British East India Company and Mysore's ruler, Tipu Sultan. British officers often noted the superior quality of such swords to European blades. The deeply curved blade is a traditional Indian style.

FULL VIEW

INDIAN STAFF
WEAPONS

Until the 17th century, the development of staff weapons in the
Indian subcontinent was broadly similar to their evolution in
Europe, although local Hindu traditions and the influence of
Muslim invaders ensured notable differences in design and
decoration. Despite the adoption of Western-style firearms by
Indian rulers, maces and axes were actively used by Indian
armies long after they had become obsolete in Europe.
This was largely because Indian warriors continued to
wear armor. At close quarters, a staff weapon was often
more effective than a musket and bayonet or rifle.

Plain knop

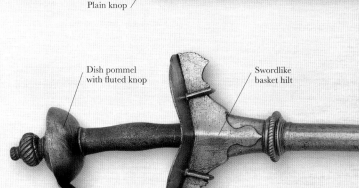

Dish pommel
with fluted knop

Swordlike
basket hilt

Shaft and blade have
sheet-silver decoration

Tubular iron shaft
contains thin knife

FULL VIEW

TABAR

DATE	18th century	WEIGHT	2¾ lb (1.29 kg)
ORIGIN	Sindh	LENGTH	28 in (71.3 cm)

The saddle ax, or *tabar*, was a standard weapon of Indian armies.
This example is from Sindh, in what is now Pakistan. The curved
cutting edge concentrated the weight of a blow at a narrow point
of impact. Unscrewing the knop at the base of the weapon reveals
a slim knife, 21¼ in (54 cm) long, inside the hollow shaft.

Iron shaft

Rounded flange ends
in bird-head design

CHILD'S MACE

DATE	18th century	WEIGHT	7.5 oz (220 g)
ORIGIN	Northern India	LENGTH	13 in (32.8 cm)

With less than a tenth of the weight of a full-sized weapon and around a third of the length, this miniature mace was designed to be used by a child. It may have been employed for early military training. The head has eight rounded flanges, and is topped by a small, ribbed knop.

Sharpened
spiral flanges

Iron shaft

FLANGED MACE

DATE	18th century	WEIGHT	5½ lb (2.55 kg)
ORIGIN	Rajasthan, India	LENGTH	33¼ in (84.2 cm)

This mace, or *gorz*, has a knuckle guard in the Hindu basket style, as often seen on *khanda* swords (*p. 289*). The spiral flanges on the head are sharpened to a cutting edge. The flanges focused the impact of a blow from this heavy weapon, making it effective even against armor.

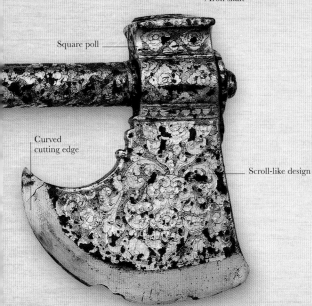
Square poll

Curved
cutting edge

Scroll-like design

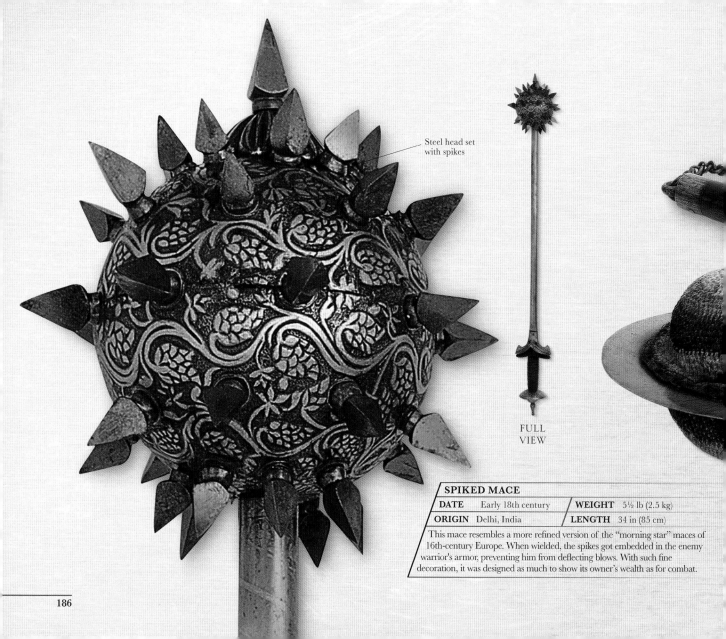

Steel head set
with spikes

FULL
VIEW

SPIKED MACE

DATE	Early 18th century	**WEIGHT**	5½ lb (2.5 kg)
ORIGIN	Delhi, India	**LENGTH**	34 in (85 cm)

This mace resembles a more refined version of the "morning star" maces of 16th-century Europe. When wielded, the spikes got embedded in the enemy warrior's armor, preventing him from deflecting blows. With such fine decoration, it was designed as much to show its owner's wealth as for combat.

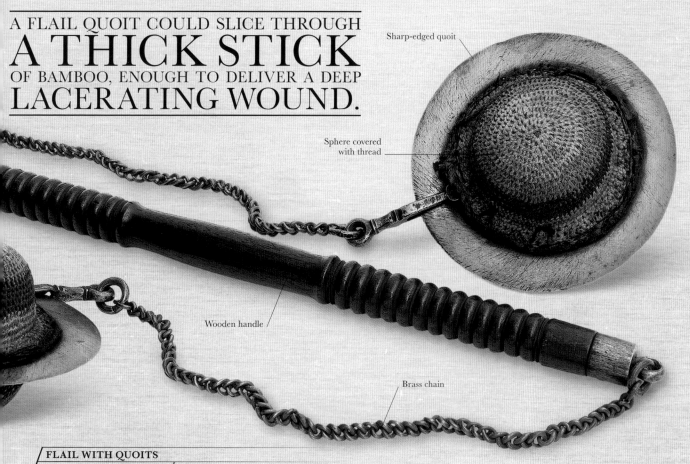

A FLAIL QUOIT COULD SLICE THROUGH A THICK STICK OF BAMBOO, ENOUGH TO DELIVER A DEEP LACERATING WOUND.

Sharp-edged quoit

Sphere covered
with thread

Wooden handle

Brass chain

FLAIL WITH QUOITS

DATE	18th century	WEIGHT	2¼ lb (1.05 kg)
ORIGIN	Gujarat, India	LENGTH	Handle: 18½ in (46.8 cm)

This flail, or *cumberjung*, was made in Gujarat when the area was under the
rule of the Hindu Maratha Empire. The handle was whirled to send the
sharp-edged quoits (flattened metal rings) scything through the air. A fearsome
weapon in close combat, it required considerable skill to use it effectively.

CUTTING AND THRUSTING

During the 18th and 19th centuries, there was much argument in military circles over the relative merits of cutting swords as opposed to thrusting blades in warfare and self-defense.

Most swords and daggers could be used for both cutting and thrusting to some degree, such as the Turkish dagger shown below. Nevertheless, specialized weapons remained popular throughout the world. Sabers (*pp. 130–31*) and *katanas*

(*pp. 190–91*) had long cutting edges that were perfect for slashing attacks, while rapiers (*pp. 138–41*) and smallswords (*pp. 142–45*) were designed primarily to injure with the point of the blade. In an 18th-century treatise on defense, Captain John Godfrey recommended that slashing swords (which he called backswords) be used in battle, where there were many targets to attack, while smallswords be confined to duels and civilian use. Godfrey proved to be correct, and, by the 19th century, the military had indeed gravitated toward the cutting saber, while the rapierlike sword was largely confined to civilian and sporting use.

TURKISH DAGGER			
DATE	c. 19th century	**WEIGHT**	c. 11 oz (300 g)
ORIGIN	Turkey	**LENGTH**	c. 12 in (30.5 cm)

This highly ornate Turkish dagger is a cut-and-thrust weapon, with a curved, double-edged blade tapering to a very fine point. The blade has cutaway sections for decoration, while the green agate handle is decorated with garnets.

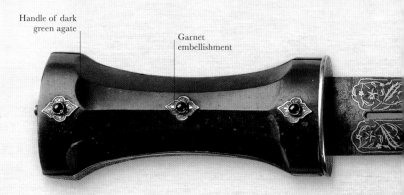

Handle of dark green agate

Garnet embellishment

TAKE NOTICE OF THE SUPERIORITY
THE BACK-SWORD
HAS OVER THE SMALL,
IN POINT OF USE.

CAPTAIN JOHN GODFREY, *A TREATISE UPON THE USEFUL SCIENCE OF DEFENCE*, 1747

CLOSE-QUARTERS COMBAT

Daggers, aside from the very slender stiletto type, are the archetypal cut-and-thrust weapons, usually designed for both piercing and laceration. In this Mogul painting from India, a warrior makes a stabbing attack on his opponent, using the point of his curved dagger.

Ornate blade with
gold inlay work

JAPANESE SAMURAI WEAPONS

Japanese sword blades are considered to be among the finest ever made. Their success was due to the combination of a hard cutting edge with a softer, more resilient core and back. After a complex process creating a soft core enfolded in hard outer layers of steel, the swordsmith covered the blade in clay, leaving only a thin layer over what was to become the cutting edge. During quenching (*pp. 98–99*), the edge cools rapidly, becoming very hard, while the back cools more slowly, remaining less hard but more flexible. The mountings for blades developed their own aesthetic finesse. In the 15th century, for example, the manufacture of *tsuba* (guards) became a separate profession, and these are now collectors' items in their own right.

Engraved metal
sayajira (sheath cap)

> **"**
> ——————————————————
> FIRST OF ALL, WHEN YOU LIFT UP THE SWORD,
> WHATEVER THE SITUATION YOUR INTENTION IS TO
> # KILL THE OPPONENT.
> ——————————————————
> SAMURAI MIYAMOTO MUSASHI (c. 1584–1645), *THE BOOK OF FIVE RINGS*, c. 1643 **"**

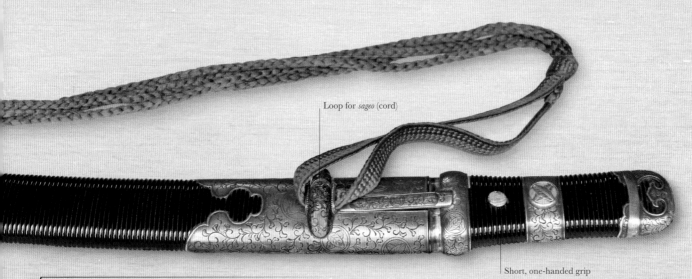

Loop for *sageo* (cord)

Short, one-handed grip

TANTO IN SCABBARD

DATE	c. 18th century	WEIGHT	19 oz (550 g)
ORIGIN	Japan	LENGTH	c. 16 in (40 cm)

The *tanto* was a short sword that came into use during the Heian period (794–1185), and its popularity waxed and waned until the 20th century. This weapon is encased in a black lacquered sheath, and it was not uncommon to see slim *kogatana* knives stored in a sheath pocket.

KATANA IN SCABBARD

DATE	18th century	WEIGHT	24 oz (680 g)
ORIGIN	Japan	LENGTH	27½ in (69.8 cm)

This long sword, or *katana*, forms a *daisho* (combination) with a matching short sword, or *wakazashi* (pp. 198–99). During the the Edo regime, the *katana* was exclusively worn by the samurai, while merchants and townsmen were allowed to carry a *wakazashi*. In combat, a samurai typically held the *katana* in a two-handed grip, which the *tsuka* (handle) easily accommodated.

Sageo for tying scabbard into belt

Tsuba (guard)

Silk braid binding

Menuki (hilt ornament)

FULL VIEW

FAN DAGGER

DATE	c. 17th century	WEIGHT	c. 11 oz (300 g)
ORIGIN	Japan	LENGTH	c. 10¼ in (25 cm)

Fans were customary items around the Japanese court, so they also provided
an ideal disguise for a self-defense weapon, such as the dagger shown here.
The fan slats are actually a solid scabbard, holding a single-edged steel dagger.
The hilt of the dagger is formed by the ridges of the fake fan slats. The loop
at the end acted as a fastening to secure the blade in the scabbard.

Single-edged blade

Scabbard disguised
as folded fan

SCABBARD

Loop-fastening
held blade in place

SHEATH

FLUTE KNIFE

DATE	c. 16th century	WEIGHT	c. 9 oz (250 g)
ORIGIN	Japan	LENGTH	c. 12 in (30.5 cm)

In Japan, bamboo flutes were occasionally used as stick-style weapons,
but this item is far more elaborate. The intricately made metal casing,
crafted to look exactly like a real bamboo flute, contains a double-edged
dagger. The fake "mouthpiece" formed the hilt, and the main body of
the "flute" was a sheath to conceal the blade.

FULL VIEW

POUCH DAGGER

DATE	c. 16th century	**WEIGHT**	c. 9 oz (250 g)
ORIGIN	Japan	**LENGTH**	c. 8 in (20 cm)

Tobacco pouches were common articles in early
modern Japan, generally worn by samurai on
the waist and fastened with a *netsuke* (toggle)
under the sash. They were natural places to conceal
weapons. Here the *netsuke* acts as a scabbard for a
simple dagger, fitted with a lacquered wood handle.

Plain, single-edged
steel blade

Lacquered
wooden handle

Pouch toggle acts
as dagger scabbard

SCABBARD

Section around mouthpiece
forms dagger hilt

Tobacco pouch

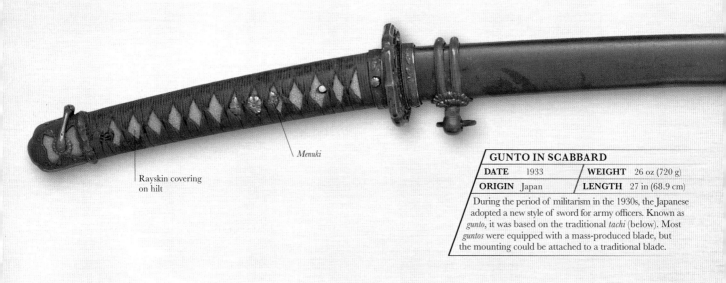

Rayskin covering
on hilt

Menuki

GUNTO IN SCABBARD

DATE	1933	WEIGHT	26 oz (720 g)
ORIGIN	Japan	LENGTH	27 in (68.9 cm)

During the period of militarism in the 1930s, the Japanese adopted a new style of sword for army officers. Known as *gunto*, it was based on the traditional *tachi* (below). Most *guntos* were equipped with a mass-produced blade, but the mounting could be attached to a traditional blade.

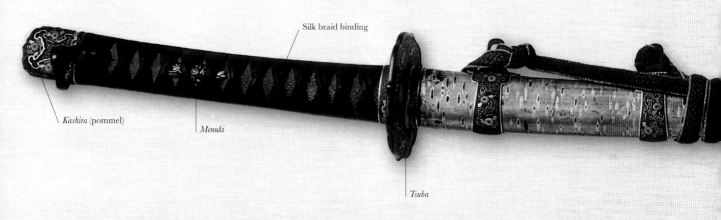

Silk braid binding

Kashira (pommel)

Menuki

Tsuba

Sayajira (scabbard tip)

Saya (scabbard)

> ## "IF AN ADVERSARY IS POSITIONED
> SUCH THAT THE TIP OF HIS SWORD IS FACING YOU,
> ## STRIKE AS HE RAISES IT."
>
> MIYAMOTO MUSASHI, *THE BOOK OF FIVE RINGS*, c. 1645

Semegane
(*saya* ring)

Sageo

TACHI IN GOLD SCABBARD			
DATE	Late 18th century	**WEIGHT**	24 oz (680 g)
ORIGIN	Japan	**LENGTH**	28¼ in (71.75 cm)

The blade of a *tachi* was traditionally over 24 in (60 cm) in length, although it was shorter than the *nodachi* field sword, which a samurai slung over his shoulder. *Tachi* hilts were equipped with a traditionally shaped *kashira* (pommel) that wrapped around the end.

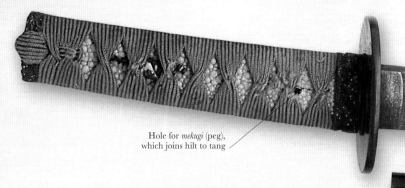

Hole for *mekugi* (peg),
which joins hilt to tang

WAKAZASHI

DATE	17th century	WEIGHT	15 oz (420 g)
ORIGIN	Japan	LENGTH	19 in (48.5 cm)

The *wakazashi* was a samurai's constant companion, worn from waking until sleeping, and even kept nearby during the night. In addition to serving as an additional fighting sword to the *katana* and as a sidearm, it was often the weapon used by the samurai to perform ritual suicide (*seppuku*), by plunging it into the abdomen.

Pocket for *kogatana*
(small blade)

Sageo

Sageo

ORNATE WAKAZASHI IN SCABBARD

DATE	c. 18th century	WEIGHT	26 oz (420 g)
ORIGIN	Japan	LENGTH	20 in (50 cm)

This modern-day replica of the *wakazashi* has been lavishly mounted. The real weapon would almost certainly have been worn on ceremonial occasions as a display of status. The sides of the ornate lacquered scabbard carry the *kogatana* and *kogai* (hair pin) associated with the *wakazashi*.

Kissaki (point)

Black lacquer coating

SCABBARD

Habaki (collar)

Kogatana in pocket
on side of scabbard

Hole in guard for
kogatana to pass through

WAKAZASHI SWORD

The *wakazashi* swords in this section are of a style popular during the Edo period in Japan (1603–1876). A *wakazashi* might have been worn by a samurai when in civilian dress, as an accompaniment to his *katana*, or on its own by rich merchants or townsmen. When indoors, a samurai would leave the *katana* by the door, but would still wear the *wakazashi*. The sword's mounting (hilt and guard) was a separate piece that was attached to the blade. The following pages show the constituent parts of both the blade and the mounting. A lavish mounting was a visible symbol of the wearer's wealth. A well-off individual would have had several mountings for a single blade, choosing the most suitable one for a given occasion.

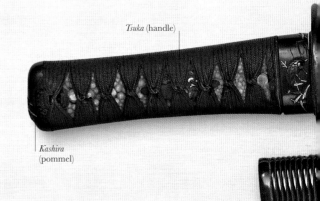

Tsuka (handle)

Kashira (pommel)

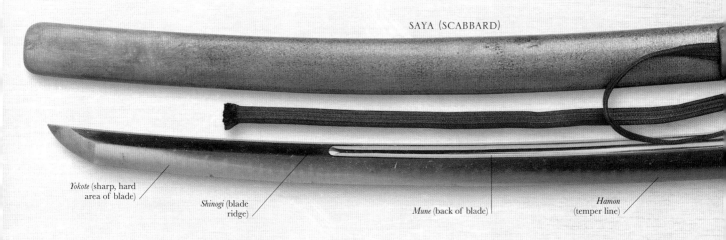

SAYA (SCABBARD)

Yokote (sharp, hard area of blade)

Shinogi (blade ridge)

Mune (back of blade)

Hamon (temper line)

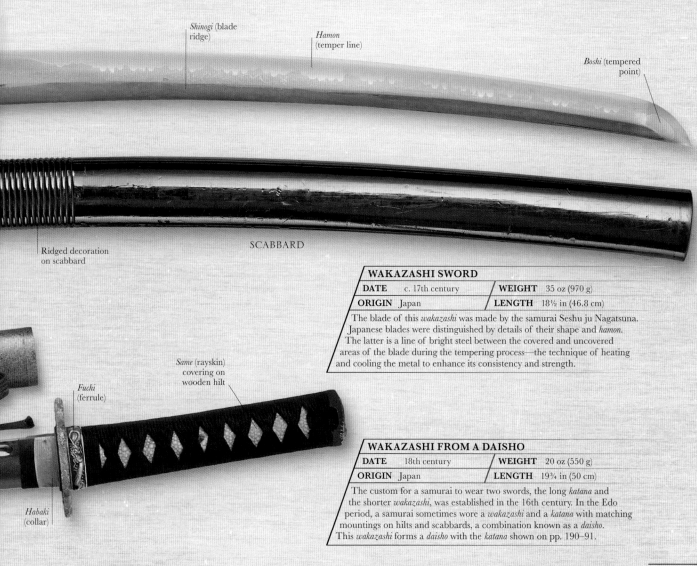

Shinogi (blade ridge)

Hamon (temper line)

Boshi (tempered point)

Ridged decoration on scabbard

SCABBARD

Same (rayskin) covering on wooden hilt

Fuchi (ferrule)

Habaki (collar)

WAKAZASHI SWORD

DATE	c. 17th century	WEIGHT	35 oz (970 g)
ORIGIN	Japan	LENGTH	18½ in (46.8 cm)

The blade of this *wakazashi* was made by the samurai Seshu ju Nagatsuna. Japanese blades were distinguished by details of their shape and *hamon*. The latter is a line of bright steel between the covered and uncovered areas of the blade during the tempering process—the technique of heating and cooling the metal to enhance its consistency and strength.

WAKAZASHI FROM A DAISHO

DATE	18th century	WEIGHT	20 oz (550 g)
ORIGIN	Japan	LENGTH	19¾ in (50 cm)

The custom for a samurai to wear two swords, the long *katana* and the shorter *wakazashi*, was established in the 16th century. In the Edo period, a samurai sometimes wore a *wakazashi* and a *katana* with matching mountings on hilts and scabbards, a combination known as a *daisho*. This *wakazashi* forms a daisho with the *katana* shown on pp. 190–91.

WAKAZASHI

DATE	17th century	**WEIGHT**	15 oz (420 g)
ORIGIN	Japan	**LENGTH**	19 in (48 cm)

The complete *wakazashi* sword shown here is a fine example of the typical samurai side arm. Light and perfectly balanced—the point of balance was just in front of the *tsuba* (guard)—it was an useful weapon for both cutting and thrusting. A *kogai*, or hair pin, is held in a special fitting on the *saya* (scabbard), which also housed a *kogatana*, or small blade. The various components of a *wakazashi* are shown here in close-up on pp. 202–03.

Tsuka

Habaki

Tsuba

Kogai

MEKUGI

The *mekugi* is a small peg that passed through a hole in the hilt and a corresponding hole in the *nakago* (tang) of the blade, securing the hilt to the tang. The *mekugi* was usually made of bamboo, but occasionally of horn or ivory.

SUNAGI

When it was not attached to a blade, the mounting of the sword was assembled on a wooden copy of a blade and tang called a *sunagi*. Separated from its mounting, the blade was stored in a wooden scabbard with a plain wooden grip called a *shirasaya*.

Hole for *mekugi*

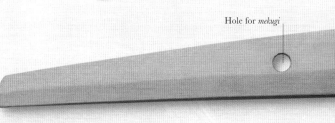

BLADE

Making the hard, sharp edge and softer, resilient core and back of the blade was a complex, skilled operation. Swordsmiths often marked the tang of the *wakazashi* with their signature; this blade is signed by Tadahiro of Hizen province on Kyushu island.

Nakago (tang) features the swordsmith's signature

Hole for *mekugi*

Hamachi (edge notch)

Munemachi (back notch)

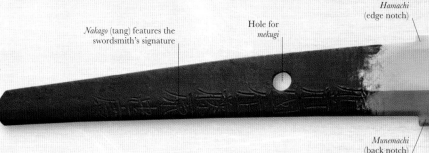

Kissaki

SCABBARD

Hamon

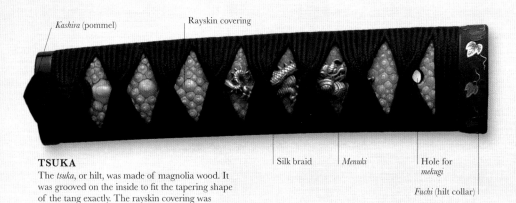

Kashira (pommel)

Rayskin covering

TSUKA

The *tsuka*, or hilt, was made of magnolia wood. It was grooved on the inside to fit the tapering shape of the tang exactly. The rayskin covering was valuable; the lozenge-shape openings in the silk braid allow it to be seen. The *menuki* ornaments were not just decorative, but also helped in enhancing the wielder's grip on the sword.

Silk braid

Menuki

Hole for *mekugi*

Fuchi (hilt collar)

HABAKI

The *habaki*, a part of the blade rather than the mounting, slid over the tang and butted up against the blade notches.

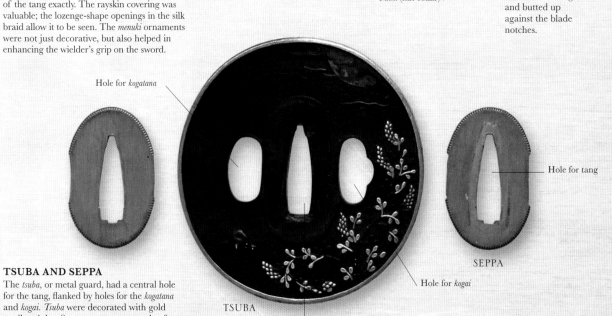

Hole for *kogatana*

Hole for tang

SEPPA

TSUBA AND SEPPA

The *tsuba*, or metal guard, had a central hole for the tang, flanked by holes for the *kogatana* and *kogai*. *Tsuba* were decorated with gold or silver inlay. Seppa, or spacers, made of copper fit onto each side of the guard.

TSUBA

Hole for tang

Hole for *kogai*

Ear cleaner

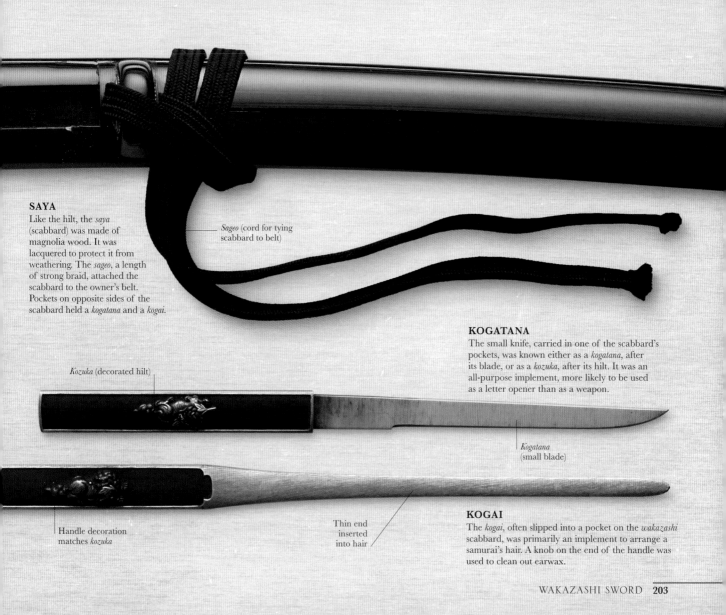

SAYA

Like the hilt, the *saya* (scabbard) was made of magnolia wood. It was lacquered to protect it from weathering. The *sageo*, a length of strong braid, attached the scabbard to the owner's belt. Pockets on opposite sides of the scabbard held a *kogatana* and a *kogai*.

Sageo (cord for tying scabbard to belt)

KOGATANA

The small knife, carried in one of the scabbard's pockets, was known either as a *kogatana*, after its blade, or as a *kozuka*, after its hilt. It was an all-purpose implement, more likely to be used as a letter opener than as a weapon.

Kozuka (decorated hilt)

Kogatana (small blade)

Handle decoration matches *kozuka*

Thin end inserted into hair

KOGAI

The *kogai*, often slipped into a pocket on the *wakazashi* scabbard, was primarily an implement to arrange a samurai's hair. A knob on the end of the handle was used to clean out earwax.

SAMURAI

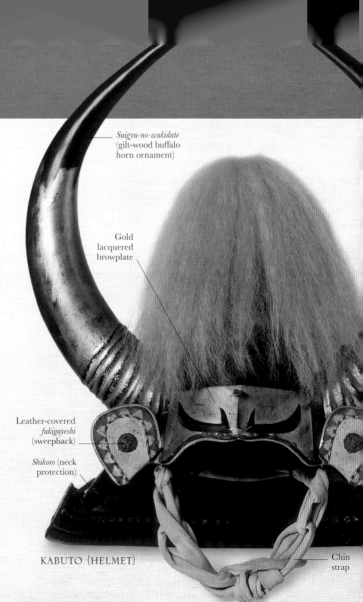

A martial elite of Japan from the medieval period to the 17th century, the samurai were mounted armored warriors known for their skills with the sword and spear. By the 12th century, they had effectively become Japan's ruling class. Although we have come to identify the samurai mainly with swords, between the 11th and 14th centuries, the bow-and-arrow was their principal weapon. Later, improvements in sword making made the *katana* and *wakazashi* the preferred weapons of combat.

Wearing an elaborate suit of armor, the samurai was a terrifying battlefield warrior. He would often kill an enemy, cut off his head, wash it, and mount it on a spike. Fierce and bloodthirsty, he was revered for his skill in swordfighting.

TOSEI GUSOKU

DATE	16th century
ORIGIN	Japan

The *tosei gusoku* was a light samurai body armor made from bamboo, cloth, and metal. Introduced during the 16th century, it was lighter than the lacquered metal armor used during the medieval period. The helmet was usually adorned with antlers or buffalo horns.

Suigyu-no-wakidate (gilt-wood buffalo horn ornament)

Gold lacquered browplate

Leather-covered *fukigayeshi* (sweepback)

Shikoro (neck protection)

KABUTO (HELMET)

Chin strap

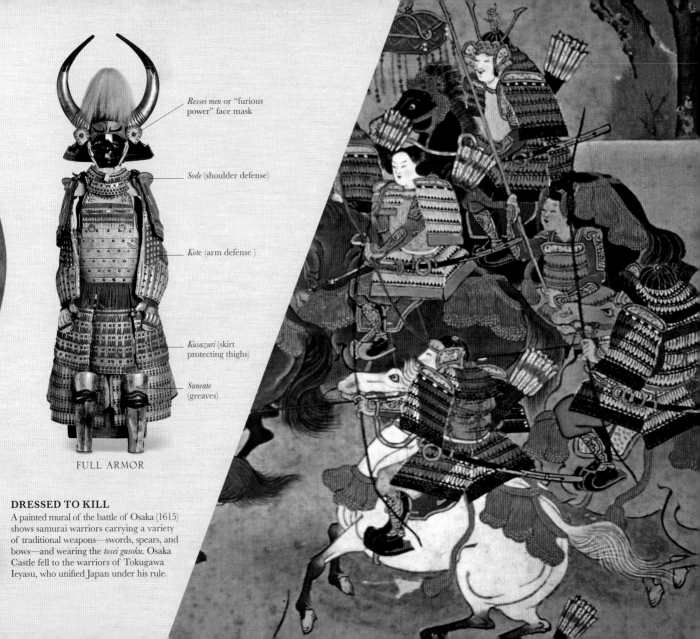

Ressei men or "furious power" face mask

Sode (shoulder defense)

Kote (arm defense)

Kusazuri (skirt protecting thighs)

Suneate (greaves)

FULL ARMOR

DRESSED TO KILL

A painted mural of the battle of Osaka (1615)
shows samurai warriors carrying a variety
of traditional weapons—swords, spears, and
bows—and wearing the *tosei gusoku*. Osaka
Castle fell to the warriors of Tokugawa
Ieyasu, who unified Japan under his rule.

ASIAN DAGGERS

From the 16th to the early 18th century, when most of India was ruled by the Mogul Empire, the daggers from the Indian subcontinent were notable for their high-quality metalwork, ornamentation, and distinctive forms. Some daggers, such as the *kard*, were Islamic imports; others, including the *katar*, had specifically Indian roots. Daggers were worn by Indian princes and nobles for self-defense, for hunting, and for display. In combat, they were essential close-quarters weapons, capable of piercing the chain-mail armor worn by Indian warriors.

FULL VIEW

Gilded chape
(metallic trimming)

Guard inlaid
with silver

Decorative tassle

PARRYING SHIELD			
DATE	18th century	**WEIGHT**	Unknown
ORIGIN	Central India	**LENGTH**	Blades: 7 in (17.7 cm)

This Indian parrying shield has five blades, each with a reinforced tip, that radiate from a central point. The grip is hidden behind a protective metal guard that curves backward around the warrior's hand.

Reinforced tip

Central ridge

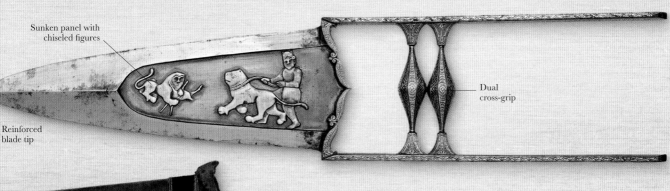

Sunken panel with
chiseled figures

Reinforced
blade tip

Dual
cross-grip

INDIAN KATAR

DATE	Early 19th century	WEIGHT	20½ oz (570 g)
ORIGIN	India	LENGTH	16½ in (42.1 cm)

To use this north Indian dagger, the warrior grasped the cross-grips,
making a fist, so that the sidebars of the hilt lay on either side of
his hand and forearm. Holding the blade horizontally, he then
stabbed with a punching motion.

Wood covered
with velvet

SCABBARD

Watered steel blade

Simple
flared tip

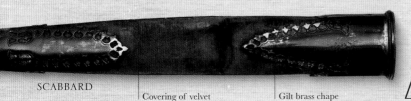

SCABBARD

Covering of velvet

Gilt brass chape

INDIAN KARD

DATE	1710–11	WEIGHT	12½ oz (340 g)
ORIGIN	India	LENGTH	15¼ in (38.5 cm)

Of Persian origin, the straight-bladed, single-edged *kard*
was in use across much of the Islamic world by the 18th
century, from Ottoman Turkey to Mogul India. The *kard*
was mostly used as a stabbing weapon.

INDIAN KATAR

DATE	1759–60	WEIGHT	18 oz (500 g)
ORIGIN	India	LENGTH	17¾ in (44.6 cm)

Decorated with depictions of animal figures in gold inlay, this impressive *katar* and its scabbard were designed to show off their owner's wealth. The *katar* was an effective weapon in close combat. The double-edged blade could penetrate chain-mail armor with a punching stab.

Binding of gold thread

Gold *koftgari* decoration

Dual cross-grip

H-shaped hilt

Hilt extension embellished with seated tiger

INDIAN BICH'HWA WITH CAST-BRASS HILT

DATE	18th century	WEIGHT	8½ oz (240 g)
ORIGIN	India	LENGTH	11¾ in (29.6 cm)

This *bich'hwa*, the Indian word for scorpion, has a cast-brass hilt decorated with a monster's head. The knuckle guard is designed to depict the beast eating its own tail. The narrow, double-curved blade has a low medial ridge on both sides. The crudely cut marks on the quillon block may be letters.

Medial ridge on blade

Mauve velvet covering

Chape decorated
with image of
parrot in foliage

SCABBARD

Reinforced
blade tip

Grip terminates
in monster-head
decoration

Brass
knuckle guard

Quillon block

Narrow
octagonal grip

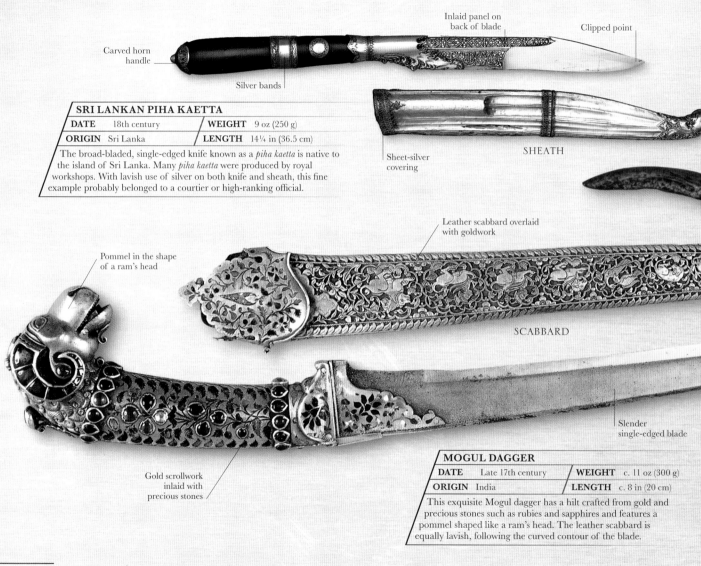

Carved horn
handle

Inlaid panel on
back of blade

Clipped point

Silver bands

SRI LANKAN PIHA KAETTA

DATE	18th century	WEIGHT	9 oz (250 g)
ORIGIN	Sri Lanka	LENGTH	14¼ in (36.5 cm)

The broad-bladed, single-edged knife known as a *piha kaetta* is native to
the island of Sri Lanka. Many *piha kaetta* were produced by royal
workshops. With lavish use of silver on both knife and sheath, this fine
example probably belonged to a courtier or high-ranking official.

Sheet-silver
covering

SHEATH

Leather scabbard overlaid
with goldwork

SCABBARD

Pommel in the shape
of a ram's head

Slender
single-edged blade

Gold scrollwork
inlaid with
precious stones

MOGUL DAGGER

DATE	Late 17th century	WEIGHT	c. 11 oz (300 g)
ORIGIN	India	LENGTH	c. 8 in (20 cm)

This exquisite Mogul dagger has a hilt crafted from gold and
precious stones such as rubies and sapphires and features a
pommel shaped like a ram's head. The leather scabbard is
equally lavish, following the curved contour of the blade.

MALAYAN DAGGER

DATE	c. 18th century	WEIGHT	c. 11 oz (300 g)
ORIGIN	Malaysia	LENGTH	c. 12 in (30.5 cm)

The shape of this Malayan dagger called a *kris* varies from region to region. The wavy blade contour delivers terrible stabbing injuries, and the rear of the blade widens at the hilt to form a type of cross-guard. The *kris* plays an important role in Malayan culture. It often has supernatural connotations, with certain blades believed to bring good or bad luck.

Ivory handle shaped like Garuda, a mythological eagle

Angled tip

BHUTANESE DAGGER

DATE	18th century	WEIGHT	13 oz (350 g)
ORIGIN	Bhutan	LENGTH	17 in (43.4 cm)

This straight-bladed dagger originates from the small Himalayan kingdom of Bhutan, which shares its borders with China and India. The hilt is chiseled with various Chinese symbols of good luck on a background of tendrils. The wooden scabbard has a border and chape of gilded iron.

Tapering single-edged blade

Scabbard bound with layers of paper and red velvet

Iron grip with gold and siver inlay

Silver mount

SCABBARD

Rosette on
knuckle guard

Loop-shaped
hilt

Floral engraving
on ricasso

Steel neck

Bone handle

BICH'HWA DAGGERS
WERE CARRIED BY
**WARRIORS,
NOBLES, AND**
ASSASSINS ALIKE.

CURVED DAGGER			
DATE	c. 18th century	**WEIGHT**	c. 7¼ oz (210 g)
ORIGIN	Southeast Asia	**LENGTH**	c. 11½ in (29 cm)

The blade of this dagger is strongly curved and sharpened on both edges,
making it a slashing as well as a stabbing weapon. The blade of the dagger
has a double fuller and floral engraving. The bone hilt is secured by three
pins, with the tang button visible at the base.

INDIAN BICH'HWA WITH IRON HILT

DATE	18th century	WEIGHT	7¼ oz (210 g)
ORIGIN	India	LENGTH	10½ in (27.2 cm)

With the shape of its blade inspired by a buffalo horn, this *bich'hwa* was a small but deadly dagger. In this example the iron hilt, decorated in silver *koftgari* (inlay), is in the form of a flattened loop, attached to the blade by two rivets. The blade is recurved (bent backward) and is reinforced at the point to increase its penetration.

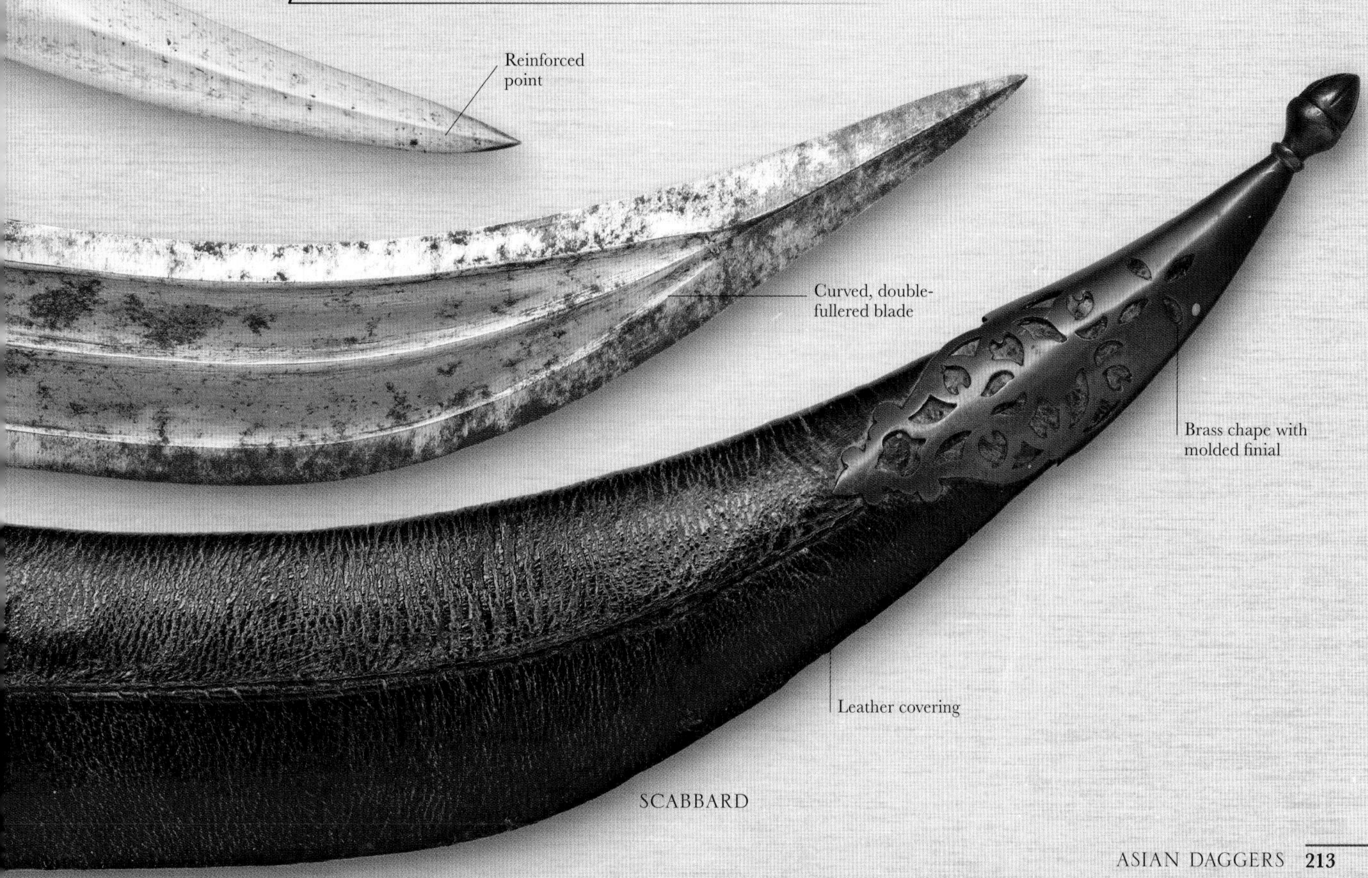

Reinforced point

Curved, double-fullered blade

Brass chape with molded finial

Leather covering

SCABBARD

COMBINATION WEAPONS

German and Italian armorers of the 16th century were particularly adept at incorporating firearms into other weapons, both blunt and edged. Many of the examples that survive today were probably intended to be showpieces, since they frequently display the most ornate decoration, and it is not clear whether they were ever meant for martial use. The tradition continued—a rifle or pistol equipped with a bayonet can be termed a combination weapon—and spread to other countries, notably to India, where more practical examples were produced during the late Mogul period.

MATCHLOCK AX/DAGGER

DATE	c. 1820	WEIGHT	2½ lb (1.12 kg)
ORIGIN	India	LENGTH	20½ in (52.3 cm)

This weapon has been designed by combining a matchlock gun, an ax, and a dagger. A matchlock was an early type of gun that was fired using a smoldering cord. This gun's barrel is closed by a tubular, crosshatched grip, which unscrews to reveal a knife. The pommel also unscrews to reveal a tiny compartment. The axhead, decorated with engraved scrollwork, is mounted on an iron shaft.

Pommel

Cock holds flint

Ramrod

Serrated wheel strikes
flint to fire the gun

Square shaft
takes the key that
winds the wheel

Trigger

Hinged
pommel

WAR HAMMER WHEELLOCK

DATE	c. 1590	WEIGHT	3¾ lb (1.70 kg)
ORIGIN	Germany	LENGTH	24¼ in (61.6 cm)

This long-shafted war hammer incorporates a wheellock pistol—an improvement on the matchlock pistol. The hammerhead of this war hammer is missing; only its beak remains. With all its fully functional parts, it seems this weapon was produced for practical rather than ceremonial purposes.

Beak

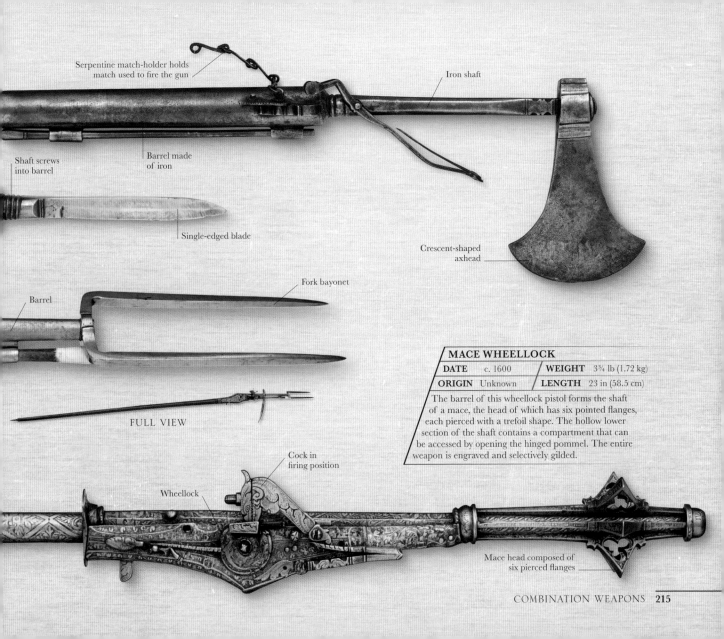

Serpentine match-holder holds match used to fire the gun

Iron shaft

Barrel made of iron

Shaft screws into barrel

Single-edged blade

Crescent-shaped axhead

Fork bayonet

Barrel

FULL VIEW

Cock in firing position

Wheellock

MACE WHEELLOCK

DATE	c. 1600	WEIGHT	3¾ lb (1.72 kg)
ORIGIN	Unknown	LENGTH	23 in (58.5 cm)

The barrel of this wheellock pistol forms the shaft of a mace, the head of which has six pointed flanges, each pierced with a trefoil shape. The hollow lower section of the shaft contains a compartment that can be accessed by opening the hinged pommel. The entire weapon is engraved and selectively gilded.

Mace head composed of six pierced flanges

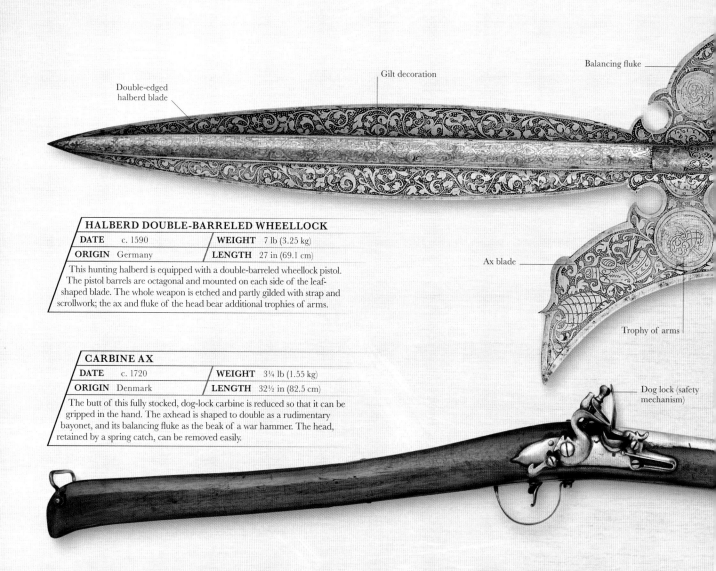

Double-edged
halberd blade

Gilt decoration

Balancing fluke

HALBERD DOUBLE-BARRELED WHEELLOCK

DATE	c. 1590	WEIGHT	7 lb (3.25 kg)
ORIGIN	Germany	LENGTH	27 in (69.1 cm)

This hunting halberd is equipped with a double-barreled wheellock pistol.
The pistol barrels are octagonal and mounted on each side of the leaf-
shaped blade. The whole weapon is etched and partly gilded with strap and
scrollwork; the ax and fluke of the head bear additional trophies of arms.

Ax blade

Trophy of arms

CARBINE AX

DATE	c. 1720	WEIGHT	3¼ lb (1.55 kg)
ORIGIN	Denmark	LENGTH	32½ in (82.5 cm)

The butt of this fully stocked, dog-lock carbine is reduced so that it can be
gripped in the hand. The axhead is shaped to double as a rudimentary
bayonet, and its balancing fluke as the beak of a war hammer. The head,
retained by a spring catch, can be removed easily.

Dog lock (safety
mechanism)

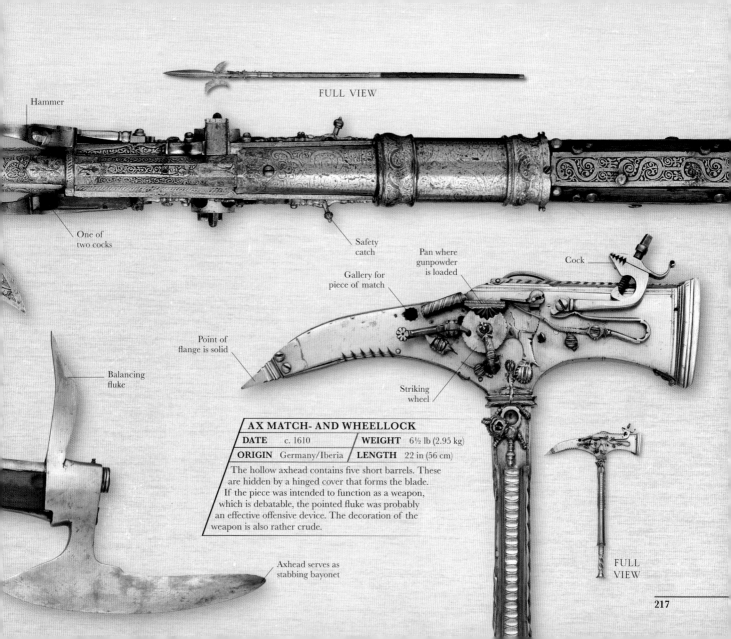

FULL VIEW

Hammer

One of
two cocks

Safety
catch

Gallery for
piece of match

Pan where
gunpowder
is loaded

Cock

Point of
flange is solid

Striking
wheel

Balancing
fluke

AX MATCH- AND WHEELLOCK

DATE	c. 1610	WEIGHT	6½ lb (2.95 kg)
ORIGIN	Germany/Iberia	LENGTH	22 in (56 cm)

The hollow axhead contains five short barrels. These
are hidden by a hinged cover that forms the blade.
If the piece was intended to function as a weapon,
which is debatable, the pointed fluke was probably
an effective offensive device. The decoration of the
weapon is also rather crude.

Axhead serves as
stabbing bayonet

FULL
VIEW

TWILIGHT OF
THE SWORD
1775–1900

THE PERIOD FROM 1775 TO 1900 CONTINUED to see swords being used in combat. In the hands of both the infantry and cavalry, swords were wielded in action from the battlefields of colonial America to those of China and India. Yet, during the 19th century, the value of the sword declined massively, as firearms became more sophisticated and powerful. By the end of the century, the sword's role in deciding the outcome of battles was negligible.

It was the widespread use of firearms that irrevocably altered the status of the sword, but this change was gradual. Firearms had been around for several centuries and by 1775 the flintlock musket became the standard infantry weapon of most European armies. Its automated mechanism allowed the infantryman to fire the gun more easily, which gave him a tactical advantage over the more traditionally armed enemy. Yet the flintlock had its limitations. Flintlock weapons were generally inaccurate and suitable only for tactics such as volley fire, when all the muskets were fired simultaenously. They also had a poor rate of fire—only two or three rounds a minute in battlefield conditions— and wet weather dampened gunpowder, rendering entire banks of muskets useless. Because of these limitations, foot soldiers still had to come close to the enemy to secure victory, and in the ensuing close-quarters battle the sword still proved useful, particularly for the cavalry. Fine examples of short swords and cavalry swords therefore remained in production throughout the 19th century, not only in Europe but also in the newly independent United States.

Prior to the arrival of the European colonists in the 16th century, the Native American population used traditional knives made of stone, bone, and horn, as well as some copper blades. Yet as colonization expanded in the 17th century, the Native Americans increasingly used daggers bought directly from European settlers. The settlers too initially used swords and daggers made in Europe, but during and following the Revolutionary War (1775–83) the homegrown sword industry began to flourish. Simple battle-ready hanger swords, cavalry sabers, and bayonets were forged, which steadily became popular across the country. During the 19th century, certain American blades such as the Bowie knife gained international recognition. By the time of the Civil War (1861–65) sword production in the United States reflected the

North-South divide. The Northern Union produced high volumes of swords, possibly because of its greater reliance on cavalry and its more powerful industrial base, while the Confederate South was forced to rely on far smaller outputs from local swordsmiths and factories.

During the 19th century, blade design more or less ceased to evolve. During their colonial expansion, British soldiers often encountered opposition from warriors wielding medieval-style swords. In Burma, for example, during the wars of 1824–86, British and allied Indian soldiers faced Burmese warriors swinging the *dha*, a single-edged blade similar in shape but not in quality to the Japanese samurai swords. In the Middle East, Turkish warriors were still seen carrying the *yataghan* sword, even as the Ottoman Empire faded. However, the prominence of swords declined further as the century wore on. By the 1890s, firearms had evolved into breech-loading guns (loaded from the rear of the barrel) fed by magazines of cartridges. A single infantryman could now fire 10–15 accurately aimed shots per minute. The introduction of automatic guns such as the multi-barreled Gatling and the self-powered Maxim machine guns turned individual firearms into weapons of mass destruction. The development of firearms meant that by the end of the century most battles were decided by exchanges of firepower, not in close-quarters engagements with the sword. This raised questions about the relevance of the sword in combat. At the same time, the civilian use of swords also dwindled and faded.

Advances in gun making transformed warfare, but did not remove blades from the battlefield. At the end of the 19th century every modern army still used hefty bayonets, and officers often wore dress swords to distinguish themselves from their men. Although firearms could kill opponents at long range, soldiers still had to fight at close quarters to take and hold ground, and here the bayonet was invaluable. New models of bayonet were issued in Europe throughout the 1890s, and promised to keep the blade-bearing warrior a reality into the 20th century.

TWILIGHT OF THE SWORD

EUROPEAN SWORDS

By the time of the French Revolution (1789–99) and Napoleonic Wars (1799–1815), cavalry swords had evolved into the long, straight, thrusting sword of the heavy cavalry, and the light cavalry's curved saber that was designed for cutting and slicing. For the infantry, the rising supremacy of firearms meant that swords were well on their way to becoming ceremonial weapons, but such was their status that they continued to be used as symbols of rank, carried by officers and senior noncommissioned officers. Having lost their practical function, infantry swords became increasingly decorative, some even harkening back to weapons of the classical era.

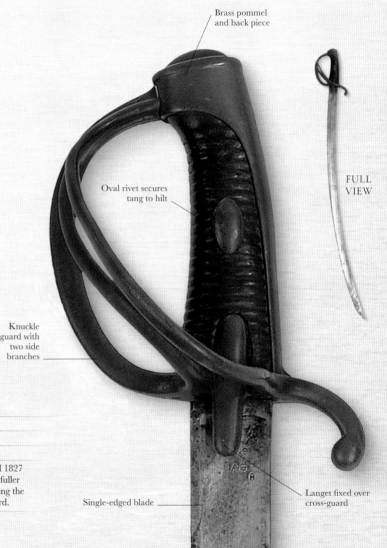

Brass pommel and back piece

FULL VIEW

Oval rivet secures tang to hilt

Knuckle guard with two side branches

Langet fixed over cross-guard

Single-edged blade

MODEL 1827 SABER		
DATE c. 1830	**WEIGHT**	2¾ lb (1.22 kg)
ORIGIN Russia	**LENGTH**	3¼ ft (1.02 m)

A copy of cavalry swords of the Napoleonic era, the Russian Model 1827 Cavalry Saber had a slightly curved, single-edged blade with a wide fuller and a brass hilt. The twin langets were not only useful in firmly securing the sword to the scabbard, but also helped in trapping an opponent's sword.

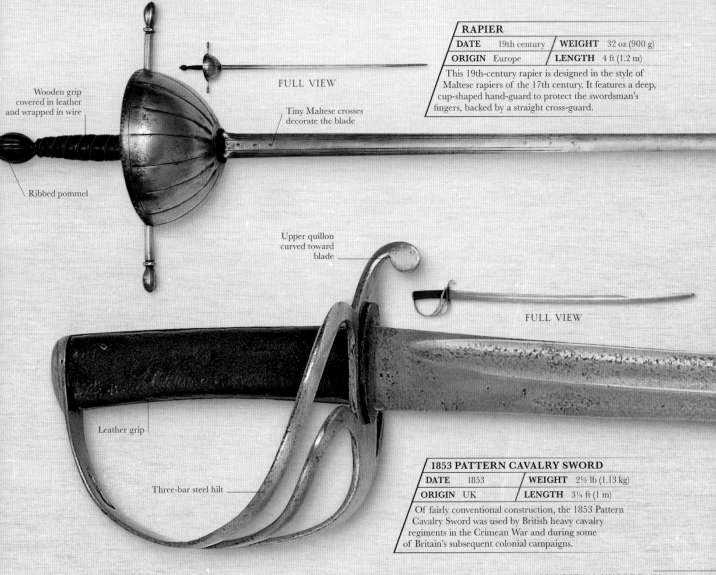

Wooden grip
covered in leather
and wrapped in wire

Ribbed pommel

FULL VIEW

Tiny Maltese crosses
decorate the blade

RAPIER

DATE	19th century	WEIGHT	32 oz (900 g)
ORIGIN	Europe	LENGTH	4 ft (1.2 m)

This 19th-century rapier is designed in the style of
Maltese rapiers of the 17th century. It features a deep,
cup-shaped hand-guard to protect the swordsman's
fingers, backed by a straight cross-guard.

Upper quillon
curved toward
blade

FULL VIEW

Leather grip

Three-bar steel hilt

1853 PATTERN CAVALRY SWORD

DATE	1853	WEIGHT	2½ lb (1.13 kg)
ORIGIN	UK	LENGTH	3¼ ft (1 m)

Of fairly conventional construction, the 1853 Pattern
Cavalry Sword was used by British heavy cavalry
regiments in the Crimean War and during some
of Britain's subsequent colonial campaigns.

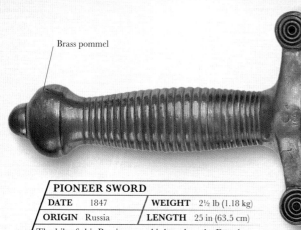

Brass pommel

Straight
quillon with
circular finial

PIONEER SWORD

DATE	1847	WEIGHT	2½ lb (1.18 kg)
ORIGIN	Russia	LENGTH	25 in (63.5 cm)

The hilt of this Russian sword is based on the French
Model 1831 infantry sword. Both weapons reflect an
interest in the classical world and clearly demonstrate the
influence of the Roman *gladius* (*pp. 34–35*). The all-brass
hilt includes a simple cross-guard, ribbed grip, and
pommel, while the short, wide blade has a single fuller.

Brass
pommel cap

Brass hilt includes
the symbol of the
Fasces, a reference
to republican Rome

D-shaped langet

1796 LIGHT CAVALRY SWORD

DATE	1796	WEIGHT	2¼ lb (1 kg)
ORIGIN	UK	LENGTH	38 in (96.5 cm)

Considered to be among the finest of cutting swords, the 1796 Light
Cavalry Sword was developed in tandem with the Heavy Cavalry
Sword (*pp. 234–35*). The broadening of the blade near the tip gave
greater power at point of impact.

Stirrup-shaped
hilt

Serrated edge for
sawing wood

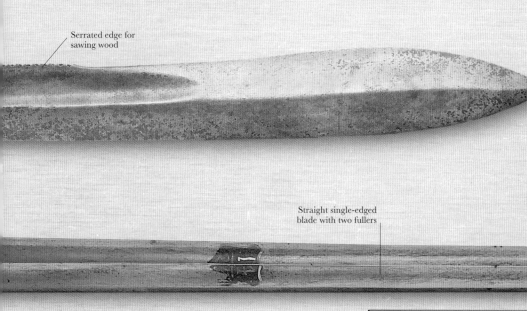

Straight single-edged
blade with two fullers

FULL VIEW

MODEL AN IV CAVALRY SWORD

DATE	1794	WEIGHT	2½ lb (1.16 kg)
ORIGIN	France	LENGTH	3½ ft (1.13 m)

Known as the Model An IV (Year 4, after the French Revolutionary calendar),
this sword equipped some French heavy cavalry and dragoons (infantrymen
trained in horse riding) during the Napoleonic period. Its long blade, like
other French cavalry swords, was narrower than its British equivalent.

Curved blade
wider at the
tip than hilt

BRITISH CAVALRYMAN

From the late 18th to the end of the 19th century, fascinating developments took place in the British cavalry. There were two types of cavalry—heavy cavalry (heavily armed and armored) and light cavalry, which used lighter arms and armor.

British cavalrymen used a mix of swords, and there was little consistent training until the intervention of Major-General John Gaspard Le Marchant, a cavalry general in the British Army.

Dissatisfied with the state of cavalry swords and swordsmanship during his campaigns with the British Army in the 1790s, Le Marchant developed a new sword and published a manual of mounted warfare techniques. His tactics focused on striking at the enemy's head with precision even when at a gallop. Le Marchant's 1796 Light Cavalry Sword (*pp. 224–25*) was a good cutting weapon adopted by the light cavalry, but the army decided that the heavy cavalry should use a straight, heavy cutting sword, like the heavy cavalry sword (below), since it made the strike more powerful. After testing various designs, a new cut-and-thrust cavalry saber was established in 1853 as standard for both light and heavy cavalry.

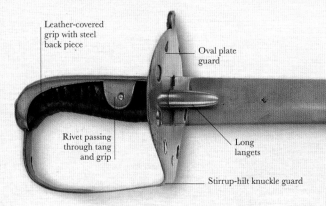

Leather-covered grip with steel back piece

Oval plate guard

Rivet passing through tang and grip

Long langets

Stirrup-hilt knuckle guard

Straight, single-edged blade

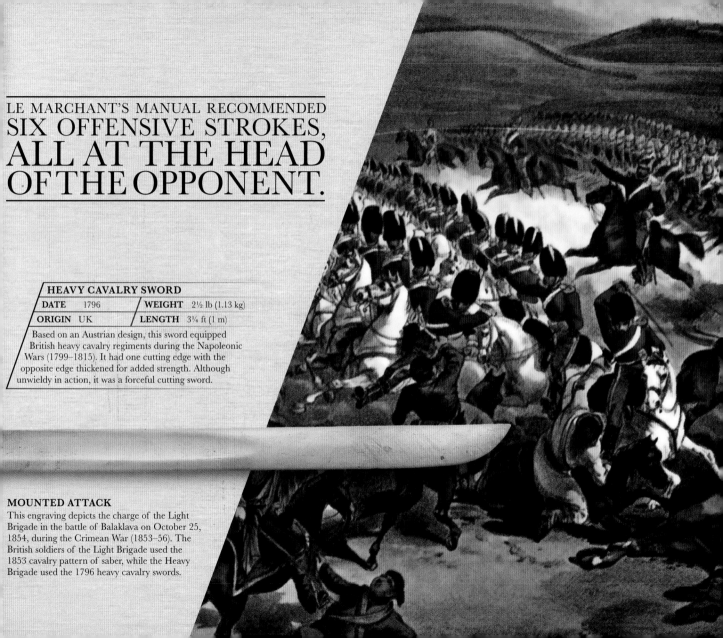

LE MARCHANT'S MANUAL RECOMMENDED

SIX OFFENSIVE STROKES, ALL AT THE HEAD OF THE OPPONENT.

HEAVY CAVALRY SWORD

DATE	1796	WEIGHT	2½ lb (1.13 kg)
ORIGIN	UK	LENGTH	3¼ ft (1 m)

Based on an Austrian design, this sword equipped British heavy cavalry regiments during the Napoleonic Wars (1799–1815). It had one cutting edge with the opposite edge thickened for added strength. Although unwieldy in action, it was a forceful cutting sword.

MOUNTED ATTACK

This engraving depicts the charge of the Light Brigade in the battle of Balaklava on October 25, 1854, during the Crimean War (1853–56). The British soldiers of the Light Brigade used the 1853 cavalry pattern of saber, while the Heavy Brigade used the 1796 heavy cavalry swords.

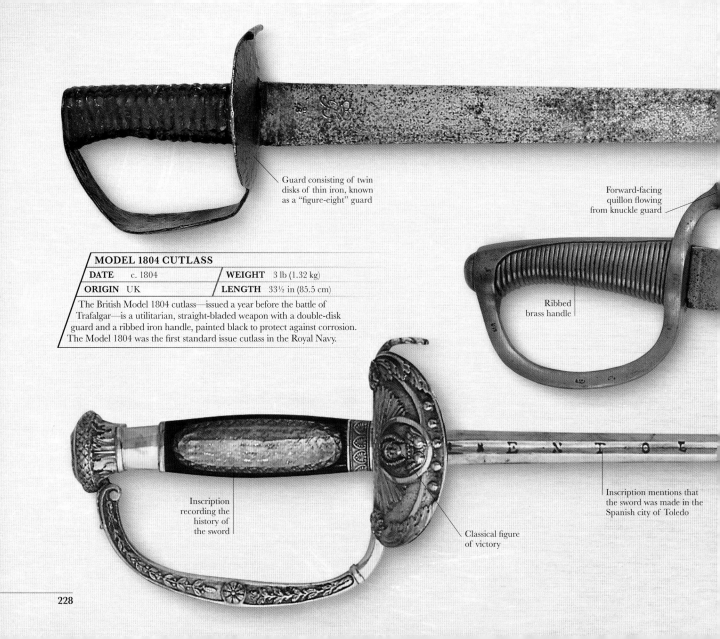

Guard consisting of twin
disks of thin iron, known
as a "figure-eight" guard

Forward-facing
quillon flowing
from knuckle guard

MODEL 1804 CUTLASS

DATE	c. 1804	WEIGHT	3 lb (1.32 kg)
ORIGIN	UK	LENGTH	33½ in (85.5 cm)

The British Model 1804 cutlass—issued a year before the battle of
Trafalgar—is a utilitarian, straight-bladed weapon with a double-disk
guard and a ribbed iron handle, painted black to protect against corrosion.
The Model 1804 was the first standard issue cutlass in the Royal Navy.

Ribbed
brass handle

Inscription
recording the
history of
the sword

Classical figure
of victory

Inscription mentions that
the sword was made in the
Spanish city of Toledo

Straight double-
edged blade

Simple ogival
(arched) point

NAPOLEONIC INFANTRY SWORD

DATE	Early 19th century	WEIGHT	32 oz (900 g)
ORIGIN	France	LENGTH	29 in (74 cm)

Carried by the ordinary foot soldier during the Napoleonic Wars, this infantry hanger was known as a "briquet." It has a simple, one-piece brass grip, which is ribbed to improve the grip, and a curved steel blade. This type of sword was also issued to French sailors in place of a naval cutlass.

FULL VIEW

Curved steel blade

Double-edged blade
with single deep fuller

SPANISH CEREMONIAL RAPIER

DATE	Early 19th century	WEIGHT	c. 2¼ lb (1 kg)
ORIGIN	Spain	LENGTH	c. 4½ ft (1.4 m)

This sword was surrendered by the French governor of Ciudad Rodrigo, in Spain, to British Lieutenant John Gurwod, who led the attack on this fortress in 1812 during the Peninsular War (1800–14). The inscription on the blade shows the sword was made in Toledo, a city famous for its high-quality metalwork.

FULL VIEW

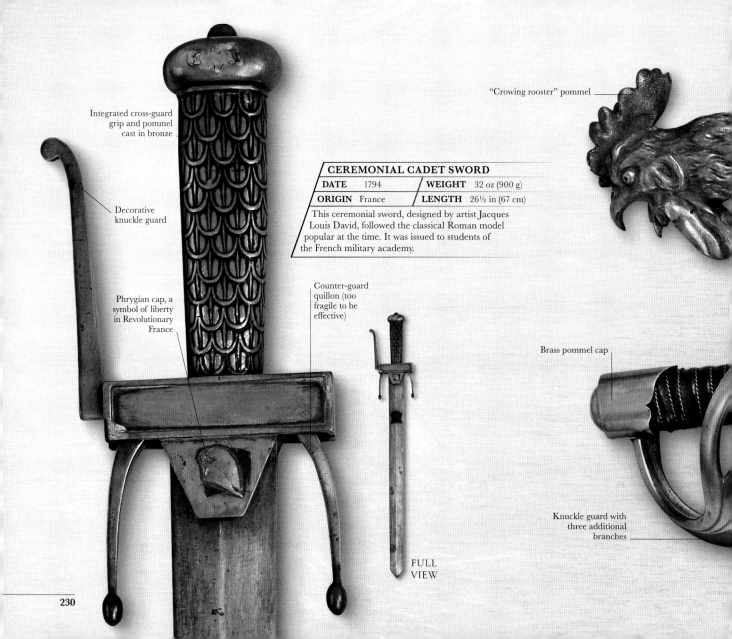

Integrated cross-guard
grip and pommel
cast in bronze

"Crowing rooster" pommel

Decorative
knuckle guard

CEREMONIAL CADET SWORD

DATE	1794	**WEIGHT**	32 oz (900 g)
ORIGIN	France	**LENGTH**	26½ in (67 cm)

This ceremonial sword, designed by artist Jacques
Louis David, followed the classical Roman model
popular at the time. It was issued to students of
the French military academy.

Phrygian cap, a
symbol of liberty
in Revolutionary
France

Counter-guard
quillon (too
fragile to be
effective)

Brass pommel cap

FULL
VIEW

Knuckle guard with
three additional
branches

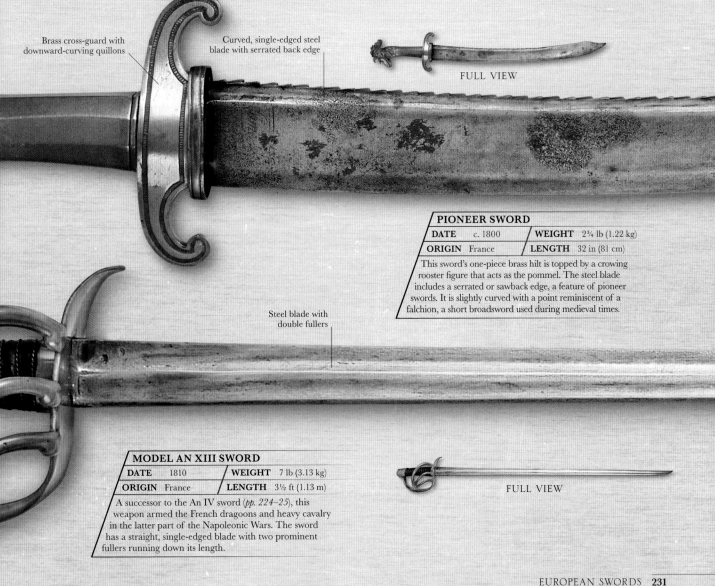

Brass cross-guard with
downward-curving quillons

Curved, single-edged steel
blade with serrated back edge

FULL VIEW

PIONEER SWORD

DATE	c. 1800	WEIGHT	2¾ lb (1.22 kg)
ORIGIN	France	LENGTH	32 in (81 cm)

This sword's one-piece brass hilt is topped by a crowing
rooster figure that acts as the pommel. The steel blade
includes a serrated or sawback edge, a feature of pioneer
swords. It is slightly curved with a point reminiscent of a
falchion, a short broadsword used during medieval times.

Steel blade with
double fullers

MODEL AN XIII SWORD

DATE	1810	WEIGHT	7 lb (3.13 kg)
ORIGIN	France	LENGTH	3½ ft (1.13 m)

A successor to the An IV sword (*pp. 224–25*), this
weapon armed the French dragoons and heavy cavalry
in the latter part of the Napoleonic Wars. The sword
has a straight, single-edged blade with two prominent
fullers running down its length.

FULL VIEW

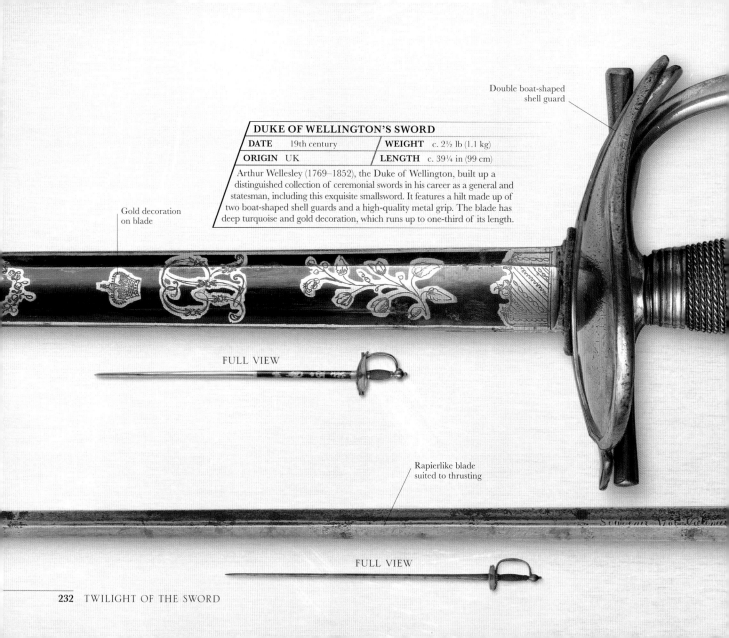

DUKE OF WELLINGTON'S SWORD

DATE	19th century	WEIGHT	c. 2½ lb (1.1 kg)
ORIGIN	UK	LENGTH	c. 39¼ in (99 cm)

Arthur Wellesley (1769–1852), the Duke of Wellington, built up a
distinguished collection of ceremonial swords in his career as a general and
statesman, including this exquisite smallsword. It features a hilt made up of
two boat-shaped shell guards and a high-quality metal grip. The blade has
deep turquoise and gold decoration, which runs up to one-third of its length.

Gold decoration
on blade

FULL VIEW

Rapierlike blade
suited to thrusting

FULL VIEW

IF THEY BE THE FIRST TO DRAW THE SWORD, I SHALL BE THE LAST TO SHEATH IT.**"**

NAPOLEON BONAPARTE, ON THE BRITISH, 1803

Spherical pommel
riveted to knuckle guard

NAPOLEON'S SWORD			
DATE	Late 18th century	**WEIGHT**	c. 2¼ lb (1.02 kg)
ORIGIN	France	**LENGTH**	c. 37¾ in (96 cm)

This simple, rapierlike sword belonged to none other than the French emperor Napoleon Bonaparte (1769–1821). It was presented to him when he was serving as a young artillery officer. The sword's double-shell cross-guard is made of brass and carries an inscription meaning "Royal Artillery" in French.

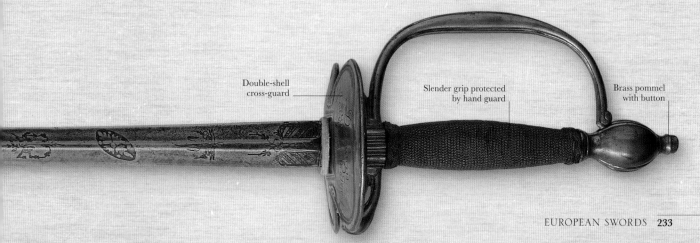

Double-shell
cross-guard

Slender grip protected
by hand guard

Brass pommel
with button

FENCING

Fencing developed in Europe in the 13th or 14th century as a form of training for duels (*pp. 136–37*) and for warfare. By the 15th century, it had evolved into a sport, with points awarded to a fencer when his sword made contact with his opponent's body. Fencing's popularity surged in the 16th century, when it became fashionable for civilians to carry swords. Fought with rapiers (*pp. 138–41*) and smallswords (*pp. 142–45*), early fencing was dangerous, and at times fatal. It became much safer in the 18th century with the introduction of the fencing mask and customized weapons—the foil and the fencing saber. These,

along with the *épée* (below), became the quintessential fencing weapons. All three corresponded to a particular style of fencing, governed by its own set of rules. The foil, a light, flexible sword with a blunt tip, was used for thrusting movements—only the tip of its blade made contact with the opponent. The saber was of a similar design, but was used for both thrusting and slashing—the tip and edges of the blade came into play. The *épée* was developed in the 19th century by a group of French students who found the foil and saber too light to give the experience of a realistic duel. Essentially a copy of the smallsword, it was used for thrusting, like the foil. While dueling was steadily banned in many countries during the 17th to 19th centuries, fencing's popularity continued. The sport featured in the first modern Olympic Games in 1896 and continues to be an integral part of the event.

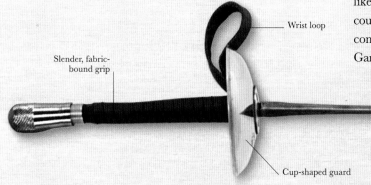

Wrist loop

Slender, fabric-bound grip

Cup-shaped guard

Blade with triangular cross-section

> " TWICE HE TOUCHED HIS CHEST, AND BY DEGREES DROVE HIM BACK, PANTING, UNTIL HE WAS AGAINST THE DOOR. "

WRITER WEIR MITCHELL DESCRIBES A FENCING MATCH IN *THE ADVENTURES OF FRANCOIS*, 1898

ÉPÉE

DATE	c. 19th century	**WEIGHT**	c. 14 oz (400 g)
ORIGIN	Britain	**LENGTH**	c. 35 in (90 cm)

The *épée* was specially developed as a sporting version of the smallsword. It has a flexible, three-sided blade, with a blunt tip that reduces the chance of injury. A shallow, cup-shaped guard protects the fencer's hand, while a wrist loop prevents the sword from being dropped.

FENCING FOR AN AUDIENCE

This illustration by artist F. Meaulle appeared in *Le Petit Journal* on June 9, 1895. It shows two men fencing at the Palais de l'Élysée, the official residence of the president of France.

SWORDS OF THE AMERICAN CIVIL WAR

The armorers of the newly independent United States of America followed patterns for sword making from a mixture of German, French, and British sources. But from the 1840s onward, US swords were based almost exclusively on French designs, and it was these swords that armed the soldiers of the American Civil War (1861–65). While the Union forces of the North were well supplied with arms and equipment, the Confederate armies in the South were short of weapons of all kinds, including swords. They were forced to rely on captured Union stocks, foreign sources, and their own home-produced weapons.

Leather grip wrapped in twisted brass wire

Guard branch

Knuckle guard

MODEL 1860 LIGHT CAVALRY SABER

DATE	c. 1860	WEIGHT	3 lb (1.36 kg)
ORIGIN	USA	LENGTH	35½ in (90 cm)

This saber, used by armies of both sides during the Civil War, was designed to replace the Model 1840 Light Cavalry Saber. The latter was a heavy, powerful sword whose weight made it unpopular with the troops, who nicknamed it "Old Wrist Breaker." The new sword was not considered much of an improvement, although it was an effective thrusting and hacking weapon.

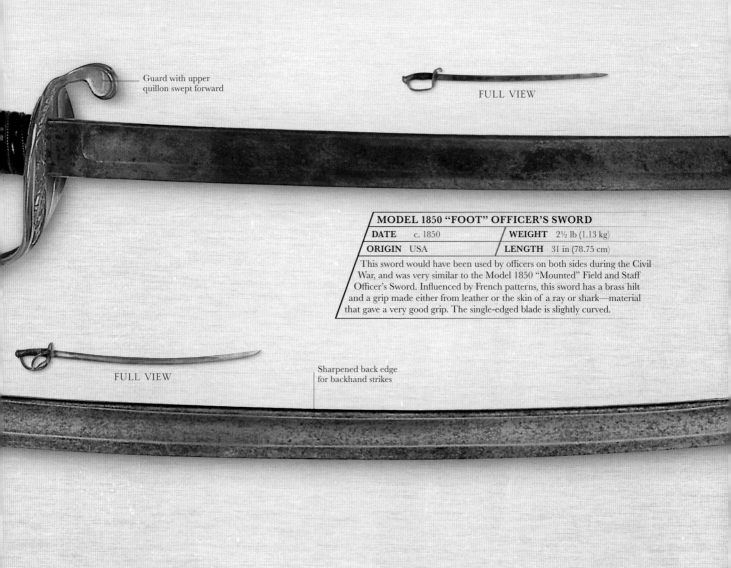

Guard with upper
quillon swept forward

FULL VIEW

MODEL 1850 "FOOT" OFFICER'S SWORD

DATE	c. 1850	WEIGHT	2½ lb (1.13 kg)
ORIGIN	USA	LENGTH	31 in (78.75 cm)

This sword would have been used by officers on both sides during the Civil War, and was very similar to the Model 1850 "Mounted" Field and Staff Officer's Sword. Influenced by French patterns, this sword has a brass hilt and a grip made either from leather or the skin of a ray or shark—material that gave a very good grip. The single-edged blade is slightly curved.

FULL VIEW

Sharpened back edge
for backhand strikes

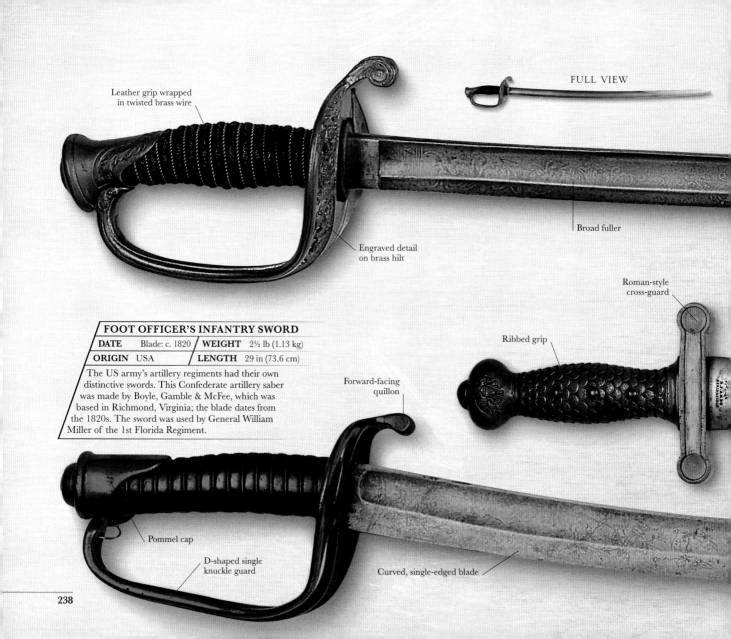

Leather grip wrapped
in twisted brass wire

Broad fuller

Engraved detail
on brass hilt

Roman-style
cross-guard

Ribbed grip

FOOT OFFICER'S INFANTRY SWORD

DATE	Blade: c. 1820	**WEIGHT**	2½ lb (1.13 kg)
ORIGIN	USA	**LENGTH**	29 in (73.6 cm)

The US army's artillery regiments had their own
distinctive swords. This Confederate artillery saber
was made by Boyle, Gamble & McFee, which was
based in Richmond, Virginia; the blade dates from
the 1820s. The sword was used by General William
Miller of the 1st Florida Regiment.

Forward-facing
quillon

Pommel cap

D-shaped single
knuckle guard

Curved, single-edged blade

MODEL 1850 INFANTRY SWORD

DATE	c. 1850	WEIGHT	2½ lb (1.13 kg)
ORIGIN	USA	LENGTH	30 in (76.8 cm)

Swords such as the example shown here equipped the majority
of infantry officers on the Union side. By the time of the Civil War,
officers would rarely have used a sword in actual combat, but such
was its potency that it continued to be worn throughout
the 19th century as a symbol of rank.

ARTILLERYMAN'S SHORT SWORD

DATE	c. 1850	WEIGHT	c. 2¾ lb (1.2 kg)
ORIGIN	USA	LENGTH	25 in (63.5 cm)

Long before the Civil War, the US Army gave artillerymen these short
swords, modeled on the blades of ancient Rome. Originally intended
for self-defense, by the time of the Civil War they were generally used
instead for cutting rope and cannon fuses.

Deep fuller

Double-
edged blade

FULL VIEW

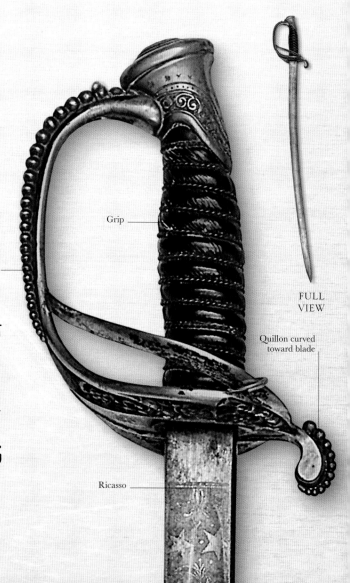

CONFEDERATE SWORD			
DATE	c. 1860	**WEIGHT**	2½ lb (1.13 kg)
ORIGIN	USA	**LENGTH**	30 in (76.2 cm)

The purchase of weapons for popular officers by their
troops was a feature of American military life. This
fine sword, made by Leech & Rigdon, was presented
in 1864 to General D. W. Adams of the Confederate
Army by the men under his command. The sword
follows the standard pattern for staff and field officers'
swords in the Confederate forces.

Grip

Knuckle guard

FULL
VIEW

Quillon curved
toward blade

Ricasso

> # A YOUNG LIEUTENANT
> ## HAD FALLEN IN TRYING TO
> # RALLY HIS MEN:
> ## HIS HAND WAS STILL FIRMLY
> ## GRASPING HIS SWORD...
>
> *POPULAR SCIENCE*, 1893

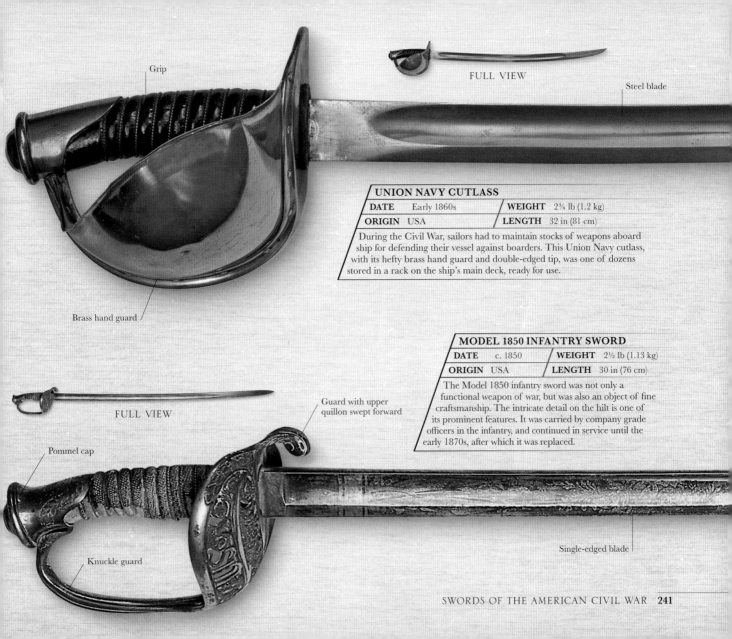

Grip

FULL VIEW

Steel blade

UNION NAVY CUTLASS

DATE	Early 1860s	WEIGHT	2¾ lb (1.2 kg)
ORIGIN	USA	LENGTH	32 in (81 cm)

During the Civil War, sailors had to maintain stocks of weapons aboard ship for defending their vessel against boarders. This Union Navy cutlass, with its hefty brass hand guard and double-edged tip, was one of dozens stored in a rack on the ship's main deck, ready for use.

Brass hand guard

MODEL 1850 INFANTRY SWORD

DATE	c. 1850	WEIGHT	2½ lb (1.13 kg)
ORIGIN	USA	LENGTH	30 in (76 cm)

The Model 1850 infantry sword was not only a functional weapon of war, but was also an object of fine craftsmanship. The intricate detail on the hilt is one of its prominent features. It was carried by company grade officers in the infantry, and continued in service until the early 1870s, after which it was replaced.

Guard with upper quillon swept forward

FULL VIEW

Pommel cap

Knuckle guard

Single-edged blade

UNITED STATES CAVALRYMAN

The American Civil War (1861–65) between the Confederate South and the Northern Union marked a transitional time for American cavalry. The increased use of musket and cannon threatened to make the cavalry obsolete, at least in open battle.

Massed cavalry actions still occurred—for example, at the battles of Brandy Station (1863) and Trevilian Station (1864). Aside from these, the cavalry was principally used for raiding, pursuit, and reconnaissance. Initially, the Confederate cavalry was regarded as a superior force because of its better horsemanship, but by 1864 the Union cavalry had achieved similar competence. The Northern cavalry used traditional sabers more for fighting, while the Southern cavalry preferred carbines and pistols, although they still wore sabers alongside their firearms, as backup weapons and as a sign of status. The classic Civil War cavalry swords were the 1840 Cavalry Saber (below) and the subsequent 1860 Light Cavalry Saber.

Brass basket hilt
and guard

CONFEDERATE 1840 CAVALRY SABER

DATE	c. 1850	WEIGHT	3¼ lb (1.56 kg)
ORIGIN	USA	LENGTH	35 in (89 cm)

This Confederate cavalry saber, designed for heavy slashing blows, features a brass basket hilt and a leather grip. The slight angling of the grip gave the swordsman greater leverage behind the blow. The cavalry of the Confederate states used sabers based on this model.

> **AS WE DASHED FIERCELY INTO THEM,**
> # SABER IN HAND,
> **THEY BROKE LIKE A WAVE ON THE BOWS OF A SHIP.**

UNION CAVALRYMAN DESCRIBING THE BATTLE
OF BRANDY STATION, VIRGINIA, 1863

CHARGING THE ENEMY

The first Battle of Bull Run (1861), also known as the first
Battle of Manassas (Virginia), was a major land battle of
the Civil War, won by the Confederate forces. In this scene,
the Confederate cavalry is shown charging Union ranks,
making downward slashing attacks with sabers similar
to the one featured here.

Slightly curved,
single-edged blade

EUROPEAN AND AMERICAN BAYONETS

The sword bayonet, with its long blade, became increasingly popular in the 19th century, replacing the hanger sword and socket bayonet of the ordinary infantryman. However, the 19th century also saw the development of mass-produced, long-range firepower that rendered the bayonet irrelevant as a military weapon. Despite this, armies continued to place great emphasis on the bayonet, not least because it was believed to encourage an aggressive, offensive spirit among the infantry. It was this attitude that, in part, led to the mass slaughters of World War I, when soldiers with bayonets fixed were pitted against quick-firing artillery and machine guns.

Locking-bolt spring

Brass handle

Leather grip

Knuckle guard

Straight quillon

FULL VIEW

VOLUNTEER INFANTRY SWORD BAYONET

DATE	1810	WEIGHT	18 oz (500 g)
ORIGIN	UK	LENGTH	30½ in (77.5 cm)

During the Napoleonic Wars (1799–1815), the regular British Army was equipped with the Baker rifle and its sword bayonet (*pp. 250–51*). Volunteer units, however, had to draw upon other sources for their rifles and bayonets. This sword bayonet, made for the London gunmaker Staudenmayer, features a gilded hilt and straight steel blade. Its knuckle guard would lock the rifle to the bayonet. This method rendered the weapon less effective than the Baker rifle and bayonet.

Ring for muzzle (open front end of barrel) with fore sight slot

I. GILL

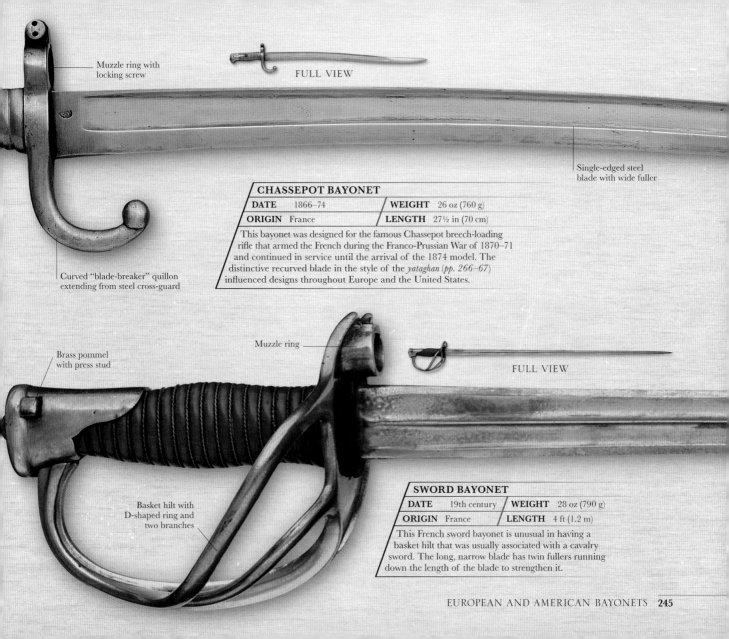

Muzzle ring with
locking screw

FULL VIEW

Single-edged steel
blade with wide fuller

CHASSEPOT BAYONET

DATE	1866–74	WEIGHT	26 oz (760 g)
ORIGIN	France	LENGTH	27½ in (70 cm)

This bayonet was designed for the famous Chassepot breech-loading
rifle that armed the French during the Franco-Prussian War of 1870–71
and continued in service until the arrival of the 1874 model. The
distinctive recurved blade in the style of the *yataghan* (*pp. 266–67*)
influenced designs throughout Europe and the United States.

Curved "blade-breaker" quillon
extending from steel cross-guard

Muzzle ring

FULL VIEW

Brass pommel
with press stud

SWORD BAYONET

DATE	19th century	WEIGHT	28 oz (790 g)
ORIGIN	France	LENGTH	4 ft (1.2 m)

This French sword bayonet is unusual in having a
basket hilt that was usually associated with a cavalry
sword. The long, narrow blade has twin fullers running
down the length of the blade to strengthen it.

Basket hilt with
D-shaped ring and
two branches

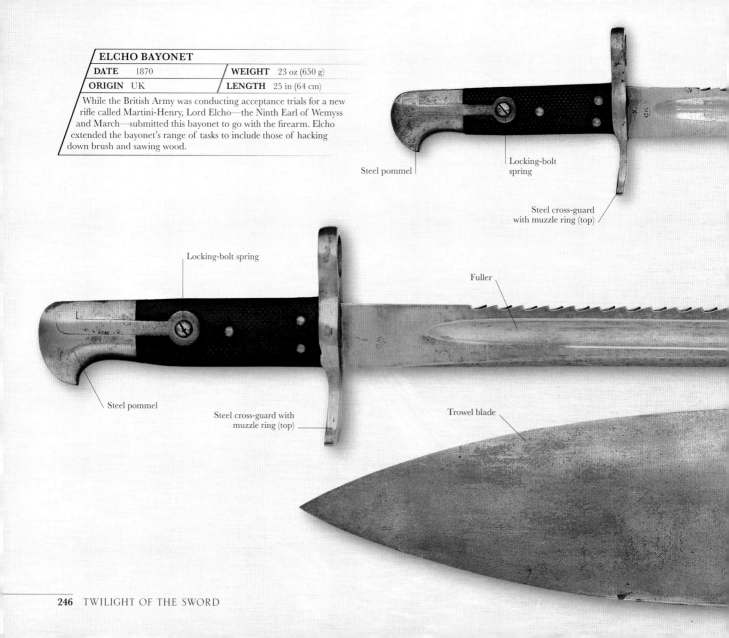

ELCHO BAYONET

DATE	1870	WEIGHT	23 oz (650 g)
ORIGIN	UK	LENGTH	25 in (64 cm)

While the British Army was conducting acceptance trials for a new rifle called Martini-Henry, Lord Elcho—the Ninth Earl of Wemyss and March—submitted this bayonet to go with the firearm. Elcho extended the bayonet's range of tasks to include those of hacking down brush and sawing wood.

Steel pommel

Locking-bolt spring

Steel cross-guard with muzzle ring (top)

Locking-bolt spring

Fuller

Steel pommel

Steel cross-guard with muzzle ring (top)

Trowel blade

Serrated edge for
sawing wood

Broadened blade to chop
through undergrowth

LATER ELCHO BAYONET

DATE	c. 1875	WEIGHT	22½ oz (640 g)
ORIGIN	UK	LENGTH	25 in (64.2 cm)

Despite initial success—and the arming of some infantry units—
the Elcho bayonet was not taken up as an official model, since it was
considered too expensive and ungainly. Even this later model, with a
more conventional blade, failed to persuade the authorities in its favor.

Serrated edge for
sawing wood

Conventional
bayonet blade

Locking collar incorporating
bridge and mortise slot (socket to
receive projecting muzzle)

TROWEL BAYONET

DATE	Late 19th century	WEIGHT	18 oz (500 g)
ORIGIN	USA	LENGTH	15 in (36.8 cm)

Designed to fit over the muzzle of the US 1873 "Trapdoor" Springfield
rifle, this ingenious implement was intended as an entrenching or general
digging tool, although it could also be used as a very broad-bladed
bayonet. Constructed from metal, it has a blued finish.

Flint

Cock

Trigger guard

Rear sling attachment

Barrel band
securing barrel to stock

Cock

Octagonal
barrel

Trigger guard releases bayonet
from closed position

POCKET PISTOL BAYONET

DATE	1800	WEIGHT	17 oz (478 g)
ORIGIN	Belgium	LENGTH	4¼ in (11 cm)

Short-barreled pistols replaced the sword as the gentleman's weapon of self-defense. Such pistols sometimes had a folded bayonet, which was released by pulling back the trigger guard. The bayonet was attached to the gun by a simple hinge, and a catch would spring open to lock the bayonet in place.

Cock

Flint clamp

CHARLEVILLE MUSKET

Barrel band

Trigger

Rear sling swivel

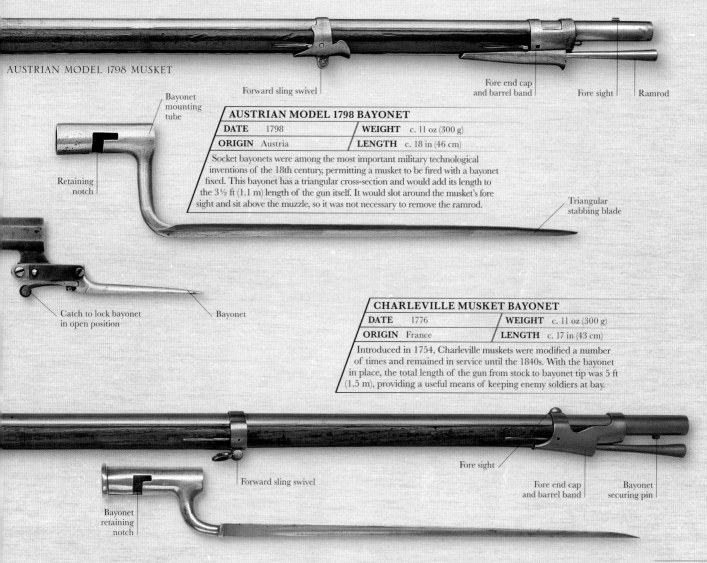

AUSTRIAN MODEL 1798 MUSKET

Forward sling swivel

Fore end cap
and barrel band

Fore sight

Ramrod

Bayonet
mounting
tube

AUSTRIAN MODEL 1798 BAYONET

DATE	1798	WEIGHT	c. 11 oz (300 g)
ORIGIN	Austria	LENGTH	c. 18 in (46 cm)

Socket bayonets were among the most important military technological
inventions of the 18th century, permitting a musket to be fired with a bayonet
fixed. This bayonet has a triangular cross-section and would add its length to
the 3½ ft (1.1 m) length of the gun itself. It would slot around the musket's fore
sight and sit above the muzzle, so it was not necessary to remove the ramrod.

Triangular
stabbing blade

Retaining
notch

Catch to lock bayonet
in open position

Bayonet

CHARLEVILLE MUSKET BAYONET

DATE	1776	WEIGHT	c. 11 oz (300 g)
ORIGIN	France	LENGTH	c. 17 in (43 cm)

Introduced in 1754, Charleville muskets were modified a number
of times and remained in service until the 1840s. With the bayonet
in place, the total length of the gun from stock to bayonet tip was 5 ft
(1.5 m), providing a useful means of keeping enemy soldiers at bay.

Fore sight

Fore end cap
and barrel band

Bayonet
securing pin

Forward sling swivel

Bayonet
retaining
notch

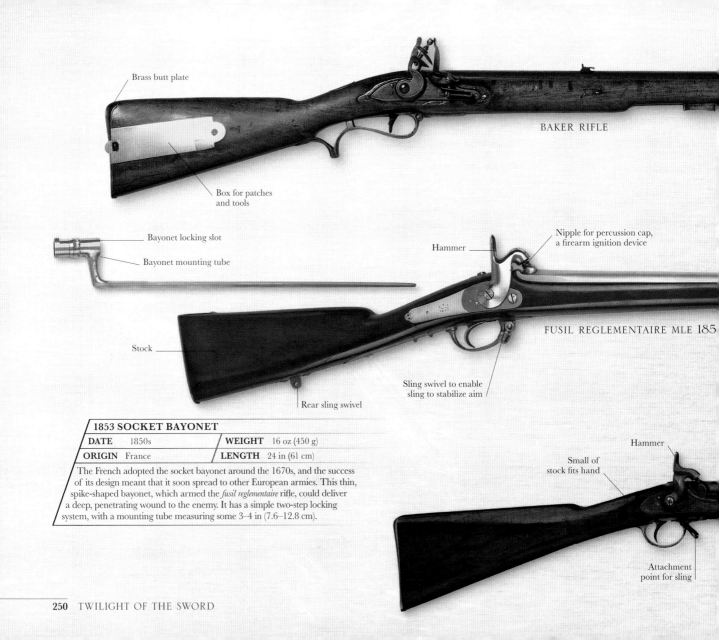

Brass butt plate

BAKER RIFLE

Box for patches
and tools

Bayonet locking slot

Nipple for percussion cap,
a firearm ignition device

Hammer

Bayonet mounting tube

Stock

FUSIL REGLEMENTAIRE MLE 185

Sling swivel to enable
sling to stabilize aim

Rear sling swivel

Hammer

Small of
stock fits hand

1853 SOCKET BAYONET

DATE	1850s	WEIGHT	16 oz (450 g)
ORIGIN	France	LENGTH	24 in (61 cm)

The French adopted the socket bayonet around the 1670s, and the success
of its design meant that it soon spread to other European armies. This thin,
spike-shaped bayonet, which armed the *fusil reglementaire* rifle, could deliver
a deep, penetrating wound to the enemy. It has a simple two-step locking
system, with a mounting tube measuring some 3–4 in (7.6–12.8 cm).

Attachment
point for sling

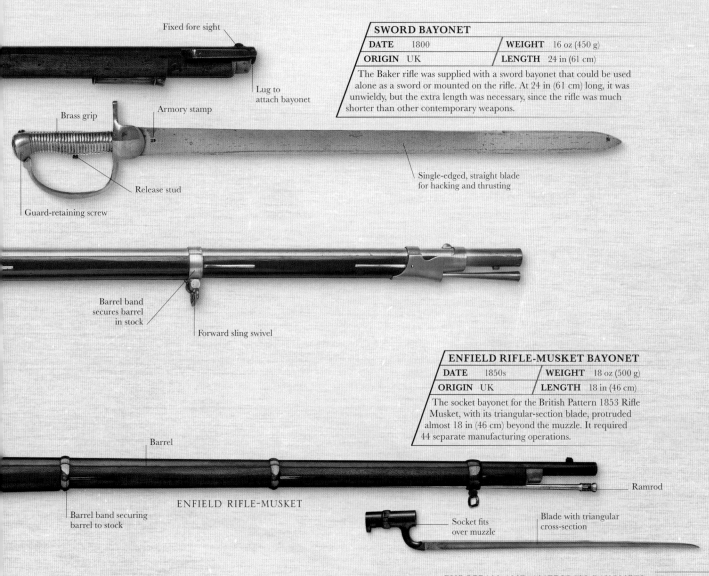

Fixed fore sight

Lug to attach bayonet

SWORD BAYONET

DATE	1800	WEIGHT	16 oz (450 g)
ORIGIN	UK	LENGTH	24 in (61 cm)

The Baker rifle was supplied with a sword bayonet that could be used alone as a sword or mounted on the rifle. At 24 in (61 cm) long, it was unwieldy, but the extra length was necessary, since the rifle was much shorter than other contemporary weapons.

Brass grip

Armory stamp

Release stud

Guard-retaining screw

Single-edged, straight blade for hacking and thrusting

Barrel band secures barrel in stock

Forward sling swivel

ENFIELD RIFLE-MUSKET BAYONET

DATE	1850s	WEIGHT	18 oz (500 g)
ORIGIN	UK	LENGTH	18 in (46 cm)

The socket bayonet for the British Pattern 1853 Rifle Musket, with its triangular-section blade, protruded almost 18 in (46 cm) beyond the muzzle. It required 44 separate manufacturing operations.

Barrel

ENFIELD RIFLE-MUSKET

Ramrod

Barrel band securing barrel to stock

Socket fits over muzzle

Blade with triangular cross-section

BAYONET TACTICS

Bayonets transformed the power of the ordinary foot soldier. By adding a bayonet to the musket, an infantryman could function both as a shooter and a pikeman (*pp. 176–77*), thereby gaining a tactical advantage over a nearly invincible cavalry.

Bayonets made an important contribution to the battefield when they appeared during the 17th century. First, they provided an offensive capability—infantrymen could make a bayonet charge at the enemy and break his lines. This was especially important since firepower alone was rarely decisive before the advent of rapid-fire weapons in the 19th century. The infantryman was typically trained to focus on parrying the enemy's thrust before driving the bayonet into his chest. Second, the bayonet could also be used as a defensive tool. Cavalry charges, for example, would be largely ineffective against tight, disciplined squares or lines of bayonet-armed infantry, since horses were reluctant to impale themselves on steel spikes.

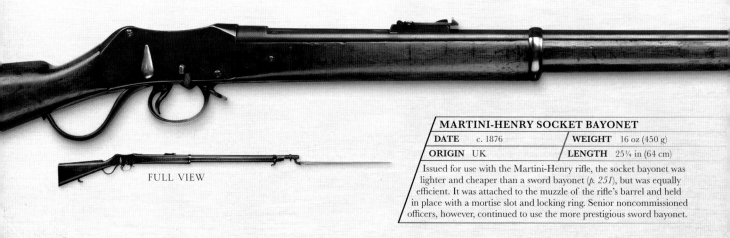

FULL VIEW

MARTINI-HENRY SOCKET BAYONET

DATE	c. 1876	WEIGHT	16 oz (450 g)
ORIGIN	UK	LENGTH	25¼ in (64 cm)

Issued for use with the Martini-Henry rifle, the socket bayonet was lighter and cheaper than a sword bayonet (*p. 251*), but was equally efficient. It was attached to the muzzle of the rifle's barrel and held in place with a mortise slot and locking ring. Senior noncommissioned officers, however, continued to use the more prestigious sword bayonet.

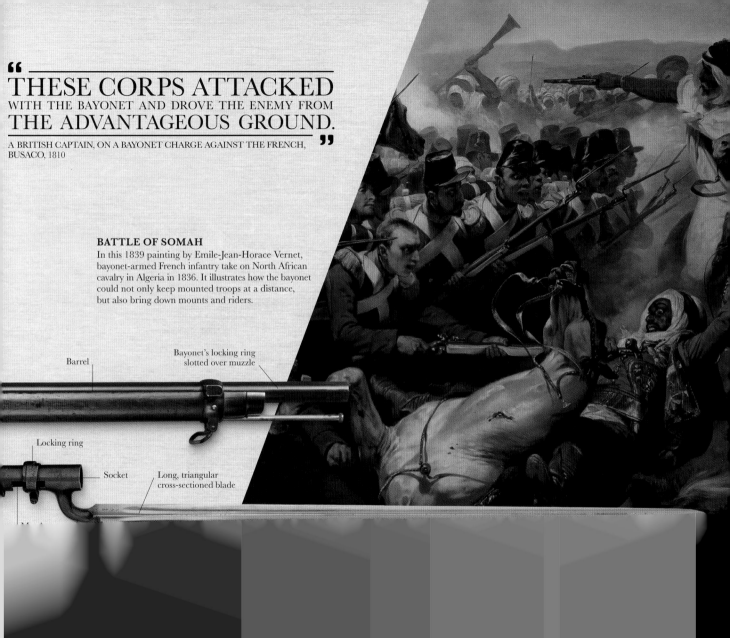

"THESE CORPS ATTACKED
WITH THE BAYONET AND DROVE THE ENEMY FROM
THE ADVANTAGEOUS GROUND."

A BRITISH CAPTAIN, ON A BAYONET CHARGE AGAINST THE FRENCH,
BUSACO, 1810

BATTLE OF SOMAH

In this 1839 painting by Emile-Jean-Horace Vernet,
bayonet-armed French infantry take on North African
cavalry in Algeria in 1836. It illustrates how the bayonet
could not only keep mounted troops at a distance,
but also bring down mounts and riders.

Barrel

Bayonet's locking ring
slotted over muzzle

Locking ring

Socket

Long, triangular
cross-sectioned blade

NORTH AMERICAN HILT WEAPONS

Although wood and stone implements remained in use, by the late 18th century, Native Americans were purchasing and using weapons with metal blades or heads of European and Euro-American origin, which they often customized with decorative motifs. Many items shown here were not primarily designed for combat, but instead had a range of practical or symbolic uses, from hunting to performing religious rites. Yet tomahawks and clubs remained fearsome weapons in the hands of a skilled warrior.

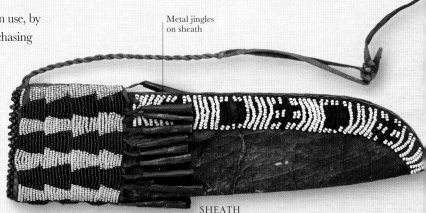

Metal jingles on sheath

SHEATH

Spearhead made into knife

Wooden handle covered with red cloth

SPEARHEAD KNIFE		
DATE c. 1900	**WEIGHT** 11 oz (300 g)	
ORIGIN USA	**LENGTH** 16 in (41 cm)	

This knife was made by attaching a wooden handle to the head of a lance or spear—a common weapon for a Native-American warrior. The rawhide sheath, finely stitched with beadwork, was probably used with this knife, but not specifically made for it, hence, the difference in shape.

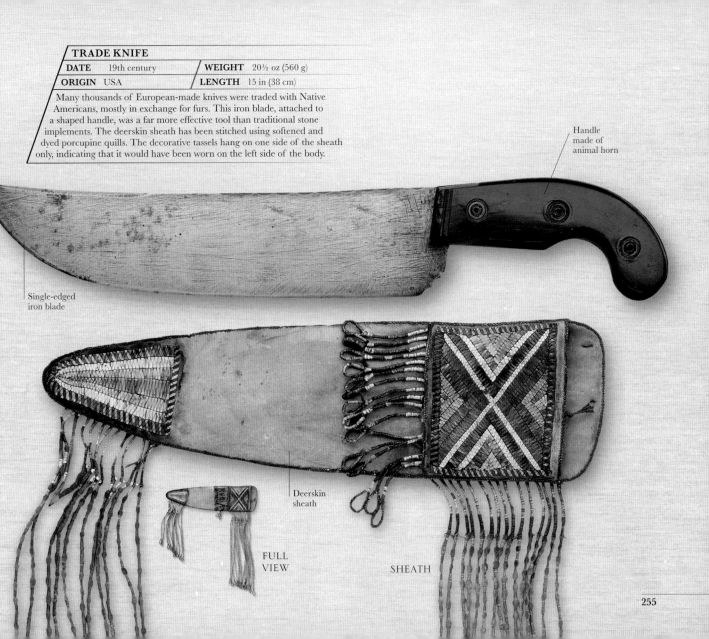

TRADE KNIFE

| **DATE** | 19th century | **WEIGHT** | 20½ oz (560 g) |
| **ORIGIN** | USA | **LENGTH** | 15 in (38 cm) |

Many thousands of European-made knives were traded with Native Americans, mostly in exchange for furs. This iron blade, attached to a shaped handle, was a far more effective tool than traditional stone implements. The deerskin sheath has been stitched using softened and dyed porcupine quills. The decorative tassels hang on one side of the sheath only, indicating that it would have been worn on the left side of the body.

Handle made of animal horn

Single-edged iron blade

Deerskin sheath

FULL VIEW

SHEATH

BOWIE KNIFE

DATE	c. 1820	WEIGHT	18 oz (500 g)
ORIGIN	USA	LENGTH	9½ in (25 cm)

The archetypal American blade, the Bowie knife was designed by Rezin P. Bowie, brother of Battle of Alamo hero James "Jim" Bowie. The knife, with its heavy butcher's type blade, was initially used as a hunting tool, but later became popular as a self-defense weapon.

Sheath made of red leather

SHEATH

Hardwood handle

Straight cross-guard

Concave clip-point (tip clipped to make it thinner and sharper)

Totem figure of raven on bear's head

TLINGIT FIGHTING KNIFE

DATE	19th century	WEIGHT	18 oz (500 g)
ORIGIN	USA	LENGTH	20 in (50 cm)

The Tlingit people of the northwest Pacific coast were skilled metalworkers, producing good-quality copper and iron blades. The handle of this knife is wrapped in leather and topped with a fine totem carving, which is inlaid with abalone shell. Fighting in close combat, the Tlingit warrior would wrap the loose leather strap around his wrist to ensure a secure hold upon the weapon.

Chape

Stylized fish carving

FULL VIEW

HAIDA CLUB

DATE	19th century	WEIGHT	c. 4½ lb (2 kg)
ORIGIN	USA	LENGTH	c. 20 in (51 cm)

Living on islands off the northwest coast of North America, the Haida people fished from canoes. This wooden club was used to stun big fish as soon as they were hauled from the water before their struggles upset the canoe. Due to the lack of metals, the Haidas crafted wood into rudimentary blades; the head of the club was flattened rather than rounded to produce a narrow impact point. Unlike regular clubs, this one had a separate, distinctive hilt.

Heavy
iron blade

Leather strap
to lash onto
wrist in combat

PIPE TOMAHAWK

DATE	c. 1890
ORIGIN	USA

The idea of combining a peace pipe (ceremonial smoking pipe) and a war ax was dreamed up by Euro-American traders, but taken on by Native Americans with enthusiasm. They bought large numbers of these pipe tomahawks, making them a part of their culture. They were carried by Native-American chiefs as symbols of prestige and exchanged as diplomatic gifts.

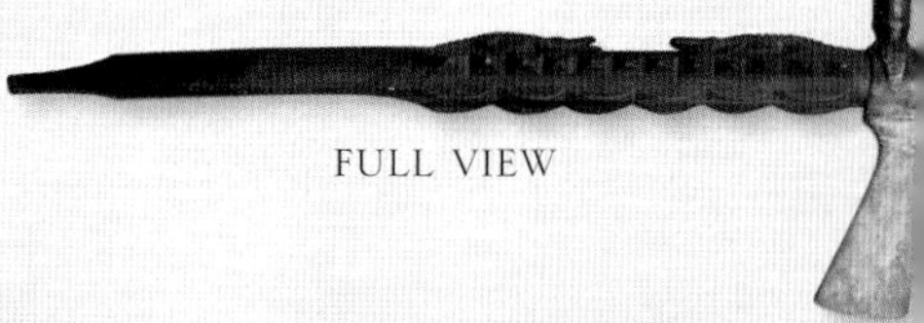

FULL VIEW

Carved wooden shaft

Birchwood club

Carving of lake scene

FULL VIEW

ANTLER SPIKE CLUB

DATE	18th/19th century
ORIGIN	USA

The North American Indians manufactured a variety of spiked clubs, with spikes made from antler (as seen here), bone, or on occasion, steel. This two-handed war club is made of birchwood and crudely decorated with a scene showing a lake with three warriors nearby. Notches at each end may have been for tallying numbers of enemies or animals killed.

Antler spike

Iron
tobacco
bowl

Shaped rock
forms club head

Rock is lashed
to the handle

PENOBSCOT STONE CLUB

| **DATE** | 19th century |
| **ORIGIN** | USA |

This stone club was used by the Penobscot Indians
of Maine, in the northeastern United States. Clubs such
as this would typically be used to finish off a wounded
moose or deer that had been brought down by an arrow
or a spear, although they may have been used in combat.

FULL
VIEW

NORTH AMERICAN WARRIOR

Prior to their contact with European colonizers, Native-American warriors chiefly used weapons such as the bow, tomahawk, spear, and club. Even after the introduction of firearms in the 16th century, the Native Americans continued to fight in the more traditional ways, favoring ambushes and hit-and-run battles over the formal, ordered tactics of the European settler armies.

The Native-American way of war was largely based upon stealth, surprise, camouflage, and concealment. Many Europeans misinterpreted such tactics as underhanded and cowardly. By employing these tactics, however, the Native Americans could avoid sacrificing their already dwindling population and fight using the same techniques they used for hunting. During the 17th and 18th centuries, firearms became popular among Native-American tribes, although traditional weapons were still used in combat until the end of 19th century.

PIPE TOMAHAWK			
DATE	c. 18th century	**WEIGHT**	c. 2¾ lb (1.2 kg)
ORIGIN	North America	**LENGTH**	c. 15 in (38 cm)

The tomahawk was a type of ax, used as both a utility tool and a weapon. Pipe tomahawks, such as the example shown here, had a tobacco bowl at the back of the axhead and a hollow handle, so they could be used as smoking pipes as well. Tomahawks were often thrown as missiles; the warriors calculated the right amount of spin to apply so that the blade, not the shaft, struck the target.

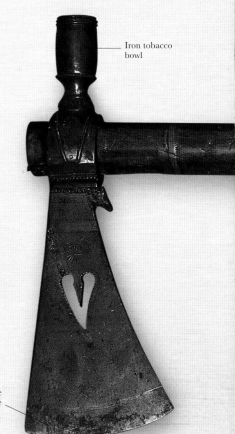

Iron tobacco bowl

Cutting edge of blade

Hollowed-out handle

FULL VIEW

TOMAHAWK FIGHT

This detail from the grave marker of American pioneer and hunter Daniel Boone (1734–1820) shows him fighting a Native American. The scene depicts both old and new weaponry—the warrior wields a tomahawk and a dagger, while Boone is armed with a hunting musket.

OTTOMAN EMPIRE SWORDS

The Ottoman Empire, at its height from the 15th to the 17th century, was founded by Turks who migrated to Anatolia (now in Turkey) from Central Asia. Their curved swords reflect these origins, being derived from the Central Asian Turko-Mongolian saber of the 13th century. Europeans first encountered these blades in wars with the Ottomans and called them scimitars (a term used to refer collectively to curved Asian swords). Many of the swords shown here date from the 19th century but are typical of the Ottoman Empire at its peak. Similar weapons were used across the Islamic world, from North Africa to Persia and India.

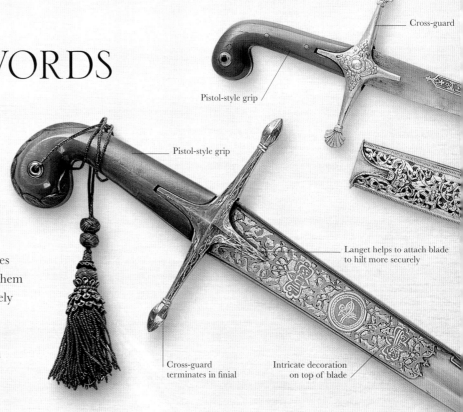

Cross-guard

Pistol-style grip

Pistol-style grip

Langet helps to attach blade to hilt more securely

Cross-guard terminates in finial

Intricate decoration on top of blade

PERSIAN KILIJ			
DATE	Early 19th century	**WEIGHT**	21 oz (600 g)
ORIGIN Persia		**LENGTH**	32 in (81 cm)

Persian craftsmen were acknowledged masters of sword-making. The *kilij* was first used in the Ottoman Empire in the 15th century. Over time, its blade showed many variations. This example has a deep curve cut away along its back edge, and has a distinctive flared tip called a *yelman*.

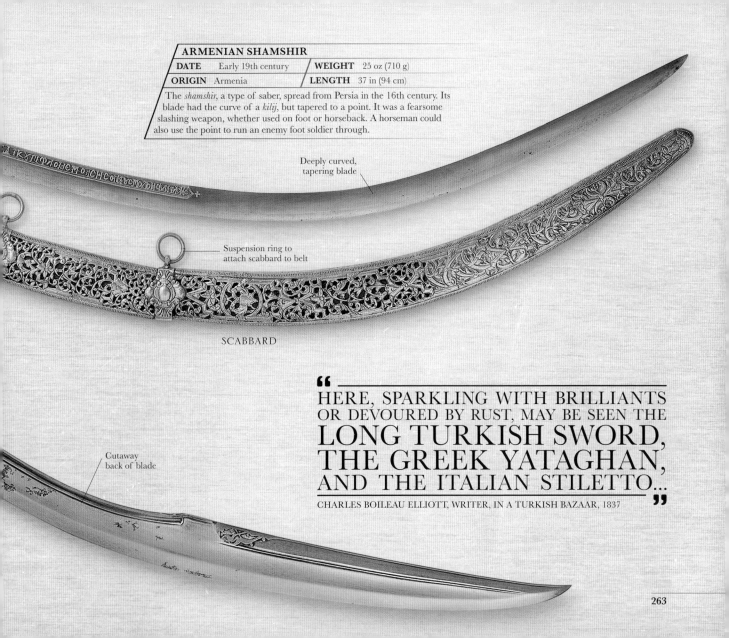

ARMENIAN SHAMSHIR

DATE	Early 19th century	**WEIGHT**	25 oz (710 g)
ORIGIN	Armenia	**LENGTH**	37 in (94 cm)

The *shamshir*, a type of saber, spread from Persia in the 16th century. Its blade had the curve of a *kilij*, but tapered to a point. It was a fearsome slashing weapon, whether used on foot or horseback. A horseman could also use the point to run an enemy foot soldier through.

Deeply curved, tapering blade

Suspension ring to attach scabbard to belt

SCABBARD

Cutaway back of blade

" HERE, SPARKLING WITH BRILLIANTS OR DEVOURED BY RUST, MAY BE SEEN THE LONG TURKISH SWORD, THE GREEK YATAGHAN, AND THE ITALIAN STILETTO... "

CHARLES BOILEAU ELLIOTT, WRITER, IN A TURKISH BAZAAR, 1837

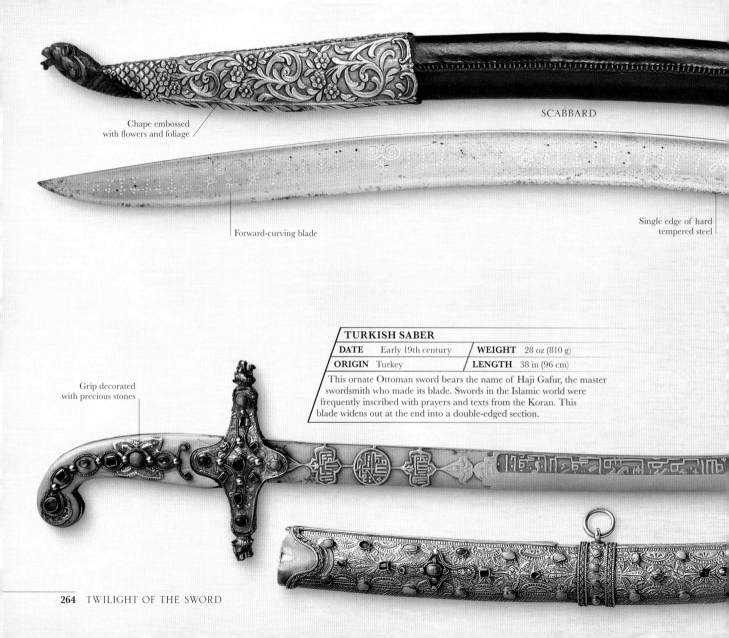

Chape embossed
with flowers and foliage

SCABBARD

Forward-curving blade

Single edge of hard
tempered steel

Grip decorated
with precious stones

TURKISH SABER

DATE	Early 19th century	WEIGHT	28 oz (810 g)
ORIGIN	Turkey	LENGTH	38 in (96 cm)

This ornate Ottoman sword bears the name of Haji Gafur, the master
swordsmith who made its blade. Swords in the Islamic world were
frequently inscribed with prayers and texts from the Koran. This
blade widens out at the end into a double-edged section.

Silver band

TURKISH YATAGHAN

| DATE | Mid-19th century | WEIGHT | 21 oz (600 g) |
| ORIGIN | Turkey | LENGTH | 29 in (74 cm) |

A *yataghan* has a forward-curving blade known as a *kopis* blade, after the ancient Greek sword of that name (*p. 29*). The *yataghan* is similar to the Indian *sosun pattah* (*p. 291*) and the Nepalese *kukri* (*pp. 334-35*). This late Ottoman example is identical in style to those used when the empire was at its height. The wooden scabbard is clad in leather.

Hilt has no guard

Distinctive grip plaques
flare into "wings" or "ears"

Gold inscription
from the Koran

Turquoise set
into scabbard

SCABBARD

OTTOMAN WARRIOR

From the 14th to the 18th centuries, the Ottoman army of the Turkish sultans was one of the most professional military forces in the world. Well trained and skilled, the Ottoman warrior used the *kilij* (a curved sword) with deadly precision.

There were many different types of soldier in the Ottoman army. The slave-soldier janissaries—part of the sultan's standing army—acted as elite infantry, in contrast to the dispensable *azab* foot soldiers. Ottoman cavalry ranged from heavy shock troops to light scouts. Yet all were bound together as a unified, disciplined, tactically intelligent whole. The Ottoman warriors were feared for their proficiency with weapons, particularly the *kilij* seen here. This curved sword had a flaring tip called a yelman or "false edge" that enhanced its cutting power and could sever a head with a single stroke. Cavalry used either these swords or long spears, and protected themselves with long coats of chain mail and helmets.

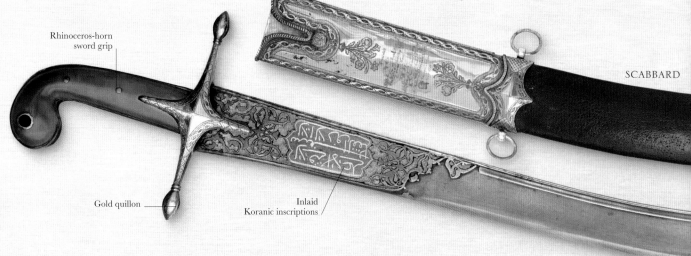

Rhinoceros-horn sword grip

SCABBARD

Gold quillon

Inlaid Koranic inscriptions

FEARLESS CAVALRY
This painting shows Ottoman troops setting out for conquest. Cavalry soldiers were experts in wielding the *kilij* as well as lances and bows. They would aim strikes at the skull, neck, and face of the enemy, using the speed of the horse to add power.

> "
> # MAY YOUR BLADE BE VICTORIOUS OVER THE NECKS OF YOUR FOES.
> "

INSCRIPTION ON A 16TH-CENTURY OTTOMAN SWORD

KILIJ			
DATE	1625	**WEIGHT**	c. 21 oz (600 g)
ORIGIN	Ottoman Empire	**LENGTH**	c. 32 in (81 cm)

This Ottoman *kilij* is representative of the classic Ottoman sword up to the 19th century. Its trademark curved blade is inscribed with a quotation from the Koran on the ricasso. It has a rounded hilt made of rhinoceros horn. The cross-guard reinforces the blade, and the wooden scabbard is overlaid with silver gilt.

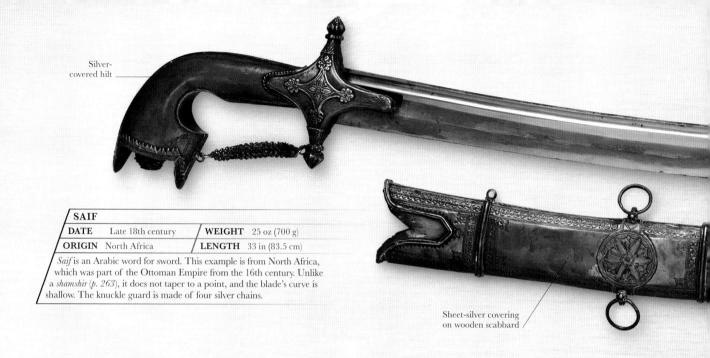

Silver-covered hilt

SAIF			
DATE	Late 18th century	**WEIGHT**	25 oz (700 g)
ORIGIN	North Africa	**LENGTH**	33 in (83.5 cm)

Saif is an Arabic word for sword. This example is from North Africa, which was part of the Ottoman Empire from the 16th century. Unlike a *shamshir* (*p. 263*), it does not taper to a point, and the blade's curve is shallow. The knuckle guard is made of four silver chains.

Sheet-silver covering on wooden scabbard

WESTERN TROOPS AND OBSERVERS WERE STILL ENCOUNTERING TURKISH BLADES IN COMBAT WELL INTO THE 20TH CENTURY.

Narrow fuller
on back of blade

SCABBARD

Silver-coated hilt inlaid
with coral and turquoise

SCABBARD

OTTOMAN QUAMA			
DATE	19th century	**WEIGHT**	25 oz (700 g)
ORIGIN	Turkey	**LENGTH**	24 in (61 cm)

Quama is a short sword, called a *kinjal* in the Caucasus and
a *kama* in Georgia. It is also known as a Cossack dagger. This
example, with its splendidly decorated hilt and scabbard, was
designed to display its owner's wealth and status.

PERSIAN SHAMSHIR

DATE	19th century
ORIGIN	Persia
LENGTH	c. 35 in (89 cm)

The classic examples of *shamshir* can be found in Persia, Turkey, India, and other parts of the Islamic world. This Persian sword is a typical *shamshir*, with an L-shaped pommel and straight quillons meeting in a diamond-shaped central plate. These swords typically had a grip made of bone or ivory, riveted to the hilt.

L-shaped
pommel

Sprung steel
covering drawing slot

Flared finial
on quillon

Straight quillon
formed into langet

KILIJ

DATE	Unknown
ORIGIN	Ottoman Empire
LENGTH	c. 35 in (89 cm)

The *kilij*, or *kilic*, is very similar to the *shamshir*, but its blade was generally broader and widened as it neared the tip. The scabbards of these swords were often specially adapted, with a slot cut into the back of the scabbard and covered with sprung steel. Without this feature, it would have been extremely difficult to draw such a highly curved blade.

Pommel features
cord loop

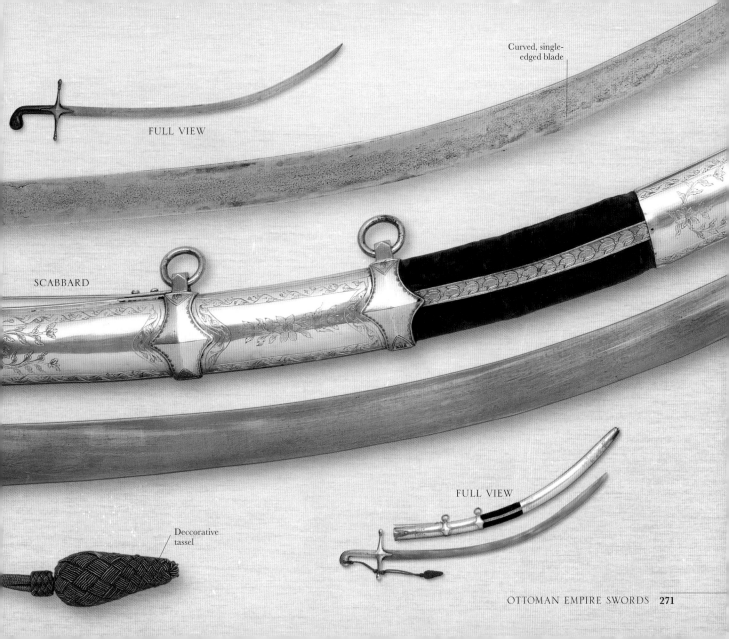

Curved, single-
edged blade

FULL VIEW

SCABBARD

Deccorative
tassel

FULL VIEW

CHINESE AND TIBETAN SWORDS

For the Chinese, the four major weapons of a warrior were the staff, the spear, and two swords—the single-edged *dao* and the double-edged *jian*. While the straight-bladed *jian* was the more prestigious of the two, the curved *dao* was more practical and easier to use. As in Europe, by the 19th century, swords in China were fast becoming ceremonial items. The military tradition of Tibet is often forgotten, but the Tibetans fought many wars and developed their own significant tradition of manufacturing swords, which were loosely related to Chinese models.

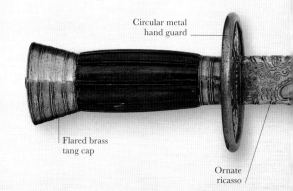

Circular metal
hand guard

Flared brass
tang cap

Ornate
ricasso

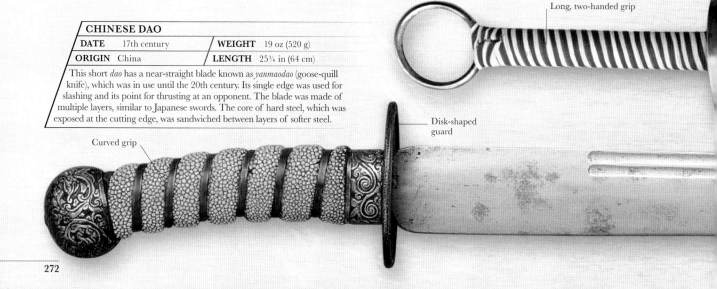

Long, two-handed grip

CHINESE DAO			
DATE	17th century	**WEIGHT**	19 oz (520 g)
ORIGIN	China	**LENGTH**	25¼ in (64 cm)

This short *dao* has a near-straight blade known as *yanmaodao* (goose-quill knife), which was in use until the 20th century. Its single edge was used for slashing and its point for thrusting at an opponent. The blade was made of multiple layers, similar to Japanese swords. The core of hard steel, which was exposed at the cutting edge, was sandwiched between layers of softer steel.

Disk-shaped
guard

Curved grip

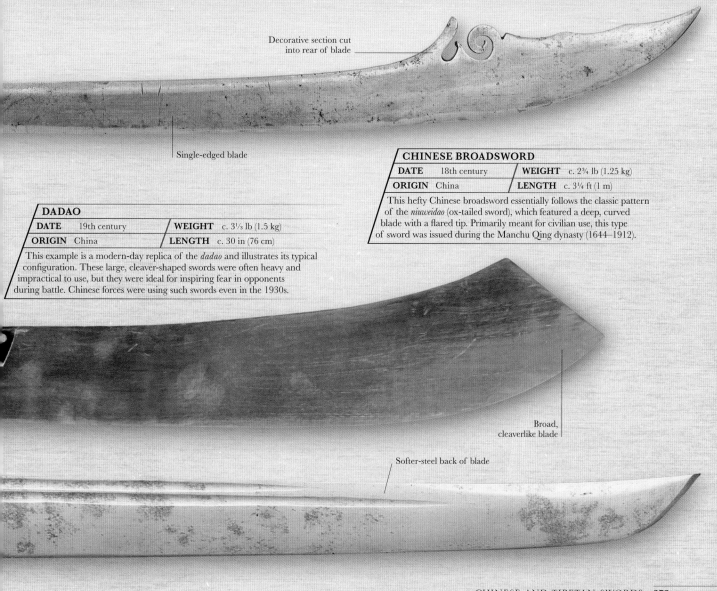

Decorative section cut
into rear of blade

Single-edged blade

CHINESE BROADSWORD

DATE	18th century	WEIGHT	c. 2¾ lb (1.25 kg)
ORIGIN	China	LENGTH	c. 3¼ ft (1 m)

This hefty Chinese broadsword essentially follows the classic pattern of the *niuweidao* (ox-tailed sword), which featured a deep, curved blade with a flared tip. Primarily meant for civilian use, this type of sword was issued during the Manchu Qing dynasty (1644–1912).

DADAO

DATE	19th century	WEIGHT	c. 3⅓ lb (1.5 kg)
ORIGIN	China	LENGTH	c. 30 in (76 cm)

This example is a modern-day replica of the *dadao* and illustrates its typical configuration. These large, cleaver-shaped swords were often heavy and impractical to use, but they were ideal for inspiring fear in opponents during battle. Chinese forces were using such swords even in the 1930s.

Broad,
cleaverlike blade

Softer-steel back of blade

CHINESE JIAN

DATE	1736–95	WEIGHT	2¾ lb (1.25 kg)
ORIGIN	China	LENGTH	3½ ft (1.07 m)

With its straight, double-edged blade, the *jian* was the
weapon chosen by Chinese swordsmen to show off
their skills. It was also worn by high officials as part of
their ceremonial regalia. This *jian* dates from the reign
of Emperor Qianlong (r. 1735–96), the fourth emperor
of the Manchu Qing dynasty (1644–1912).

Lacquer coating
on scabbard

Lobe-shaped quillon

Ivory grip

Pommel attached
to tang of blade

Gilded
collar

TIBETAN SWORD

DATE	18th century	WEIGHT	34 oz (950 g)
ORIGIN	Tibet	LENGTH	3¼ ft (1 m)

The long blade of this Tibetan sword exhibits
elaborate, swirled patterns of mixed steel on both
faces. The highly decorated pommel and the grip
wrapped in silver wire indicate that the sword was
meant for an individual of high status.

Turquoise bead
on pommel

Hand guard
made of iron

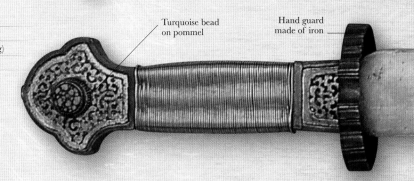

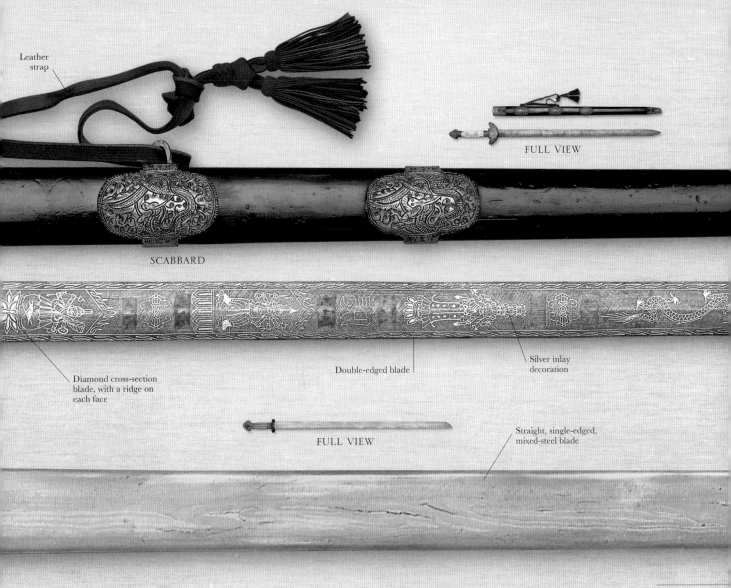

Leather strap

SCABBARD

FULL VIEW

Diamond cross-section blade, with a ridge on each face

Double-edged blade

Silver inlay decoration

FULL VIEW

Straight, single-edged, mixed-steel blade

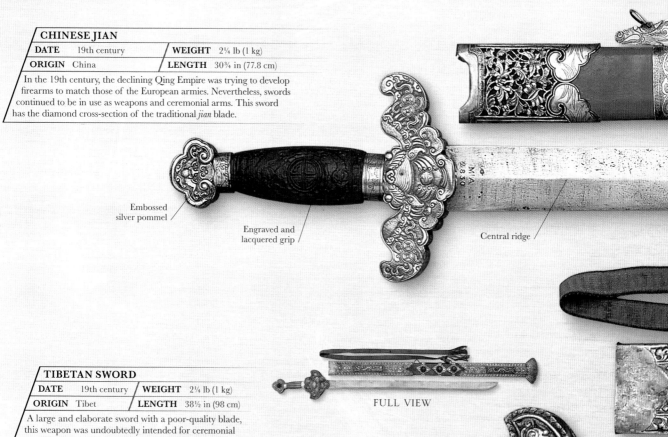

CHINESE JIAN

DATE	19th century	WEIGHT	2¼ lb (1 kg)
ORIGIN	China	LENGTH	30¾ in (77.8 cm)

In the 19th century, the declining Qing Empire was trying to develop firearms to match those of the European armies. Nevertheless, swords continued to be in use as weapons and ceremonial arms. This sword has the diamond cross-section of the traditional *jian* blade.

Embossed
silver pommel

Engraved and
lacquered grip

Central ridge

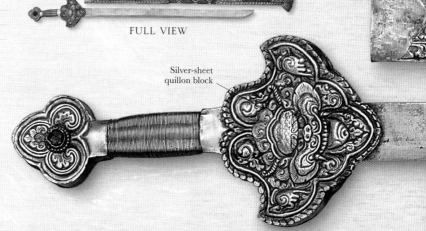

TIBETAN SWORD

DATE	19th century	WEIGHT	2¼ lb (1 kg)
ORIGIN	Tibet	LENGTH	38½ in (98 cm)

A large and elaborate sword with a poor-quality blade, this weapon was undoubtedly intended for ceremonial use. The scabbard, which is made of wood and covered in brown leather, is finely decorated with silver, gilding, and coral.

FULL VIEW

Silver-sheet
quillon block

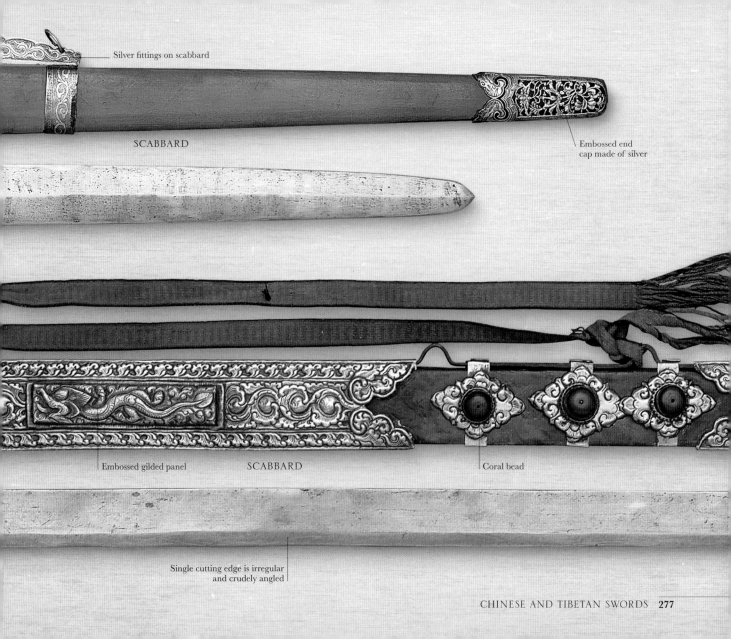

Silver fittings on scabbard

SCABBARD

Embossed end
cap made of silver

Embossed gilded panel

SCABBARD

Coral bead

Single cutting edge is irregular
and crudely angled

Black lacquered grip

Small, circular
ring guard

LIUYEDAO

DATE	c. 17th–18th century	WEIGHT	c. 32 oz (900 g)
ORIGIN	China	LENGTH	c. 36⅖ in (93 cm)

The *liuyedao* was a gently curved, saberlike weapon used in China from the 14th to the 20th centuries. A single-edged weapon generally wielded by cavalry, it was primarily a slashing rather than a thrusting weapon. However, in some *liuyedaos*, the back-edge near the tip was also sharpened for penetration.

SHUANJIAN

DATE	18th century	WEIGHT	c. 11 oz (300 g)
ORIGIN	China	LENGTH	c. 16 in (40.5 cm)

This blade was actually one of a set of paired swords, or *shuangjian*, both contained in the same scabbard. The fighter would wield the two swords at the same time, one in each hand. Such a style of fighting required cutting and thrusting qualities from the sword, so the blade is double-edged but also has a fairly sharp point.

Short, backward-facing
quillon

Diamond
cross-section blade

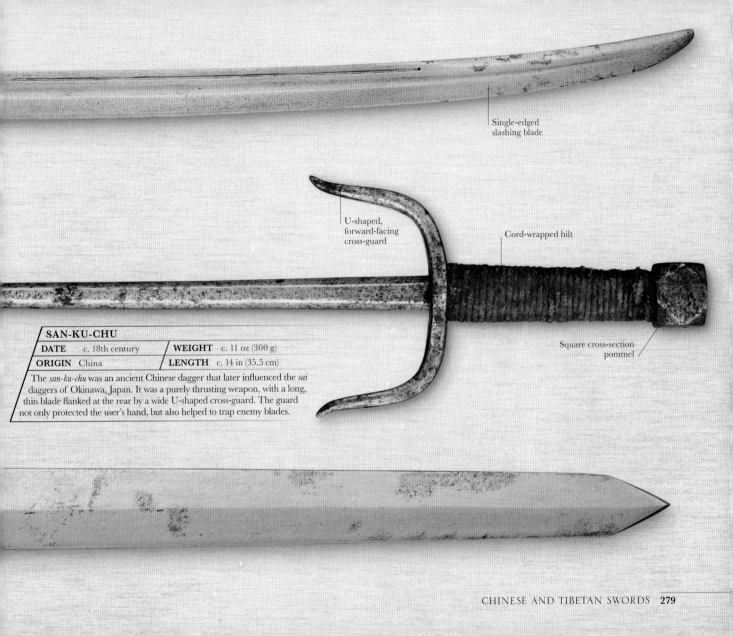

Single-edged
slashing blade

U-shaped,
forward-facing
cross-guard

Cord-wrapped hilt

Square cross-section
pommel

SAN-KU-CHU

DATE	c. 18th century	**WEIGHT**	c. 11 oz (300 g)
ORIGIN	China	**LENGTH**	c. 14 in (35.5 cm)

The *san-ku-chu* was an ancient Chinese dagger that later influenced the *sai* daggers of Okinawa, Japan. It was a purely thrusting weapon, with a long, thin blade flanked at the rear by a wide U-shaped cross-guard. The guard not only protected the user's hand, but also helped to trap enemy blades.

NINJA

The origins of the ninja—specially trained covert agents of feudal Japan—are lost in time and legend. Few texts mention them before the 15th century, but from then on, these shadowy figures played a central role in the world of Japanese politics and warfare. They were employed by feudal lords in a variety of roles, ranging from sabotage to supporting military campaigns. The last mention of ninja in battle was during the time of Tokugawa Iemitsu (1604–51), a *shogun* (commander) of the Tokugawa clan. Ninja continued to operate covertly until the end of the 18th century, by which time political stability in Japan meant that there was little use for their lethal skills. Yet their techniques lived on, in various manuals of covert warfare written in the 17th and 18th centuries. These techniques were later codified in *ninjutsu*, a form of martial arts characterized by stealth and camouflage.

The ninja utilized an unusual range of weaponry that reflected their covert roles. This included classic Japanese swords, such as the *tachi (pp. 194–95)*, as well as a variety of specialized weapons such as *shurikens (pp. 284–85)*. Some weapons, such as the *ninjato* shown below, are possibly the invention of modern Hollywood, but have become an integral part of modern *ninjutsu*.

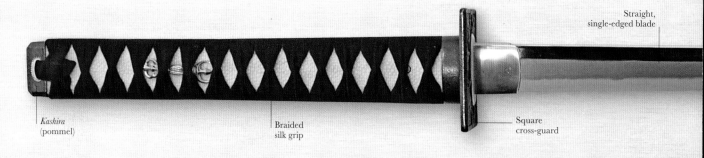

Straight, single-edged blade

Kashira (pommel)

Braided silk grip

Square cross-guard

NINJA BECAME MYTHOLOGIZED IN LATER HISTORY,
GRANTED MYSTICAL SKILLS
RANGING FROM INVISIBILITY TO
POWERS OF FLIGHT.

NINJATO			
DATE	Unknown	**WEIGHT**	c. 15 oz (420 g)
ORIGIN	Japan	**LENGTH**	c. 19 in (48 cm)

One of several swords attributed to the ninja, the *ninjato* was probably a shorter and cheaper version of the *wakazashi* (*pp. 198–203*) and had a slightly curved blade. Modern replicas, such as this example, often have straight blades and square cross guards. Many believe that these features are Hollywood inventions, although the modern ninjato swords do resemble the medieval Japanese *chokuto* straight sword.

ASSASSINATION BY STEALTH

The origin of the term ninja has sometimes been attributed to the semi-legendary 4th-century Japanese prince, Yamato Takeru, of the Yamato dynasty. This 19th-century painting shows Yamato attacking a man with a short, straight-edged blade, which is similar to the modern *ninjato* blade.

JAPANESE SPECIAL WEAPONS

The covert operations of the Ninja (*pp. 280–81*) required a variety of specialized weapons beyond the classic sword. Throwing weapons such as *shuriken*, meaning hand-hidden blade, were used as basic missiles and could be tipped with poison to make them lethal—without this, these weapons would actually cause only minor injuries. Chain weapons combined lengths of chain with blades, iron balls, or hardwood shafts, enabling them to cut, entangle, or strike. This gave the warrior some tactical advantage if confronted with a conventionally armed samurai.

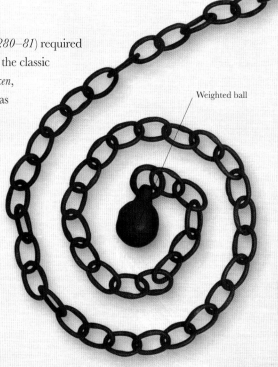

Hooked blade

Weighted ball

Iron finger guard

Thick hardwood shaft

KUSARIGAMA

DATE	18th century
ORIGIN	Japan

The chain and blade, or *kusarigama*, was used to entangle the enemy or his weapon, making it possible to draw him in and stab him. The weighted end of the chain was swung over the head, and then whipped toward the enemy. Sometimes the weight itself proved lethal. The weapon shown here also features a thick iron finger guard and brass reinforcing rings along the shaft.

THE CHAIN WRAPPED
AROUND THE ENEMY'S ARM ... THE BLADE
THEN KILLED HIM.

Cord binding provides a grip

Flared center for
extra penetration

BO SHURIKEN

DATE	c. 18th century
ORIGIN	Japan

Thrown from a distance, a *bo shuriken*, meaning stick blade, was a long metal spike with one or both ends sharpened. It could be thrown in a variety of ways: underarm, overarm, sideways, or backward; and with or without spin.

HARIGATA SHURIKEN

DATE	c. 18th century
ORIGIN	Japan

Harigata means needle-shaped, and these *shuriken* were probably so called due to their resemblance to the thick needles used for stitching leather armor. Although they had the potential to be thrown, they were more often gripped and used as easily concealed stabbing weapons.

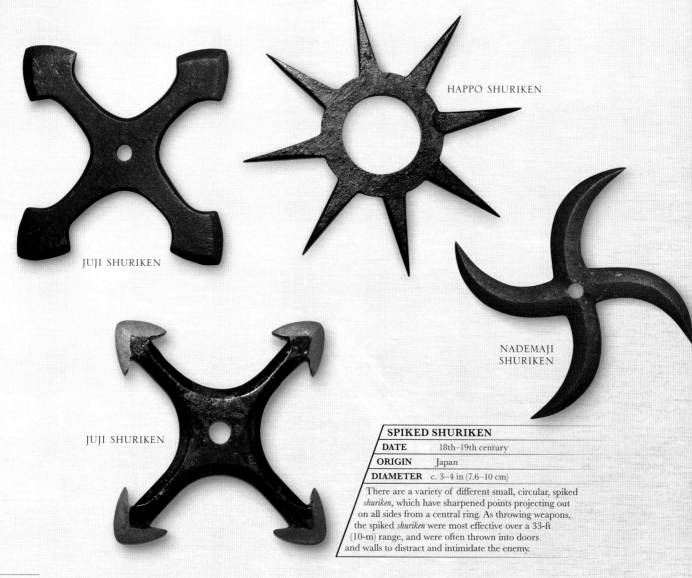

JUJI SHURIKEN

HAPPO SHURIKEN

NADEMAJI
SHURIKEN

JUJI SHURIKEN

SPIKED SHURIKEN	
DATE	18th–19th century
ORIGIN	Japan
DIAMETER	c. 3–4 in (7.6–10 cm)

There are a variety of different small, circular, spiked *shuriken*, which have sharpened points projecting out on all sides from a central ring. As throwing weapons, the spiked *shuriken* were most effective over a 33-ft (10-m) range, and were often thrown into doors and walls to distract and intimidate the enemy.

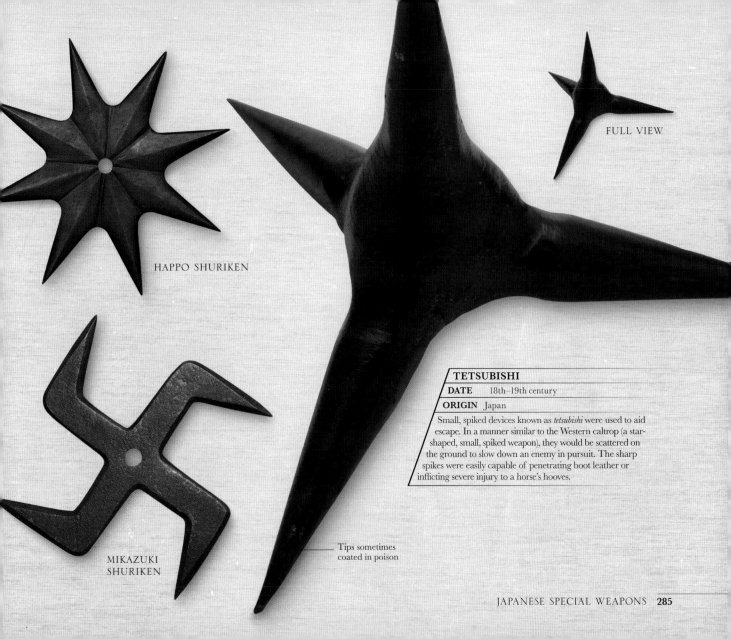

HAPPO SHURIKEN

FULL VIEW

MIKAZUKI
SHURIKEN

Tips sometimes
coated in poison

TETSUBISHI

DATE	18th–19th century
ORIGIN	Japan

Small, spiked devices known as *tetsubishi* were used to aid escape. In a manner similar to the Western caltrop (a star-shaped, small, spiked weapon), they would be scattered on the ground to slow down an enemy in pursuit. The sharp spikes were easily capable of penetrating boot leather or inflicting severe injury to a horse's hooves.

KENJUTSU

Literally meaning the art of the sword, *kenjutsu* refers to the traditional Japanese art of swordfighting, practiced by the samurai since the 4th century CE. The proponents of *kenjutsu* set up several major schools between the 14th and 16th centuries, but during the later Edo period (1603–1868), the number of schools spread dramatically, as the warrior class sought to preserve its skills with swords, such as the *katana* shown here.

During the 19th century, practitioners of *kenjutsu* began to train with wooden swords—known as *bokken*—which were roughly the same size, weight, and shape of the *katana*. This move enabled the fighters to engage one another more realistically, delivering full-power blows without the risk of death or serious injury. In the late 1860s, public interest in *kenjutsu* began to decline, possibly because of the growing domination of firearms. However, the Japanese military and police revived interest in swordfighting skills, ensuring that the ancient art form survived into the 20th century.

Kenjutsu or *kendo*—its modern-day equivalent—emphasizes speed, fluidity, and balance in its techniques. Footwork is essential for both movement and the power of the cut. A fighter's goal is to end the combat as quickly as possible, targeting areas such as the neck, forearms, head, and abdomen. Practice mainly consists of *kihon* (basic techniques) and *kata* (sequences of techniques), either solo or in pairs, graduating to free-form *kumite* (sparring).

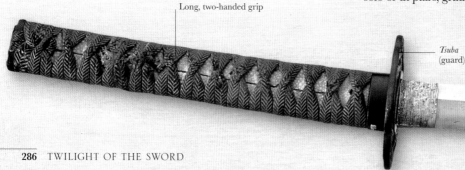

Long, two-handed grip

Tsuba
(guard)

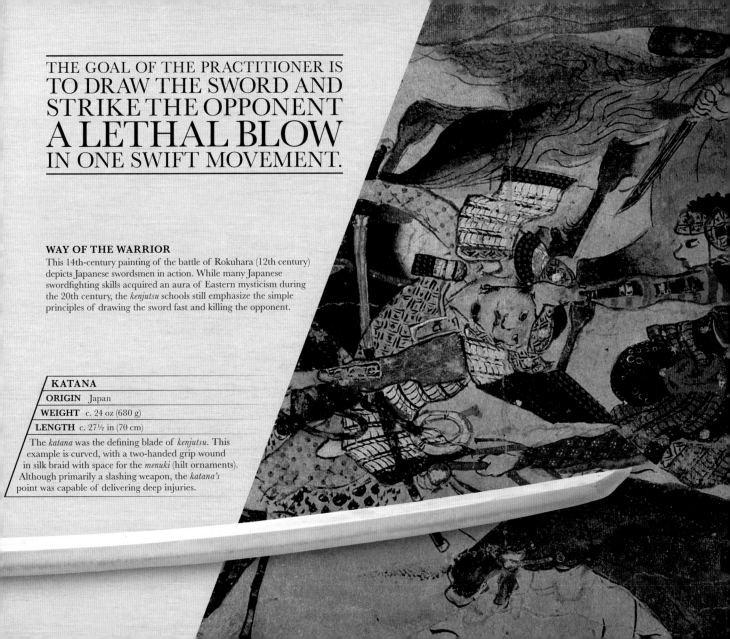

THE GOAL OF THE PRACTITIONER IS
TO DRAW THE SWORD AND
STRIKE THE OPPONENT
A LETHAL BLOW
IN ONE SWIFT MOVEMENT.

WAY OF THE WARRIOR

This 14th-century painting of the battle of Rokuhara (12th century) depicts Japanese swordsmen in action. While many Japanese swordfighting skills acquired an aura of Eastern mysticism during the 20th century, the *kenjutsu* schools still emphasize the simple principles of drawing the sword fast and killing the opponent.

KATANA	
ORIGIN	Japan
WEIGHT	c. 24 oz (680 g)
LENGTH	c. 27½ in (70 cm)

The *katana* was the defining blade of *kenjutsu*. This example is curved, with a two-handed grip wound in silk braid with space for the *menuki* (hilt ornaments). Although primarily a slashing weapon, the *katana's* point was capable of delivering deep injuries.

INDIAN SWORDS

During the late 18th and early 19th centuries, the British East India Company extended its control over most of India, paving the way for the establishment of the British Raj. These political changes had a limited impact upon Indian swordsmiths, who continued to produce swords in a great diversity of forms. These included not only mainstream swords in the Muslim and Hindu traditions—chiefly forms of *talwar* and *khanda*, made for the Indian princely courts that survived under British patronage—but also many regional or tribal variants, some distinctly strange to Western eyes. British officers often took swords home with them as souvenirs, many of which are now on display in museums.

Cutting edge

Large, gilded langet

Dish-shaped pommel

Long pommel spike

Knuckle guard lined with velvet

Embroidered wrist strap

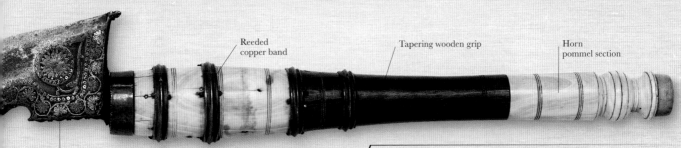

Reeded
copper band

Tapering wooden grip

Horn
pommel section

Brass rosette
on ricasso

VECHEVORAL

DATE	19th century	**WEIGHT**	2¾ lb (1.3 kg)
ORIGIN	India	**LENGTH**	24 in (62.1 cm)

The Indian subcontinent abounded in varieties of cutting implements for warfare and general agricultural use. This ornate *vechevoral* has a handle of wood and ivory, a sickle-shaped blade with a concave cutting edge, and a band of brass and decorative scrolling along the back.

Reinforcement decorated
with floral pattern

FULL VIEW

KHANDA

DATE	19th century	**WEIGHT**	2¾ lb (1.3 kg)
ORIGIN	India	**LENGTH**	39 in (99.3 cm)

Influenced by the Hindu Maratha culture, this *khanda* has a straight, pattern-welded blade that widens toward the tip. As is common in *khandas* of this period, the lightweight, flexible blade is stiffened by reinforcements that run two-thirds of the length of one edge and a shorter way up the other.

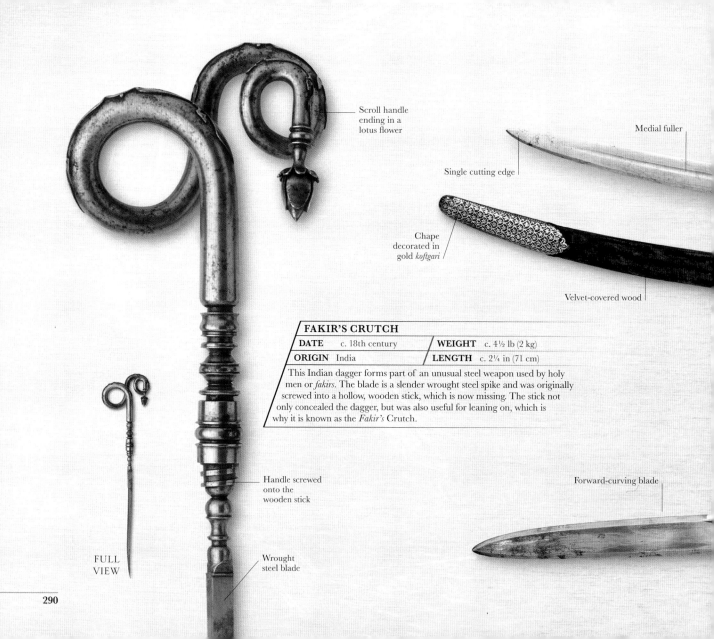

Scroll handle
ending in a
lotus flower

Medial fuller

Single cutting edge

Chape
decorated in
gold *koftgari*

Velvet-covered wood

FAKIR'S CRUTCH

DATE	c. 18th century	WEIGHT	c. 4½ lb (2 kg)
ORIGIN	India	LENGTH	c. 2¼ in (71 cm)

This Indian dagger forms part of an unusual steel weapon used by holy
men or *fakirs*. The blade is a slender wrought steel spike and was originally
screwed into a hollow, wooden stick, which is now missing. The stick not
only concealed the dagger, but was also useful for leaning on, which is
why it is known as the *Fakir's* Crutch.

Handle screwed
onto the
wooden stick

Forward-curving blade

FULL
VIEW

Wrought
steel blade

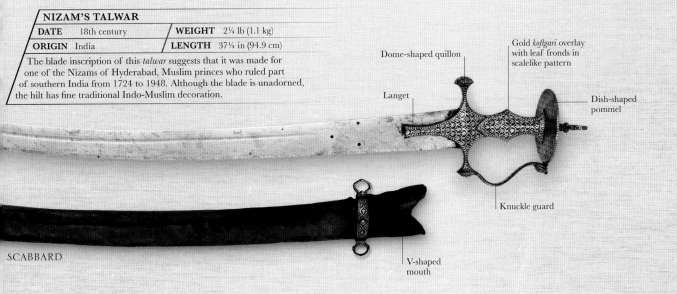

NIZAM'S TALWAR

DATE	18th century	**WEIGHT**	2¼ lb (1.1 kg)
ORIGIN	India	**LENGTH**	37¼ in (94.9 cm)

The blade inscription of this *talwar* suggests that it was made for one of the Nizams of Hyderabad, Muslim princes who ruled part of southern India from 1724 to 1948. Although the blade is unadorned, the hilt has fine traditional Indo-Muslim decoration.

Dome-shaped quillon

Langet

Gold *koftgari* overlay with leaf fronds in scalelike pattern

Dish-shaped pommel

Knuckle guard

SCABBARD

V-shaped mouth

SOSUN PATTAH

DATE	19th century	**WEIGHT**	2¼ lb (1.05 kg)
ORIGIN	India	**LENGTH**	34 in (87 cm)

A traditional form of Indian sword, a *sosun pattah* has a forward-curving blade—the reverse of, for example, the curve of a *talwar*. This type of sword exists in both Islamic and Hindu variants. The *sosun pattah* shown here has an Indo-Muslim-style hilt.

Iron hilt decorated with silver inlay

Fuller

CEREMONIAL AX

DATE	19th century	WEIGHT	c. 2¼ lb (1 kg)
ORIGIN	India	LENGTH	c. 23½ in (60 cm)

This ax comes from Assam in northeastern India.
Its purpose was almost certainly ceremonial, since the
single-edged blade is of a fairly rough-quality iron, and
the hilt and shaft are heavily decorated with colored
human hair—not the most practical material with which
to decorate a combat weapon.

Human hair
decorates hilt

Tubular, leather-
covered grip

FULL VIEW

Ruler of
Oudh's arms

EXECUTIONER'S SWORD

DATE	19th century	WEIGHT	2¼ lb (1.05 kg)
ORIGIN	India	LENGTH	28 in (71 cm)

By the 19th century, the ruler of Oudh in northern India
was under the effective control of the British, but
executions were still an area in which he had full say
and were carried out on his order. This sword, bearing
the ruler's arms, would have severed a neck at a blow.

Flat tip ends in
central point

Double-edged blade

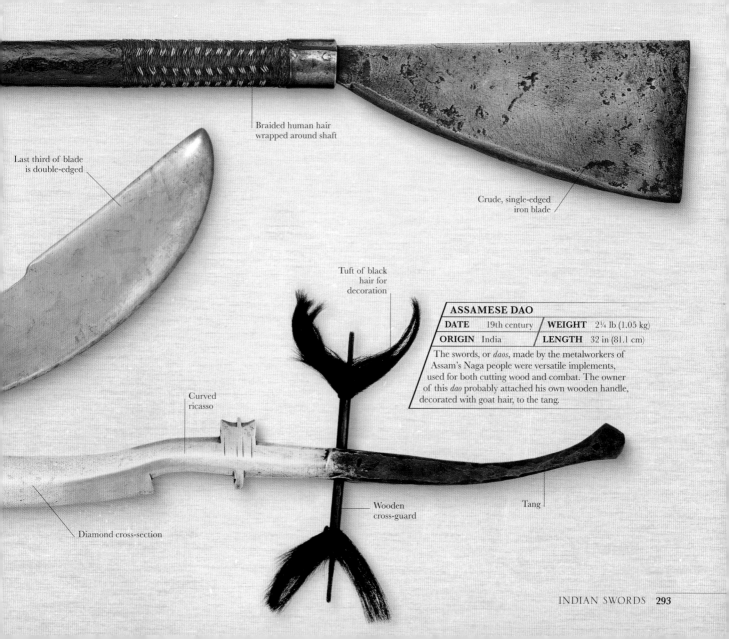

Braided human hair
wrapped around shaft

Last third of blade
is double-edged

Crude, single-edged
iron blade

Tuft of black
hair for
decoration

ASSAMESE DAO

DATE	19th century	**WEIGHT**	2¼ lb (1.05 kg)
ORIGIN	India	**LENGTH**	32 in (81.1 cm)

The swords, or *daos*, made by the metalworkers of
Assam's Naga people were versatile implements,
used for both cutting wood and combat. The owner
of this *dao* probably attached his own wooden handle,
decorated with goat hair, to the tang.

Curved
ricasso

Diamond cross-section

Wooden
cross-guard

Tang

INDIAN BLADES

Throughout the 19th century, the Indian subcontinent was the source of some of the world's most effective and original *melée* weapons (weapons used in close combat). These included a range of fearsome sharp-pointed knives with double-curved blades such as the *bich-hwa*, meaning scorpion, and various forms of fist dagger that allowed the warrior to deliver a stabbing blow to an enemy with a punching movement. Long metal sticks called parrying sticks were weapons that Indian armies had in common with African tribal fighting units. These sticks, sometimes combined with daggers, were used to fend off enemy attacks.

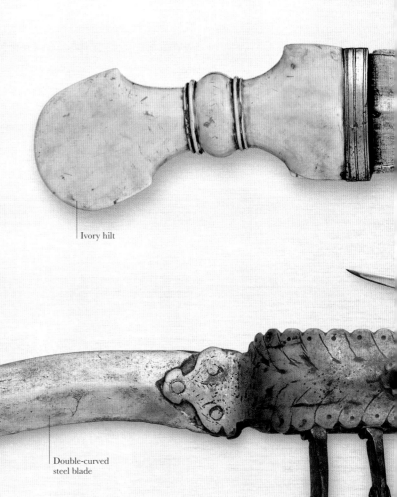

Ivory hilt

Double-curved steel blade

Diamond cross-section at point

Steel ring with claw

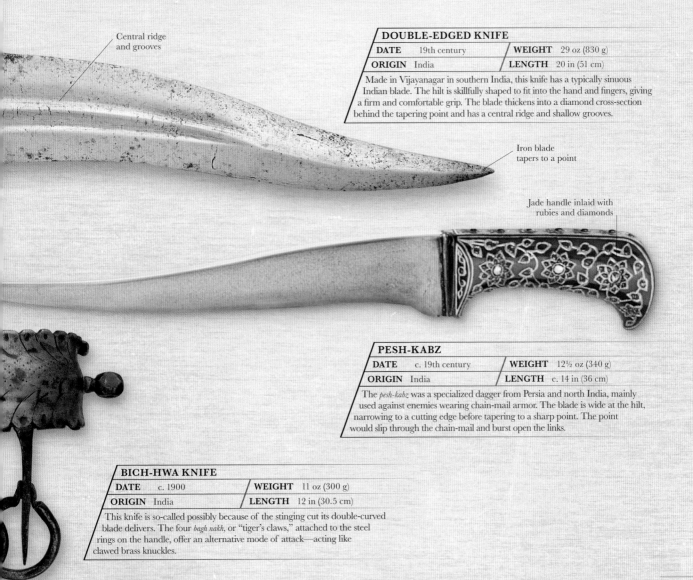

Central ridge
and grooves

DOUBLE-EDGED KNIFE

DATE	19th century	WEIGHT	29 oz (830 g)
ORIGIN	India	LENGTH	20 in (51 cm)

Made in Vijayanagar in southern India, this knife has a typically sinuous
Indian blade. The hilt is skillfully shaped to fit into the hand and fingers, giving
a firm and comfortable grip. The blade thickens into a diamond cross-section
behind the tapering point and has a central ridge and shallow grooves.

Iron blade
tapers to a point

Jade handle inlaid with
rubies and diamonds

PESH-KABZ

DATE	c. 19th century	WEIGHT	12½ oz (340 g)
ORIGIN	India	LENGTH	c. 14 in (36 cm)

The *pesh-kabz* was a specialized dagger from Persia and north India, mainly
used against enemies wearing chain-mail armor. The blade is wide at the hilt,
narrowing to a cutting edge before tapering to a sharp point. The point
would slip through the chain-mail and burst open the links.

BICH-HWA KNIFE

DATE	c. 1900	WEIGHT	11 oz (300 g)
ORIGIN	India	LENGTH	12 in (30.5 cm)

This knife is so-called possibly because of the stinging cut its double-curved
blade delivers. The four *bagh nakh*, or "tiger's claws," attached to the steel
rings on the handle, offer an alternative mode of attack—acting like
clawed brass knuckles.

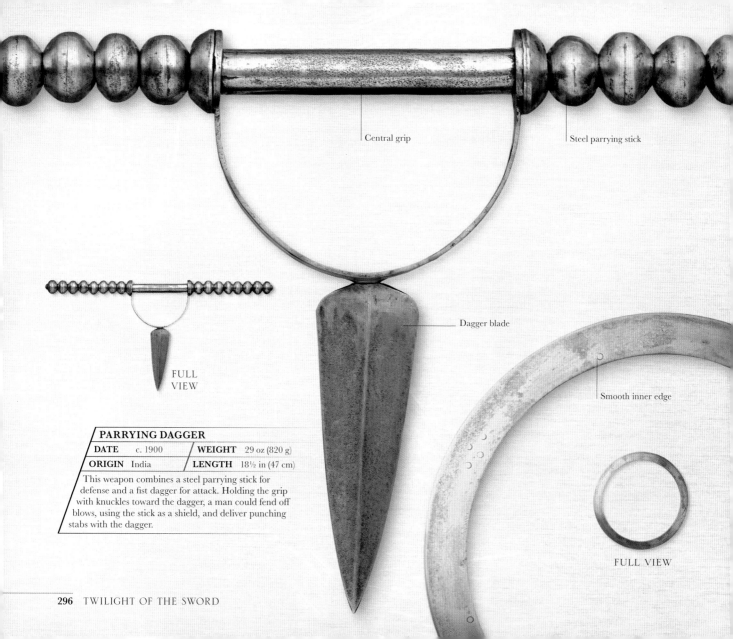

Central grip

Steel parrying stick

Dagger blade

Smooth inner edge

FULL VIEW

PARRYING DAGGER

DATE	c. 1900	**WEIGHT**	29 oz (820 g)
ORIGIN	India	**LENGTH**	18½ in (47 cm)

This weapon combines a steel parrying stick for
defense and a fist dagger for attack. Holding the grip
with knuckles toward the dagger, a man could fend off
blows, using the stick as a shield, and deliver punching
stabs with the dagger.

FULL VIEW

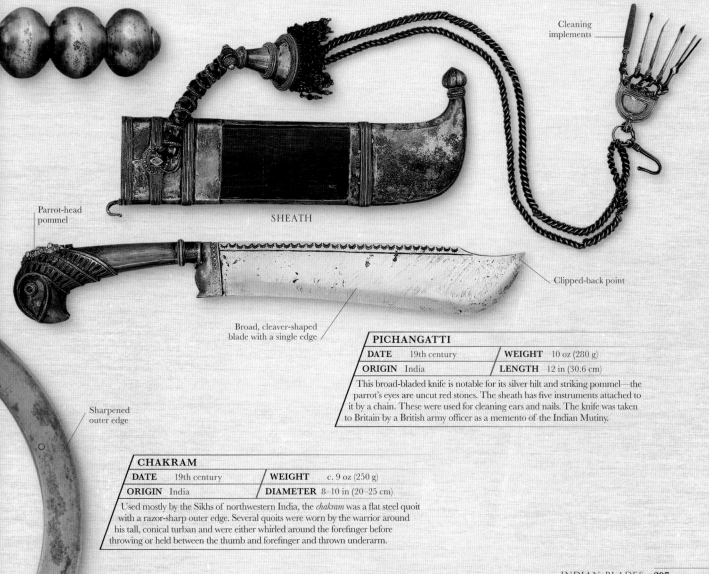

Cleaning
implements

Parrot-head
pommel

SHEATH

Clipped-back point

Broad, cleaver-shaped
blade with a single edge

PICHANGATTI

DATE	19th century	WEIGHT	10 oz (280 g)
ORIGIN	India	LENGTH	12 in (30.6 cm)

This broad-bladed knife is notable for its silver hilt and striking pommel—the parrot's eyes are uncut red stones. The sheath has five instruments attached to it by a chain. These were used for cleaning ears and nails. The knife was taken to Britain by a British army officer as a memento of the Indian Mutiny.

Sharpened
outer edge

CHAKRAM

DATE	19th century	WEIGHT	c. 9 oz (250 g)
ORIGIN	India	DIAMETER	8–10 in (20–25 cm)

Used mostly by the Sikhs of northwestern India, the *chakram* was a flat steel quoit with a razor-sharp outer edge. Several quoits were worn by the warrior around his tall, conical turban and were either whirled around the forefinger before throwing or held between the thumb and forefinger and thrown underarm.

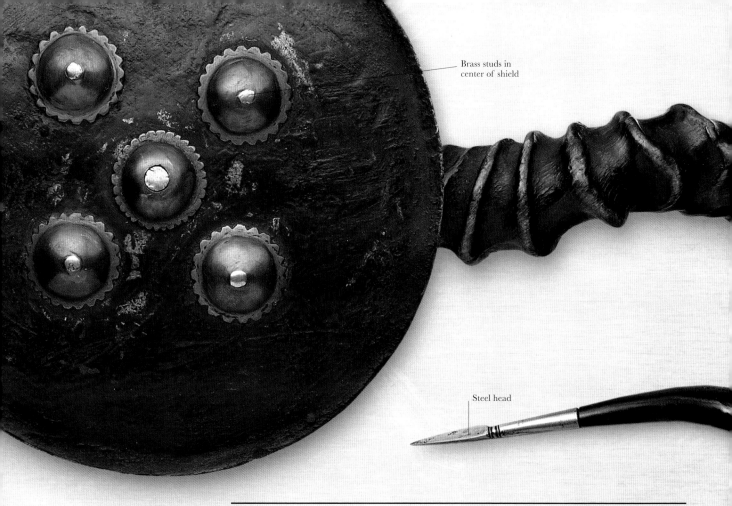

Brass studs in
center of shield

Steel head

ANImal HORN WAS A NATURAL WEAPON—
ROCK HARD BUT FLEXIBLE
ENOUGH TO WITHSTAND POWERFUL STABBING BLOWS.

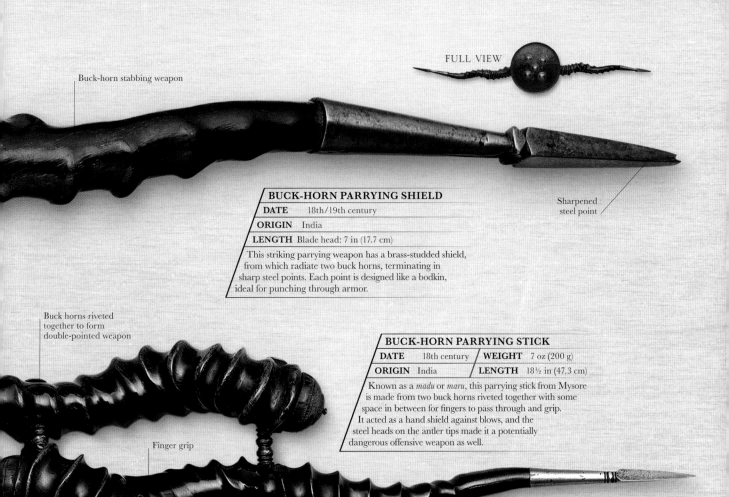

Buck-horn stabbing weapon

FULL VIEW

BUCK-HORN PARRYING SHIELD

DATE	18th/19th century
ORIGIN	India
LENGTH	Blade head: 7 in (17.7 cm)

This striking parrying weapon has a brass-studded shield, from which radiate two buck horns, terminating in sharp steel points. Each point is designed like a bodkin, ideal for punching through armor.

Sharpened steel point

Buck horns riveted together to form double-pointed weapon

BUCK-HORN PARRYING STICK

DATE	18th century	**WEIGHT**	7 oz (200 g)
ORIGIN	India	**LENGTH**	18½ in (47.3 cm)

Known as a *madu* or *maru*, this parrying stick from Mysore is made from two buck horns riveted together with some space in between for fingers to pass through and grip. It acted as a hand shield against blows, and the steel heads on the antler tips made it a potentially dangerous offensive weapon as well.

Finger grip

INDIAN STAFF WEAPONS

The domination of India by British forces in the late 18th and 19th centuries, armed at first with muskets and later with rifles, rendered staff weapons increasingly obsolete on the subcontinent. To be effective, Indian armies had to deploy artillery and firearms. Traditional varieties of battle-ax and mace continued to be found in the armories of Hindu and Muslim princes, and among the weaponry of tribal peoples. Many of these weapons were, however, more ceremonial than practical.

Decoration shows beast emerging from tiger's mouth

ANKUS

DATE	19th century	WEIGHT	21 oz (590 g)
ORIGIN	India	LENGTH	14½ in (37 cm)

This *ankus*, or elephant goad (a long stick with a pointed end used for prodding animals), is of traditional form, with the spike and hook designed to control the animal by applying pressure on the hide. The goad is so splendidly decorated, however, that it was probably meant for display and ceremonial purposes rather than for practical use.

Gilded brass pommel unscrews to reveal a hidden blade

BHUJ

DATE	19th century	WEIGHT	31 oz (870 g)
ORIGIN	India	LENGTH	28 in (70.4 cm)

The knifelike battle-axe known as a *bhuj* was used from earliest times in tribal India and adopted by Hindu and Muslim armies. It is often called an "elephant's head" because of the characteristic decoration between shaft and blade.

Metal shaft

Brass elephant's-head decoration

Silver and gold inlay

FULL VIEW

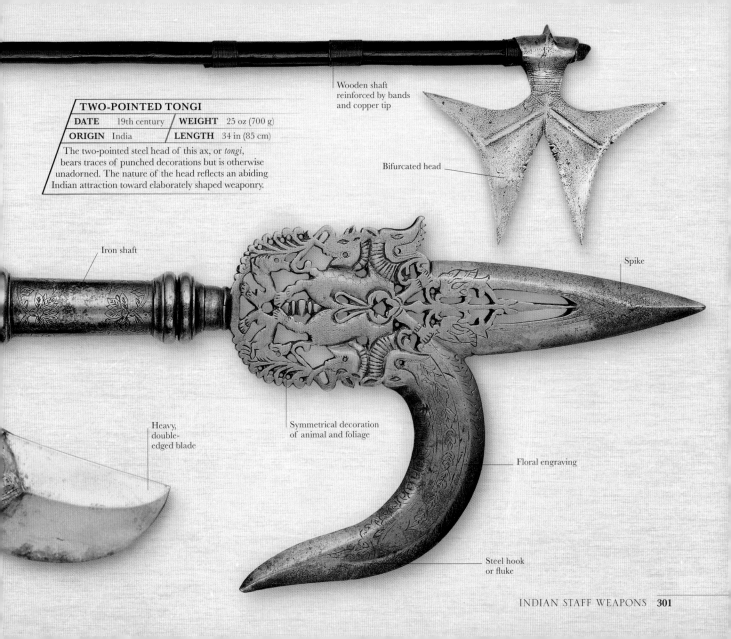

TWO-POINTED TONGI

DATE	19th century	**WEIGHT**	25 oz (700 g)
ORIGIN	India	**LENGTH**	34 in (85 cm)

The two-pointed steel head of this ax, or *tongi*, bears traces of punched decorations but is otherwise unadorned. The nature of the head reflects an abiding Indian attraction toward elaborately shaped weaponry.

Wooden shaft reinforced by bands and copper tip

Bifurcated head

Iron shaft

Spike

Heavy, double-edged blade

Symmetrical decoration of animal and foliage

Floral engraving

Steel hook or fluke

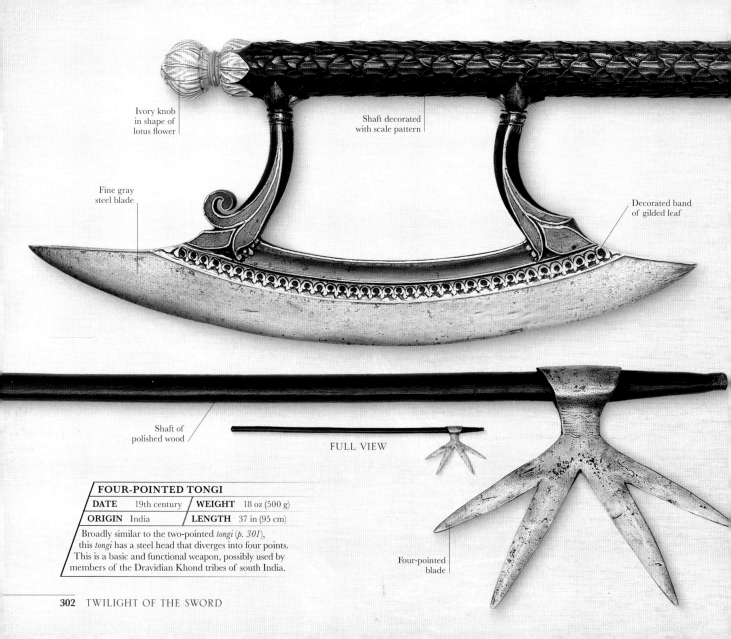

Ivory knob
in shape of
lotus flower

Shaft decorated
with scale pattern

Fine gray
steel blade

Decorated band
of gilded leaf

Shaft of
polished wood

FULL VIEW

FOUR-POINTED TONGI

DATE	19th century	**WEIGHT**	18 oz (500 g)
ORIGIN	India	**LENGTH**	37 in (95 cm)

Broadly similar to the two-pointed *tongi* (*p. 301*),
this *tongi* has a steel head that diverges into four points.
This is a basic and functional weapon, possibly used by
members of the Dravidian Khond tribes of south India.

Four-pointed
blade

TABAR

DATE	19th century	WEIGHT	25 oz (700 g)
ORIGIN	India	LENGTH	26 in (65 cm)

The carved wooden shaft of this battle-ax, or *tabar*, is covered in green velvet at the grip and tipped with carved ivory at each end. The broad steel blade was effective in combat, but the fine decoration suggests that display was its primary function.

Spikes arranged in seven horizontal bands

SPIKED MACE

DATE	18th century	WEIGHT	5¾ lb (2.7 kg)
ORIGIN	India	LENGTH	30 in (76.9 cm)

Bearing 118 individual spikes, this mace would have delivered a devastating blow to an opponent. This particular mace is a Maratha weapon. The Marathas' greatest triumph was the victory over the forces of the British East India Company at Wadgaon in 1779.

Quadrangular top spike

FULL VIEW

AFRICAN BLADES

The blades of Africa displayed a greater diversity of shapes and purposes than those in the West and in Asia. Toward the north of the Sahara and along the eastern coast, which were under Arab and Ottoman Turkish influence, weapons broadly resembled those found across the Islamic world. However, to the south of the Sahara, the prevailing traditions produced distinctive weapons that ranged from a simple stick with pointed branches to elaborately decorated metal paddles. Many of these weapons were in use long after European colonial powers took over parts of Africa during the 19th century.

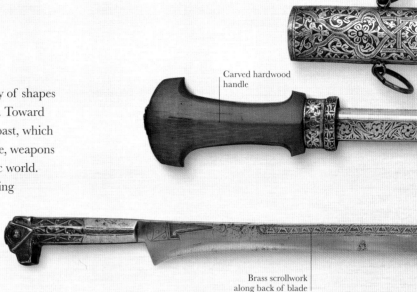

Carved hardwood handle

Brass scrollwork along back of blade

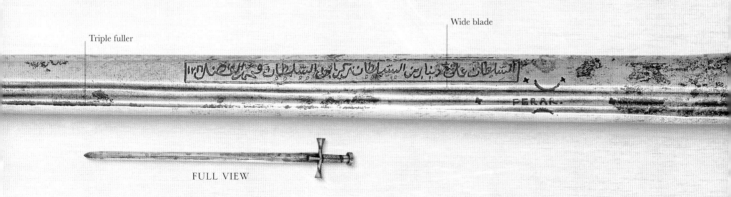

Wide blade

Triple fuller

FULL VIEW

Polished wood

SCABBARD

Engraved silver chape

CEREMONIAL DAGGER

DATE	19th century	WEIGHT	c. 11 oz (300 g)
ORIGIN	North Africa	LENGTH	c. 16 in (40.6 cm)

This extremely ornate ceremonial dagger features a simple African hardwood hilt but has rich gold work on nearly half of the blade's length. The pattern on both blade and scabbard is typical Islamic scrollwork.

Single-edged blade with gold decoration

Long, thin blade

FLYSSA SWORD

DATE	19th century	WEIGHT	c. 2½ lb (1 kg)
ORIGIN	Morocco	LENGTH	38½ in (97.7 cm)

This sword was designed to break open chain-mail armor, which was worn in parts of Africa well into the 19th century. The steel blade features elaborate inlaid brass decoration, and the hilt terminates in an animal motif.

Brass-engraved wrapping around grip

KASKARA

DATE	19th century	WEIGHT	c. 21 oz (600 g)
ORIGIN	Sudan/Chad	LENGTH	c. 35 in (90 cm)

The *kaskara*, with its straight, double-edged blade, is a type of broadsword with a recognizable connection to medieval European broadswords. Arabic script runs along the edge of the blade, which has a triple fuller to lighten it.

Circular steel pommel

Straight quillon with diamond cross-section

ZULU WARRIOR

A cattle-herding tribe in southern Africa, the Zulus developed into a military power in the 19th century—a transformation attributed to their chief Shaka (r. 1816–1828).

During Shaka's reign, the Zulus became the dominant military power in the region. Shaka introduced new weapons and tactics, and transformed the military structure. He recruited men between 18 and 20 years old for military service and organized them into regiments, each with separate dresses and shield colors. The Zulus had earlier relied heavily on the *assegai*, a throwing spear, but Shaka encouraged them to use the *iklwa*, a deadly stabbing spear shown below. The *iklwa* and the *knobkerrie* club were effective close-quarters weapons. Protected by long cowhide shields, Zulu armies would attack en masse, attempting to encircle the enemy. First, they would advance at a steady pace, banging their shields with their spears. At about 100 ft (30 m) from the enemy, they would throw the *assegai* and run at full pace to fight with the *iklwa* and club. Though aggressive, these tactics proved costly against Europeans equipped with firearms.

Hardwood shaft cut from
single piece of wood

IKLWA		
DATE 19th century	**WEIGHT** c. 2¼ lb (1 kg)	
ORIGIN Southern Africa	**LENGTH** c. 4 ft (1.2 m)	

The *iklwa* had a long, flat blade, about 14–18 in (35–45 cm) in length, attached to a staff. It was plunged into the enemy with an underhand motion, maximizing the force of the thrust. The *iklwa* is apparently named after the noise made when pulling it out from the enemy's body.

"WE KILLED EVERY WHITE MAN LEFT IN THE CAMP AND THE HORSES AND CATTLE, TOO."

A ZULU WARRIOR ON THE MASSACRE OF THE BRITISH
AT THE NTOMBE RIVER IN NORTHERN ZULULAND, 1879

Cowhide grip

Broad, flat
blade

ZULU CEREMONY

A group of Zulus gather to perform a warrior ceremony, brandishing their *iklwas* and cowhide shields. Although the Zulus used throwing spears, most of their weaponry suited close-range combat, a fact that left them open to massacre in their wars against the Europeans.

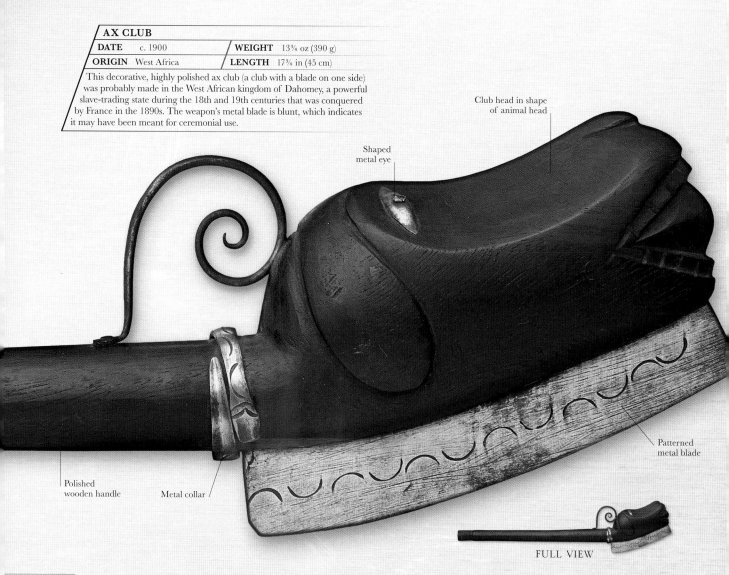

AX CLUB

DATE	c. 1900	**WEIGHT**	13¾ oz (390 g)
ORIGIN	West Africa	**LENGTH**	17¾ in (45 cm)

This decorative, highly polished ax club (a club with a blade on one side) was probably made in the West African kingdom of Dahomey, a powerful slave-trading state during the 18th and 19th centuries that was conquered by France in the 1890s. The weapon's metal blade is blunt, which indicates it may have been meant for ceremonial use.

Club head in shape of animal head

Shaped metal eye

Polished wooden handle

Metal collar

Patterned metal blade

FULL VIEW

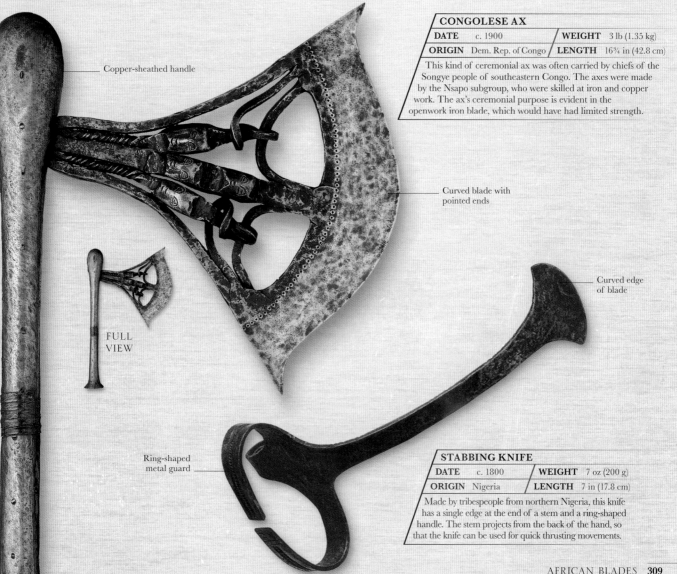

Copper-sheathed handle

CONGOLESE AX

DATE	c. 1900	WEIGHT	3 lb (1.35 kg)
ORIGIN	Dem. Rep. of Congo	LENGTH	16¾ in (42.8 cm)

This kind of ceremonial ax was often carried by chiefs of the Songye people of southeastern Congo. The axes were made by the Nsapo subgroup, who were skilled at iron and copper work. The ax's ceremonial purpose is evident in the openwork iron blade, which would have had limited strength.

Curved blade with pointed ends

Curved edge of blade

FULL VIEW

Ring-shaped metal guard

STABBING KNIFE

DATE	c. 1800	WEIGHT	7 oz (200 g)
ORIGIN	Nigeria	LENGTH	7 in (17.8 cm)

Made by tribespeople from northern Nigeria, this knife has a single edge at the end of a stem and a ring-shaped handle. The stem projects from the back of the hand, so that the knife can be used for quick thrusting movements.

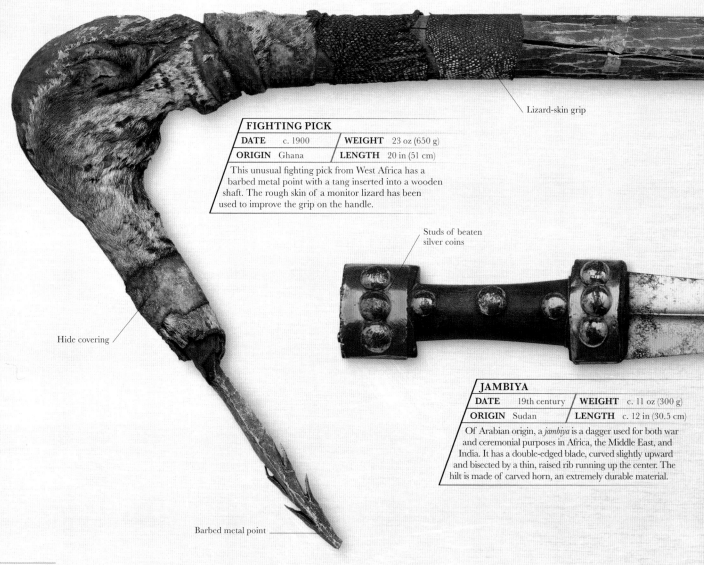

Lizard-skin grip

FIGHTING PICK

DATE	c. 1900	WEIGHT	23 oz (650 g)
ORIGIN	Ghana	LENGTH	20 in (51 cm)

This unusual fighting pick from West Africa has a barbed metal point with a tang inserted into a wooden shaft. The rough skin of a monitor lizard has been used to improve the grip on the handle.

Studs of beaten silver coins

Hide covering

JAMBIYA

DATE	19th century	WEIGHT	c. 11 oz (300 g)
ORIGIN	Sudan	LENGTH	c. 12 in (30.5 cm)

Of Arabian origin, a *jambiya* is a dagger used for both war and ceremonial purposes in Africa, the Middle East, and India. It has a double-edged blade, curved slightly upward and bisected by a thin, raised rib running up the center. The hilt is made of carved horn, an extremely durable material.

Barbed metal point

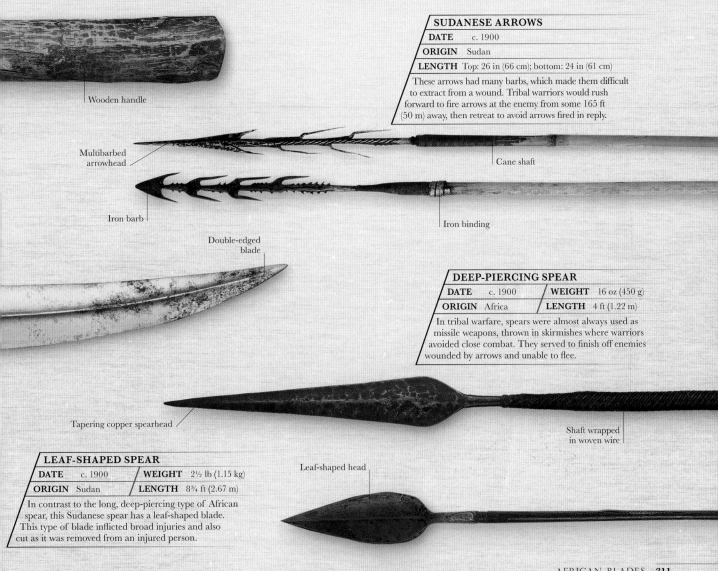

Wooden handle

SUDANESE ARROWS

DATE	c. 1900
ORIGIN	Sudan
LENGTH	Top: 26 in (66 cm); bottom: 24 in (61 cm)

These arrows had many barbs, which made them difficult to extract from a wound. Tribal warriors would rush forward to fire arrows at the enemy from some 165 ft (50 m) away, then retreat to avoid arrows fired in reply.

Multibarbed arrowhead

Cane shaft

Iron barb

Iron binding

Double-edged blade

DEEP-PIERCING SPEAR

DATE	c. 1900	**WEIGHT**	16 oz (450 g)
ORIGIN	Africa	**LENGTH**	4 ft (1.22 m)

In tribal warfare, spears were almost always used as missile weapons, thrown in skirmishes where warriors avoided close combat. They served to finish off enemies wounded by arrows and unable to flee.

Tapering copper spearhead

Shaft wrapped in woven wire

Leaf-shaped head

LEAF-SHAPED SPEAR

DATE	c. 1900	**WEIGHT**	2½ lb (1.15 kg)
ORIGIN	Sudan	**LENGTH**	8¾ ft (2.67 m)

In contrast to the long, deep-piercing type of African spear, this Sudanese spear has a leaf-shaped blade. This type of blade inflicted broad injuries and also cut as it was removed from an injured person.

DAGGERS OF OCEANIA

The Polynesians and other peoples who occupied the islands of the Pacific before the arrival of Europeans in the 17th century were much given to warfare. They engaged in forms of combat ranging from revenge raids and ritualized skirmishes to wars of conquest and extermination. Their weaponry was limited, consisting largely of wooden clubs, cleavers, daggers, and spears, sometimes edged with sharpened bone, shell, coral, stone, or obsidian. These weapons were intricately decorated and often held as objects of religious significance and valued as heirlooms.

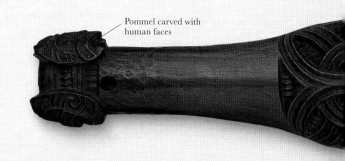

Pommel carved with human faces

MAORI PATUKI

DATE	c. 1860	WEIGHT	11 oz (310 g)
ORIGIN	New Zealand	LENGTH	14½ in (37 cm)

The Maori, Polynesians who colonized New Zealand around 1200 CE, were among the most warlike of Pacific peoples. This two-edged club, known as a *patuki*, comes from New Zealand's North Island and may have been taken as plunder by the British after their victory in the Maori War of 1860–69. It is decorated with iridescent haliotis shells, as well as elaborate carvings.

Plain wooden handle

POLYNESIAN CUTLASS

DATE	19th century	WEIGHT	3¼ lb (1.5 kg)
ORIGIN	Polynesia	LENGTH	30½ in (77.5 cm)

The shape of this weapon, either a club or a cleaver, is most unusual, perhaps modeled on the cutlasses that were carried by European sailors. The Polynesian craftsman has blended that exotic shape with intricate indigenous carving—triangular sections and geometric motifs—that covers the head of the weapon.

FULL VIEW

Haliotis shell

Decorative carving

Obsidian blade, flaked to a point

Central ridge on obsidian spearhead

Club swells to spatula shape

Remains of wooden shaft

Characteristic local design

Handle painted with red ocher

OBSIDIAN SPEARHEAD

DATE	c. 1900	**WEIGHT**	8 oz (220 g)
ORIGIN	Papua New Guinea	**LENGTH**	15 in (38 cm)

This spearhead is from the Admiralty Islands, off New Guinea, where obsidian, a volcanic glass, occurs naturally. The Melanesians discovered how to flake obsidian to a razor-sharp edge. The head is flat on one side and ridged on the other. Only part of the ocher-painted, decorated wooden shaft remains. It is fixed to the obsidian head with resin.

Head carved with geometric motifs

DAGGER WITH OBSIDIAN BLADE

DATE	c. 1900	**WEIGHT**	2 oz (60 g)
ORIGIN	Papua New Guinea	**LENGTH**	11 in (28 cm)

Like the spearhead above, this dagger was made by the Melanesian people of the Admiralty Islands. The obsidian has been flaked to make sharp edges and a point. The blade of this dagger is flat on one side and raised to a ridge on the other. The pointed wooden handle is decorated with designs characteristic of this region.

MAORI WARRIOR

Originally farmers and sailors in Polynesia, the Maori settled in New Zealand between 800 and 1300 CE and soon established a reputation as ferocious fighters. Warfare was a central part of their culture and, until the advent of the British in the 19th century, Maori clans frequently fought among themselves over land rights, feuds, and slighted honor, and for vengeance.

Maori battles were extremely bloody and merciless, with dead enemies sometimes eaten in an act of ritualistic cannibalism. All male Maori were trained from boyhood to be *toa* (warriors).

They would band together in times of conflict, typically in groups of 70–140 men. Combat ranged from ambushes and surprise attacks on enemy villages to open, prearranged battles. Maori weapons typically included stone axes, wooden spears, and clubs, sometimes with a cutting edge made of sharpened stone, bone, coral, or shell. Traditional Maori warfare was transformed when Europeans introduced firearms. Maori tribes, now armed with muskets, fought a series of highly destructive wars among themselves, called the Musket Wars (c. 1810–30). These, combined with wars against the colonists, decimated the Maori as a military force by the late 19th century.

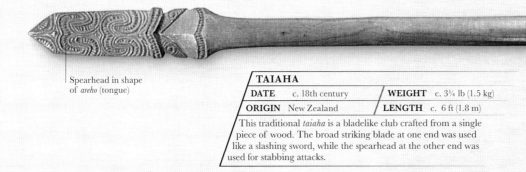

Spearhead in shape of *areho* (tongue)

TAIAHA		
DATE c. 18th century	**WEIGHT** c. 3¼ lb (1.5 kg)	
ORIGIN New Zealand	**LENGTH** c. 6 ft (1.8 m)	

This traditional *taiaha* is a bladelike club crafted from a single piece of wood. The broad striking blade at one end was used like a slashing sword, while the spearhead at the other end was used for stabbing attacks.

IN BATTLE, SOME MAORI ACTED AS CHASING WARRIORS, BRINGING DOWN FLEEING ENEMY, WHO WERE THEN FINISHED OFF BY EXECUTION SQUADS THAT FOLLOWED BEHIND.

Broad striking blade

PAINTED WARRIORS

Tattooed Maori perform their traditional dance, called the *haka*, which is meant to intimidate the enemy. Maori tattoos indicated the ancestry, status, and fighting skills of the warrior. These modern Maori are armed with traditional paddlelike *taiaha* staff weapons. A short club was usually tucked into the belt as a backup weapon.

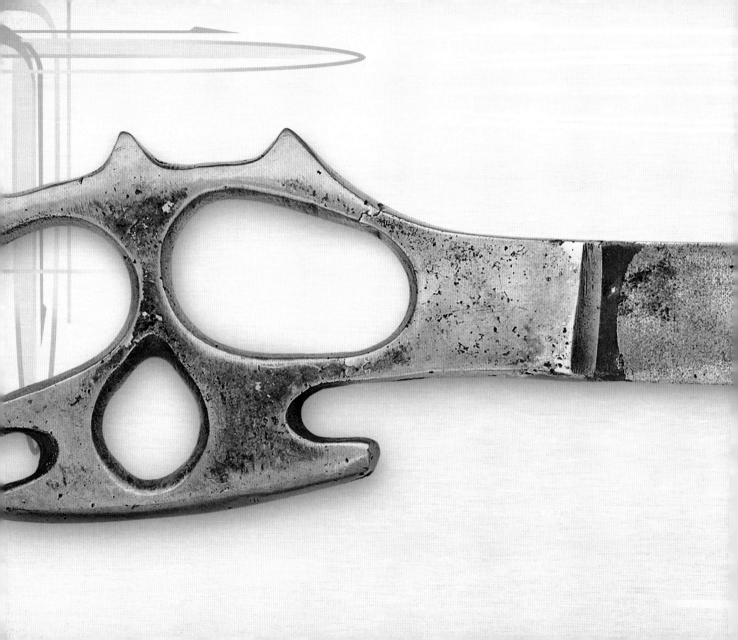

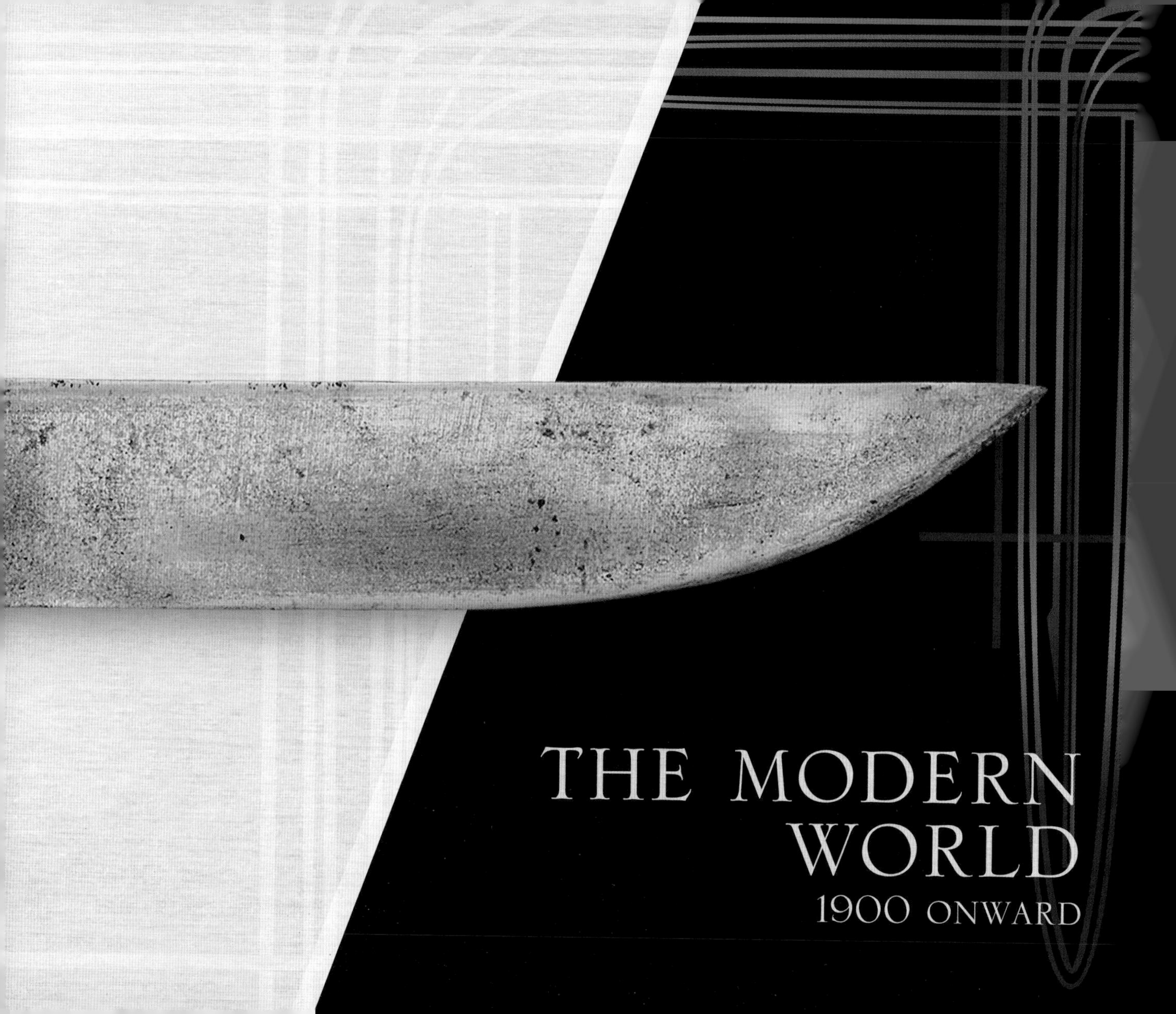

THE MODERN WORLD
WORLD
1900 ONWARD

SOLDIERS TODAY FIGHT almost exclusively with guns, artillery, missiles, and bombs, not cold steel. Yet, the fact remains that even in the age of modern warfare, knives are still found on the belts of most soldiers. During the Vietnam War (1955–75), for example, fighting knives were used by US special forces in close-quarters combat against the Viet Cong. Similarly, in the Iran–Iraq war (1980–88), both sides launched bayonet charges against enemy trench lines. Even during the Second Gulf War (2003–09), Scottish soldiers of the Argyll & Sutherland Highlanders made a bayonet charge in southern Iraq. Such events remind us that the blade still has a lurking and primitive presence in warfare.

The 20th century saw the final demise of the full-blown sword as a combat weapon. However, there were still some lingering traditionalists. In 1908, for example, the British Army officially introduced a brand-new cavalry sword—an excellent blade that fell out of use as the cavalry switched from horses to mechanized vehicles. In Eastern Europe, however, the Russian cavalries continued to make feisty sword-drawn charges against the German forces in World War I (1914–18) and even in World War II

(1939–45). Predictably, however, they suffered terrible losses against defenders armed with machine guns with an extremely high rate of fire. Toward the end of World War II, Allied soldiers in the Pacific and Southeast Asian regions faced suicidal rushes from Japanese soldiers armed with bayonets and *katana* swords. The *katana* was sometimes used by Japanese officers for committing ritual suicide when facing certain defeat.

Although the sword was fast becoming obsolete, the bayonet—an essential weapon of the infantry in the 18th and 19th centuries—showed its worth once again during the two world wars. During World War I, after the artillery had stopped pounding the enemy lines with gun fire, soldiers on the Western Front often had to cross no-man's land and launch bayonet charges at enemy trenches. The typical bayonet at this time was formidably long—the blade of British M1907 sword bayonet measured 17 in (43 cm)—and came in single-edged, double-edged, or spiked varieties. Yet the extreme length of these bayonets was a hindrance in the closed confines of a trench. This, therefore, led to broad innovations in terms of more practical fighting knives. Soldiers even sharpened entrenching tools such as the metal spades or posts that supported barbed-wire columns to use as weapons, or used vicious-looking brass-knuckle knives. Such weapons were crude but lethal in close quarters.

Soldiers were still equipped with bayonets during World War II, but by this time blades began to be used for other purposes as well, such as chopping firewood or cutting through forest undergrowth. In Germany, knives took on a special ceremonial significance among the ranks of the *Wehrmacht* (navy, army, and air force) and the *Schutzstaffel* (SS) and similar Nazi formations. Their blades were often inscribed with Nazi oaths such as "My Honor is Loyalty." In the Allied armies, by contrast, the growth of special forces units such as the British commandos, the US and British airborne forces, and the secret service agencies demanded dedicated combat and assassination weapons. This led to the development of blades such as the Fairbairn–Sykes (FS) fighting knife and the US KA-BAR, which were specially designed for close combat. Their value as last-resort weapons meant that fighting knives continued to be considered as desirable tools of war long after World War II ended. Military bayonets, however, were shortened considerably post-World War II, and tended to combine fighting and practical tools such as wire cutters in one unit.

In Africa and parts of Southeast Asia, blades were not only used for fighting, but also performed a variety of ceremonial roles. Elaborate curved daggers were used in initiation and puberty rituals, while long, cheap machetes acted as improvised weapons. Elsewhere in the world, the sword remains confined to more formal purposes. No longer the weapon of choice on the battlefield, it still enjoys a special status in the ceremonial practices of most military forces, and is often a standard part of officers' dress uniform. The sword represents individual martial skill at its purest, and for that reason alone it will continue to embody the warrior spirit, if only on the parade ground rather than on the battlefield.

THE MODERN WORLD

GERMAN AND
ITALIAN BLADES

European armies entered World War I with faith in the
bayonet charge as the key to victory in infantry combat. Reality
proved different: troops advancing with bayonets fixed were
mowed down by machine guns and rifle fire. The soldiers
cynically claimed that bayonets were more useful for opening
cans than for combat. However, bayonets have remained in
use, although, typically, with shorter blades. Fighting knives,
which proved their worth in the trenches
during the 1914–18 war, were used by
special forces in World War II and
were useful close-combat arms for the
general infantry. Bayonets also retained
a certain ceremonial status, particularly
in Germany and other Axis countries.

GERMAN S84/98 BAYONET

DATE	1940s	WEIGHT	14½ oz (420 g)
ORIGIN	Germany	LENGTH	15 in (38.2 cm)

This bayonet was introduced in 1915 as a cheap and
sturdy attachment for the Mauser Gewehr 1898 rifle. It
has no muzzle ring and is held to the rifle by a long groove
in the pommel. The grip has a flash guard to deflect hot
gases from the muzzle post-firing. This model was produced
up to World War II, which is when this example was made.

Steel flash
guard

Wooden hilt

Groove for
attaching to rifle

Ogival (pointed arch) tip

Wide fuller

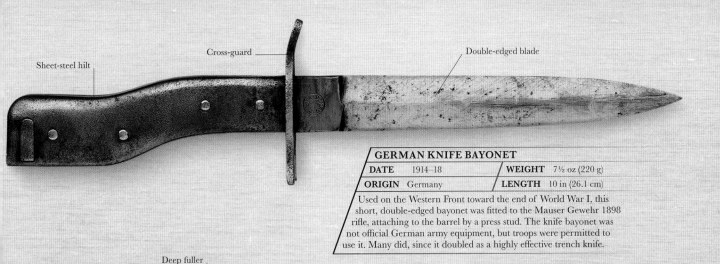

Sheet-steel hilt

Cross-guard

Double-edged blade

GERMAN KNIFE BAYONET

DATE	1914–18	WEIGHT	7½ oz (220 g)
ORIGIN	Germany	LENGTH	10 in (26.1 cm)

Used on the Western Front toward the end of World War I, this short, double-edged bayonet was fitted to the Mauser Gewehr 1898 rifle, attaching to the barrel by a press stud. The knife bayonet was not official German army equipment, but troops were permitted to use it. Many did, since it doubled as a highly effective trench knife.

Deep fuller

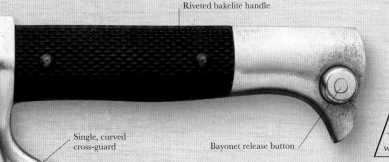

Riveted bakelite handle

GERMAN WEHRMACHT DRESS BAYONET

DATE	c. 1940	WEIGHT	14½ oz (420 g)
ORIGIN	Germany	LENGTH	14½ in (35.5 cm)

This Wehrmacht short dress bayonet was intended as a parade accompaniment for the Mauser 98k rifle, although the bayonet was never mounted. It features a black bakelite handle riveted to the steel hilt, and the bayonet release button is visible at the base of the grip. The blade is single-edged. In general, dress bayonets were unsharpened, having no combat purpose.

Single, curved cross-guard

Bayonet release button

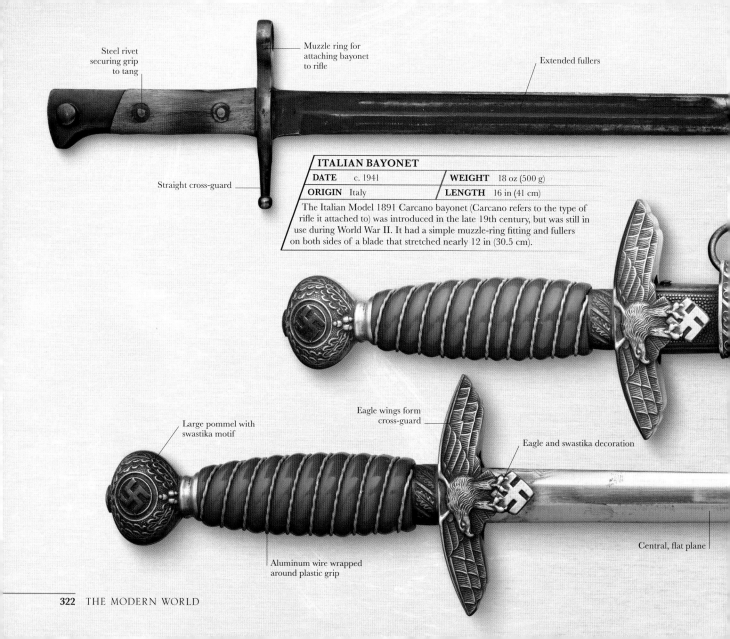

Steel rivet
securing grip
to tang

Muzzle ring for
attaching bayonet
to rifle

Extended fullers

Straight cross-guard

ITALIAN BAYONET			
DATE	c. 1941	**WEIGHT**	18 oz (500 g)
ORIGIN	Italy	**LENGTH**	16 in (41 cm)

The Italian Model 1891 Carcano bayonet (Carcano refers to the type of rifle it attached to) was introduced in the late 19th century, but was still in use during World War II. It had a simple muzzle-ring fitting and fullers on both sides of a blade that stretched nearly 12 in (30.5 cm).

Eagle wings form
cross-guard

Large pommel with
swastika motif

Eagle and swastika decoration

Aluminum wire wrapped
around plastic grip

Central, flat plane

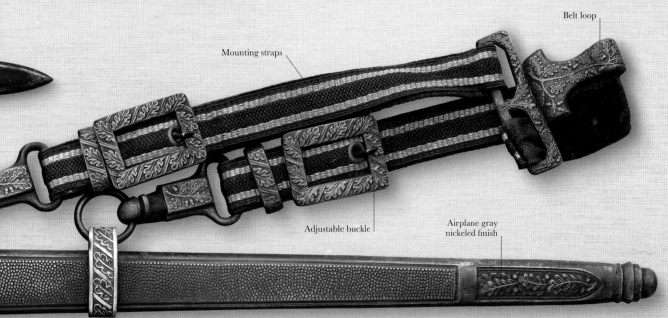

Belt loop

Mounting straps

Adjustable buckle

Airplane gray
nickeled finish

DAGGER IN
SCABBARD

GERMAN AIR OFFICER'S DAGGER

DATE	Late 1930s	**WEIGHT**	19⅓ oz (540 g)
ORIGIN	Germany	**LENGTH**	16½ in (42 cm)

The 2nd Model Luftwaffe dagger, worn only by officers, was introduced into
the German forces in 1937. It had a stiletto-type blade (a thin, long blade with
no cutting edge) with a distinctive flat plane running along the center on both
sides. The dominant decoration was a Luftwaffe-type eagle and swastika.

Pointed end

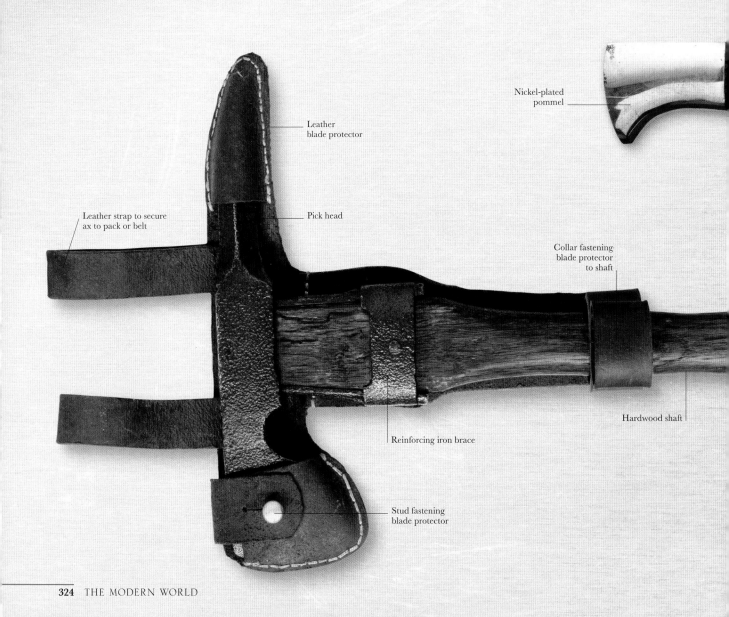

Nickel-plated
pommel

Leather
blade protector

Pick head

Leather strap to secure
ax to pack or belt

Collar fastening
blade protector
to shaft

Reinforcing iron brace

Hardwood shaft

Stud fastening
blade protector

Hitler Youth
swastika motif

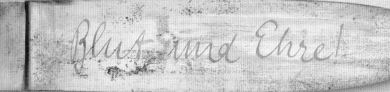

Nickel-plated,
curved cross-guard

Painted leather

SCABBARD

GERMAN TRENCH AX

DATE	c. 1915	WEIGHT	c. 3¼ lb (1.5 kg)
ORIGIN	Germany	LENGTH	21 in (53.3 cm)

Trench axes were essential pieces of gear on both sides
during World War I, useful for chopping firewood
and preparing bunkers, emplacements for military
equipment, and other structures. When necessary, they
could also be effective combat weapons—particularly
for small-party, trench-raiding operations.

HITLER YOUTH DAGGER

DATE	c. 1937	WEIGHT	c. 11 oz (300 g)
ORIGIN	Germany	LENGTH	10½ in (26.6 cm)

Although introduced around 1935, the Hitler Youth
dagger shown here is of a c. 1937 design, indicated by the
Blut und Ehre ("Blood and Honor") motto etched into the
blade, a feature that was discontinued soon after. The hilt
has a grip made of checkered bakelite, with a swastika
motif and a nickel-plated pommel and cross-guard.

ALLGEMEINE-SCHUTZSTAFFEL DAGGER

DATE	1930s	WEIGHT	11 oz (300 g)
ORIGIN	Germany	LENGTH	13 in (33 cm)

This dagger belonged to a branch of the *Schutzstaffel* (SS), or the "Protection Echelon" of the Nazi party. Called *Allgemeine-SS*, or the "General-SS," this branch had a noncombative role. The dagger has a dark wood grip, dyed with vegetable pigments to achieve the requisite black, with the motto "My Honor is Loyalty" etched on the blade. The hilt features the Nazi eagle and SS runes.

Lacquered black oxide finish

Double-edged blade

SS motto "My Honor is Loyalty"

STURMABTEILUNG DAGGER

DATE	c. 1934	WEIGHT	11 oz (300 g)
ORIGIN	Germany	LENGTH	13 in (33 cm)

This dagger was issued to the *Sturmabteilung* (SA), or the "Assault Section"— the paramilitary forces of the Nazi party. The hilt, which was made from various woods such as oak, pear, and walnut, features the Nazi swastika and eagle motif. The runic SA initials are also visible at the base of the hilt, and the motto "Everything for Germany" runs down the center of the blade.

Double-edged carbon-steel blade

Solid nickel fitting

SS BLADES COMBINED NAZI SYMBOLS WITH
RUNIC IMAGERY,
EVOKING THE WARRIOR
PEOPLES OF PAGAN NORTHERN EUROPE.

Runic SS symbol

Nazi eagle
and swastika

Nazi eagle
and swastika

Runic SA symbol

für Deutschland

SA motto "Everything
for Germany"

WWII BRITISH COMMANDO

The term "commando" was first used for citizens of the Boer republics in South Africa, who were commandeered by law to fight during the Boer War (1899–1902). It was revived during World War II to address the elite, specially trained, amphibious forces of the British army, who, alongside the Special Air Service (SAS), conducted clandestine raids in enemy-occupied territories.

Formed in June 1940, commando units drew personnel from all corners of the British forces. What set them apart from other soldiers was their training, plus the missions they undertook. They were taken to remote locations and instructed in unusual fighting techniques. Their training typically included outdoor survival, map-reading, mountain climbing, signaling, amphibious warfare, covert surveillance, and demolitions. Recruits also learned unarmed combat and knife-fighting skills. The commandos adopted the Fairbairn–Sykes knife (right), using it for disposing sentries and for hand-to-hand combat. William Fairbairn—a former police chief of Shanghai, China, and one of the knife's designers—taught them how to use his knife in the most destructive way against human targets. The commandos

fought in almost every theater of war from 1940 to 1945, and in major operations such as the attack on Dieppe, France, in 1942 and the D-Day landings at Normandy in 1944. While the British Army's commando units were disbanded after the war, the Navy's Royal Marine Commandos continued in service. They serve to this day as a small elite within Britain's armed forces.

FAIRBAIRN–SYKES FIGHTING KNIFE		
DATE	1941–45	WEIGHT	8 oz (230 g)
ORIGIN	UK	LENGTH	12 in (30 cm)

Modeled on daggers used by Chinese gangsters, this knife was developed in the 1930s by William Fairbairn and his colleague Eric Sykes. British commandos used it for hand-to-hand combat, since the sharp edge of this slender knife could easily penetrate the rib cage. The knife was light and well balanced, making it suitable for throwing as well.

"IN CLOSE-QUARTERS FIGHTING, THERE IS NO MORE DEADLY WEAPON THAN A KNIFE."

WILLIAM FAIRBAIRN (1885–1960) IN HIS BOOK *GET TOUGH*, 1942

Short ricasso leads to
double-edged blade

Oval
cross-guard

POISED TO STRIKE

This photograph shows a British Commando
in France during World War II, wearing British
battledress uniform with a French helmet and
clutching a combat dagger. Commandos
were taught to use knives against soft, vital
parts of the body, particularly the neck,
abdomen, groin, and kidneys.

BRITISH, AMERICAN, AND ALLIED BLADES

The Allies during both world wars were just as deeply wedded to the retention of bayonets as the Axis nations. Yet times were changing. During World War I, a bayonet charge was still a feature of combat, but by World War II it had largely become an anachronism. The later war was characterized by mobility, firepower, and frequent urban warfare, and mounting a lengthy bayonet was awkward and inappropriate. Yet the rise of special forces and paratroopers in World War II created the need for pure close-quarters fighting knives, while bayonets were put to other uses, such as cutting through foliage.

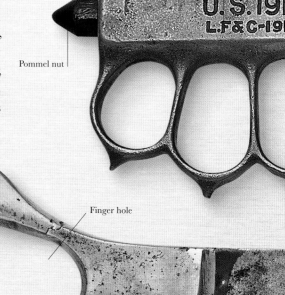

Maker's initials

U.S. 191
L.F&C-191

Pommel nut

Knuckle stud

Finger hole

T-shape fits in palm

Blade welded into hilt

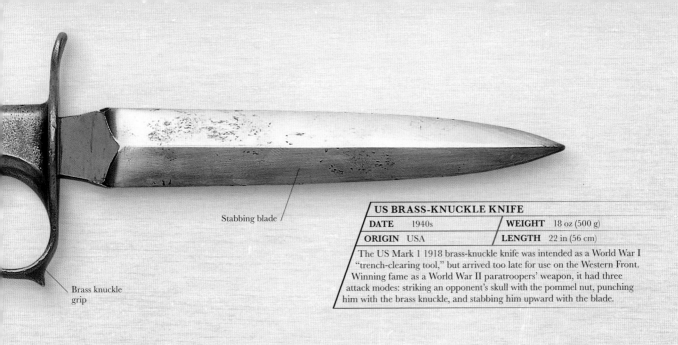

Stabbing blade

Brass knuckle
grip

US BRASS-KNUCKLE KNIFE

DATE	1940s	WEIGHT	18 oz (500 g)
ORIGIN	USA	LENGTH	22 in (56 cm)

The US Mark 1 1918 brass-knuckle knife was intended as a World War I
"trench-clearing tool," but arrived too late for use on the Western Front.
Winning fame as a World War II paratroopers' weapon, it had three
attack modes: striking an opponent's skull with the pommel nut, punching
him with the brass knuckle, and stabbing him upward with the blade.

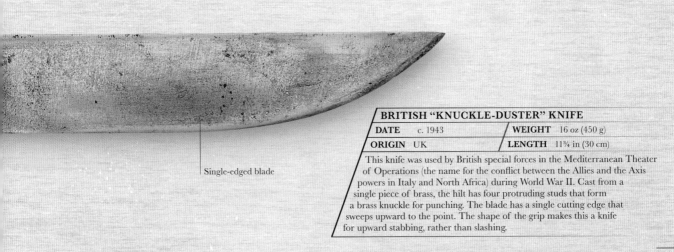

Single-edged blade

BRITISH "KNUCKLE-DUSTER" KNIFE

DATE	c. 1943	WEIGHT	16 oz (450 g)
ORIGIN	UK	LENGTH	11¾ in (30 cm)

This knife was used by British special forces in the Mediterranean Theater
of Operations (the name for the conflict between the Allies and the Axis
powers in Italy and North Africa) during World War II. Cast from a
single piece of brass, the hilt has four protruding studs that form
a brass knuckle for punching. The blade has a single cutting edge that
sweeps upward to the point. The shape of the grip makes this a knife
for upward stabbing, rather than slashing.

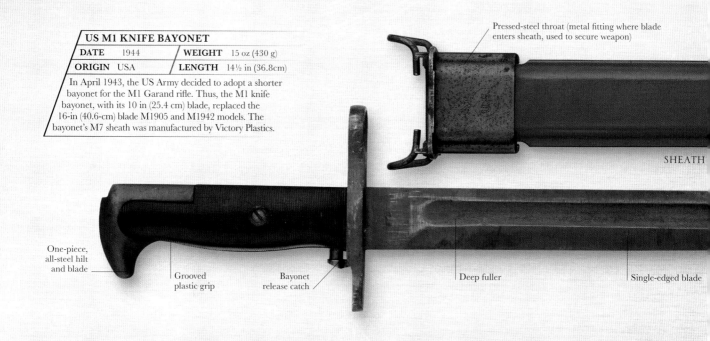

US M1 KNIFE BAYONET

DATE	1944	WEIGHT	15 oz (430 g)
ORIGIN	USA	LENGTH	14½ in (36.8cm)

In April 1943, the US Army decided to adopt a shorter bayonet for the M1 Garand rifle. Thus, the M1 knife bayonet, with its 10 in (25.4 cm) blade, replaced the 16-in (40.6-cm) blade M1905 and M1942 models. The bayonet's M7 sheath was manufactured by Victory Plastics.

Pressed-steel throat (metal fitting where blade enters sheath, used to secure weapon)

One-piece, all-steel hilt and blade

Grooved plastic grip

Bayonet release catch

Deep fuller

Single-edged blade

Leather washers form grip

Recurved quillon

Blade with diamond cross-section

Molded plastic

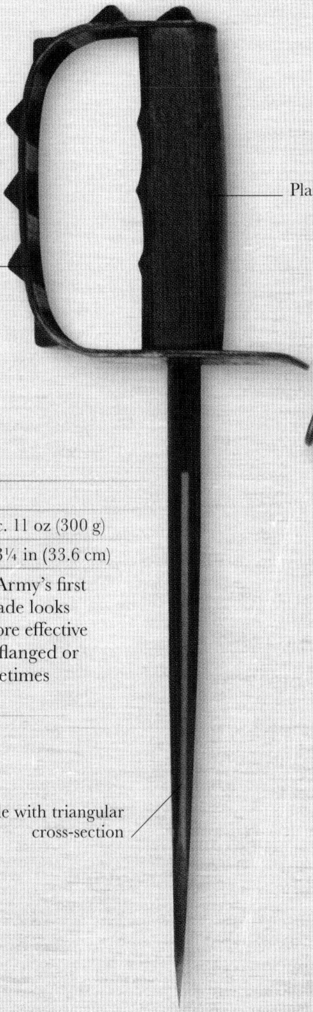

Plain hardwood grip

Brass-knuckle
guard

Steel throat

US M1917 TRENCH KNIFE

DATE	1917	**WEIGHT**	c. 11 oz (300 g)
ORIGIN	USA	**LENGTH**	13¼ in (33.6 cm)

The US M1917 trench knife was the US Army's first
trench-fighting knife. Although the pick blade looks
impressive, it was rather fragile in action. More effective
was the brass-knuckle hilt, which had either flanged or
rounded projections. The leather sheaths sometimes
had metal throats, as seen here.

Blade with triangular
cross-section

Plain leather

AMERICAN MK3 FIGHTING KNIFE

DATE	c. 1950	**WEIGHT**	9 oz (240 g)
ORIGIN	USA	**LENGTH**	12 in (29.5cm)

In 1943, the US Army introduced the Mk3 knife, designed for
hand-to-hand fighting. It was rapidly put into mass production, with
2.5 million manufactured by 1944. The hilt and blade were influenced
by the British Fairbairn–Sykes fighting knife (*pp. 328–29*).

SHEATH

Ridged hardwood grip
with flared base

Pommel with slot for
fixing bayonet to rifle

Muzzle ring

Notched blade to divert fluids,
such as blood and tree sap

Single-edged,
curved blade

Narrow fuller

One of two small knives
for utility purposes

Leather pouch

SHEATH

Single-edged
blade

Deep fuller

BRITISH 1907-PATTERN SWORD BAYONET

DATE	1914–18	WEIGHT	18 oz (500 g)
ORIGIN	UK	LENGTH	22 in (56 cm)

Designed for the Short Magazine Lee-Enfield rifle, the 1907-Pattern was based on the Japanese Arisaka bayonet. Its long blade was intended to give a soldier extra reach, but, in the trench warfare of 1914–18, its length made it unusable when detached as a sword, since the blade glittered at night and the cross-section made penetration difficult. It was awkward to remove the sword from the enemy's body, especially if it was embedded deep. As a bayonet, it changed the rifle's shooting capabilities and made it difficult to hold the rifle steady.

Steel chape

NEPALESE KUKRI

DATE	c. 1940	WEIGHT	32 oz (900 g)
ORIGIN	Nepal	LENGTH	c. 18 in (45.7 cm)

This Nepalese blade became the signature weapon of the Royal Gurkha Rifles, which gained a fearsome reputation for its use during World War II. The blade is angled at about 20 degrees, a feature that increases the knife's effectiveness as a chopping weapon. A narrow fuller is visible at the back edge of the blade. This part is also very thick, providing strength and weight.

Hole for
wrist cord

Handle riveted
to tang

Hip mounting

Loop binding
to hold handle

THE MACHETE WAS THE BASIC TOOL OF
JUNGLE OPERATIONS,
PERMITTING TRAVEL THROUGH
TANGLED VEGETATION
AWAY FROM THE TRAILS.

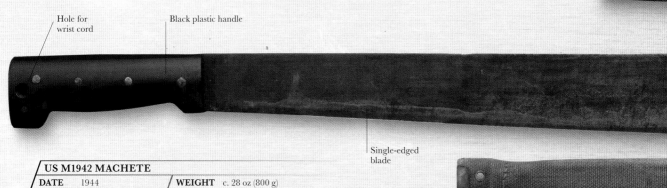

Hole for
wrist cord

Black plastic handle

Single-edged
blade

Brass
protector strip

US M1942 MACHETE			
DATE 1944		**WEIGHT** c. 28 oz (800 g)	
ORIGIN USA		**LENGTH** 22 in (56 cm)	

The M1942 machete had an 18-in (45.7-cm) blade and was based on
a commercial model manufactured by the Collins company. Like the British
example above, this machete has a hole in the handle for a wrist cord,
which prevented the machete from being dropped or lost when in use.

Heavy, counter-
balanced blade

Single
cutting edge

SHEATH

Stitched
seam

Blade flares at end
to maximize cutting edge

SHEATH

Water-repellent
canvas material

GURKHA

The Gurkhas are a people originally from Nepal and northern India, known for their indomitable courage. During the 19th century, they were recruited by the British East India Company, and continue to serve the British forces to this day. The Indian Army retains six Gurkha regiments and the Nepalese Army has two Gurkha battalions. The Gurkhas' best-known weapon is the *kukri*. Capable of removing an enemy's head in a single swipe, the *kukri* was particularly feared by the Japanese during World War II. The notch in the blade may have religious significance (resembling the hoof of the cow, a sacred animal for the primarily Hindu Gurkhas) or it may simply help to drain fluids away from the handle.

Notch at base of blade

Single-edged, curved blade

Ridged hardwood grip with flared base

KUKRI			
DATE c. 1940		**WEIGHT** c. 32 oz (900 g)	
ORIGIN Nepal		**LENGTH** c. 18 in (45.7 cm)	

The wooden handle and broad, curved blade with a notch make this a typical example of the Gurkha's *kukri*. It is large enough to be wielded two-handed, and is effective for cutting through jungle undergrowth as well as in battle.

> # "IF A MAN SAYS HE IS NOT AFRAID OF DYING, HE IS EITHER LYING OR HE IS A GURKHA."
>
> FIELD MARSHAL SAM MANEKSHAW (1914–2008),
> FORMER CHIEF OF STAFF OF THE INDIAN ARMY

Weight concentrated at front of blade

SKILLED FIGHTER

A soldier of the 1st Battalion of the Royal Gurkha Rifles displays his *kukri* skills. The *kukri's* effectiveness derives from its razor-sharp edge and heavy weight. In combat, it would be used with a chopping action, the main targets being the head, neck, and forearms.

JAPANESE BLADES

Although they were no longer practical on the World War II battlefields of the Pacific, China, and Southeast Asia, swords were still commonly worn by Japanese officers for ceremonial purposes, and were even drawn during infantry charges against the enemy or for executing prisoners. Japan's wartime shortages in raw materials meant that the quality of these swords left a lot to be desired. Their blades tended to be of standard machine steel. This, along with their poor construction quality, soon rendered these swords ineffective in hot and humid jungle or island conditions.

Crude, improvised handle

SHIN-GUNTO			
DATE	Late 1930s	**WEIGHT**	24 oz (680 g)
ORIGIN	Japan	**LENGTH**	27½ in (70 cm)

This *shin-gunto*, or army officer's sword, is based upon the traditional design of the *wakazashi (pp. 198–203)*. It has a painted metal scabbard, unlike later wartime examples (c. 1944 onward), which had lacquered wooden scabbards, sometimes called marine mounts.

Cord-wrapped hilt

Tsuba

Suspension ring to attach scabbard to belt loop or straps

| DATE | 1940s | WEIGHT | c. 2¼ lb (1 kg) |
| ORIGIN | Japan | LENGTH | 14 in (35.5 cm) |

Cane knives, as their name describes, were traditionally used by Japanese-American laborers to harvest sugar cane in Hawaii during the late 19th century. They found a new purpose among soldiers during World War II, when they were used for clearing jungle foliage.

Rudimentary iron blade

Sheath made of leather

Belt loop

SHEATH

Painted metal

SCABBARD

MODERN AFRICAN BLADES

By the early 20th century, most of the industrial world had given up on blades as combat weapons in favor of firearms. However, the use of knives and swords for combat in Africa persisted for longer. Many were in use long after the European colonial powers took over most parts of Africa. The types of blade and the design of various knives and swords reflected the cultures from which they came. Post 1945, the sale of firearms to Africa increased as the communists and capitalists wanted to fuel proxy wars. This spread of firearms pushed elaborate, expensive blades into largely ceremonial roles.

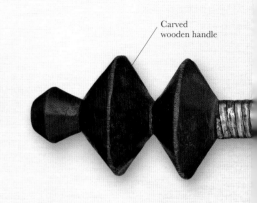

Carved wooden handle

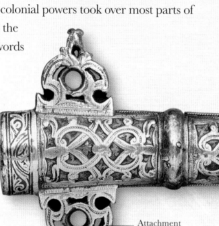

SCABBARD

Silver overlay

Attachment for baldric

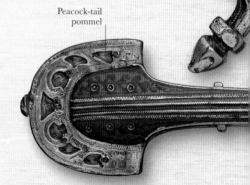

Peacock-tail pommel

WOODEN-HILTED DAGGER

DATE	19th century	WEIGHT	8 oz (230 g)
ORIGIN	North Africa	LENGTH	14¾ in (37.5 cm)

The peacock-tail shape of this dagger's pommel is functional as well as decorative, providing protection for the back of the hand. It is typical of a *koummya*, a curved dagger used by peoples of northern Africa, especially Morocco. The elaborate sheath, overlaid with silver on one side, was hung on a baldric (an ornamental belt made of silk or leather) and worn on the left hip.

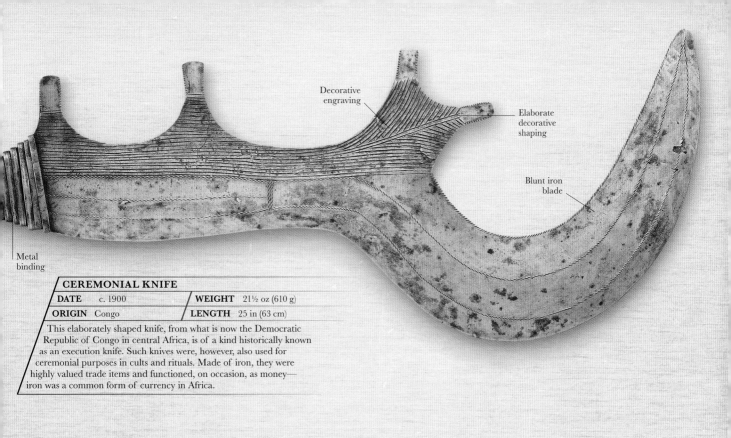

Decorative
engraving

Elaborate
decorative
shaping

Blunt iron
blade

Metal
binding

CEREMONIAL KNIFE

DATE	c. 1900	WEIGHT	21½ oz (610 g)
ORIGIN	Congo	LENGTH	25 in (63 cm)

This elaborately shaped knife, from what is now the Democratic
Republic of Congo in central Africa, is of a kind historically known
as an execution knife. Such knives were, however, also used for
ceremonial purposes in cults and rituals. Made of iron, they were
highly valued trade items and functioned, on occasion, as money—
iron was a common form of currency in Africa.

Double-edged blade

Blade curved to
resemble a boar's tusk

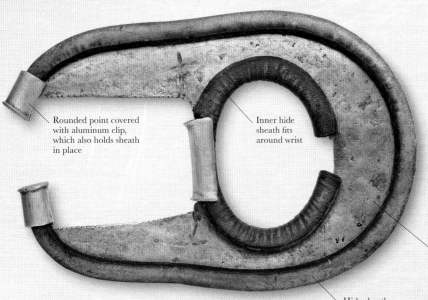

Circular knife blade

Rounded point covered with aluminum clip, which also holds sheath in place

Inner hide sheath fits around wrist

Thin sheet-iron blade

Hide sheath attached around outside edge of blade

LARIM FIGHTING BRACELET

DATE	20th century	**WEIGHT**	2½ oz (70 g)
ORIGIN	Sudan	**LENGTH**	5½ in (14 cm)

Known to the Larim people of southern Sudan as a *nyepel*, this unusual weapon is a two-pointed knife worn on the wrist. Before entering a fight, the warrior would remove the outer sheath, uncovering the sharp edge and slightly rounded tips of the hammered iron blade. Similar fighting bracelets and sheaths were used by other Sudanese peoples.

UGANDAN FINGER KNIFE

DATE	c. 1890–1950	**WEIGHT**	1¾ oz (50 g)
ORIGIN	Uganda	**LENGTH**	3¾ in (9.5 cm)

This small, almost circular knife probably comes from the Labwor people of northeastern Uganda. Made of iron, it was worn on a finger. Aside from fighting, it could also be used for everyday purposes such as cutting meat. Its advantage as a weapon lay in its diminutive size—it could be easily concealed in the hand.

Triangular pattern decoration

Straight back of blade

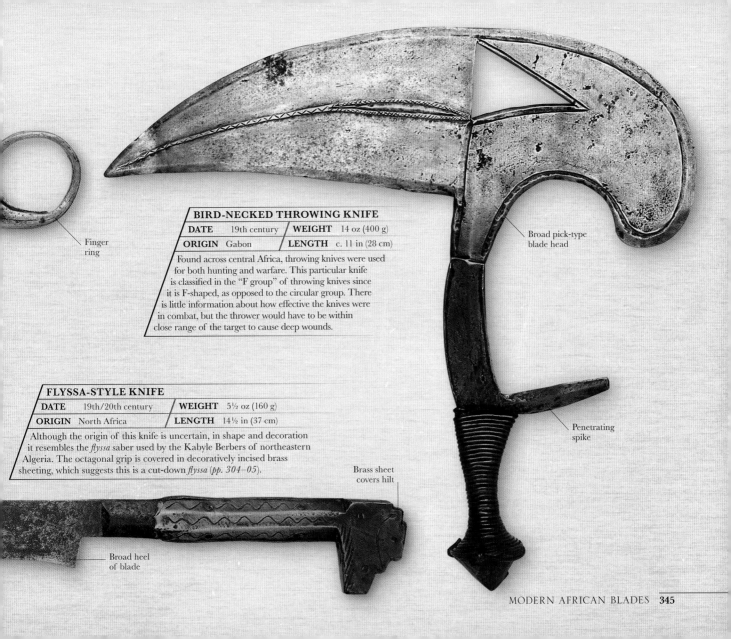

Finger
ring

BIRD-NECKED THROWING KNIFE

DATE	19th century	WEIGHT	14 oz (400 g)
ORIGIN	Gabon	LENGTH	c. 11 in (28 cm)

Found across central Africa, throwing knives were used
for both hunting and warfare. This particular knife
is classified in the "F group" of throwing knives since
it is F-shaped, as opposed to the circular group. There
is little information about how effective the knives were
in combat, but the thrower would have to be within
close range of the target to cause deep wounds.

Broad pick-type
blade head

Penetrating
spike

FLYSSA-STYLE KNIFE

DATE	19th/20th century	WEIGHT	5½ oz (160 g)
ORIGIN	North Africa	LENGTH	14½ in (37 cm)

Although the origin of this knife is uncertain, in shape and decoration
it resembles the *flyssa* saber used by the Kabyle Berbers of northeastern
Algeria. The octagonal grip is covered in decoratively incised brass
sheeting, which suggests this is a cut-down *flyssa (pp. 304–05)*.

Brass sheet
covers hilt

Broad heel
of blade

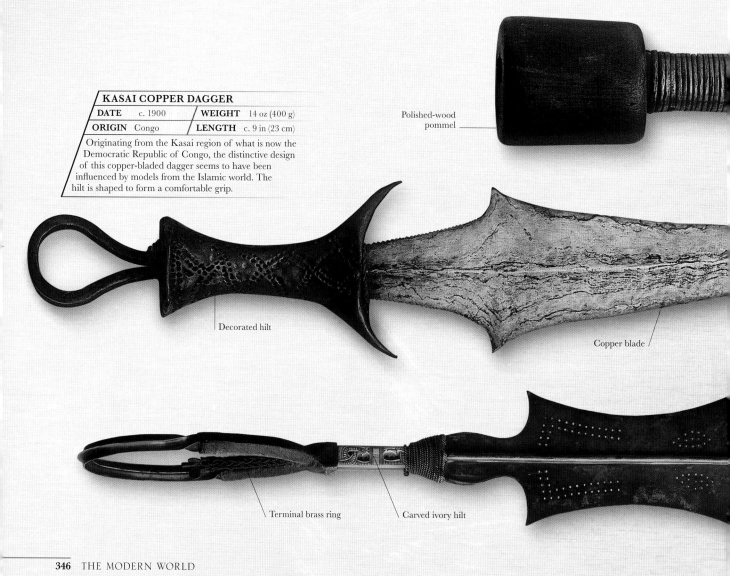

KASAI COPPER DAGGER

DATE	c. 1900	**WEIGHT**	14 oz (400 g)
ORIGIN	Congo	**LENGTH**	c. 9 in (23 cm)

Originating from the Kasai region of what is now the Democratic Republic of Congo, the distinctive design of this copper-bladed dagger seems to have been influenced by models from the Islamic world. The hilt is shaped to form a comfortable grip.

Polished-wood pommel

Decorated hilt

Copper blade

Terminal brass ring

Carved ivory hilt

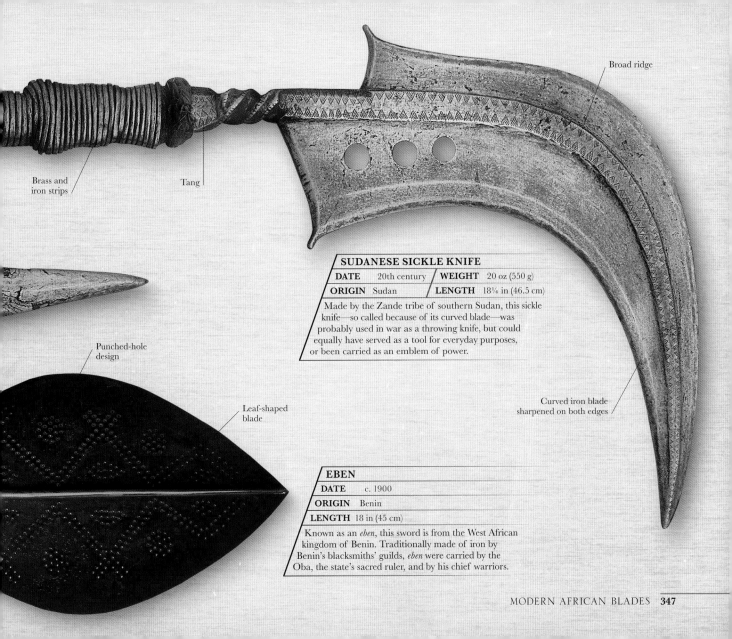

Broad ridge

Brass and
iron strips

Tang

Punched-hole
design

Leaf-shaped
blade

SUDANESE SICKLE KNIFE

DATE	20th century	**WEIGHT**	20 oz (550 g)
ORIGIN	Sudan	**LENGTH**	18¼ in (46.5 cm)

Made by the Zande tribe of southern Sudan, this sickle
knife—so called because of its curved blade—was
probably used in war as a throwing knife, but could
equally have served as a tool for everyday purposes,
or been carried as an emblem of power.

Curved iron blade
sharpened on both edges

EBEN

DATE	c. 1900
ORIGIN	Benin
LENGTH	18 in (45 cm)

Known as an *eben*, this sword is from the West African
kingdom of Benin. Traditionally made of iron by
Benin's blacksmiths' guilds, *eben* were carried by the
Oba, the state's sacred ruler, and by his chief warriors.

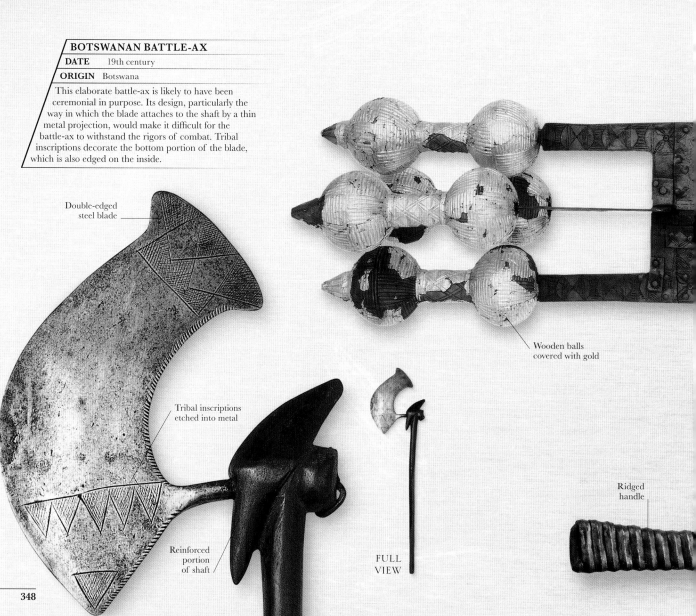

BOTSWANAN BATTLE-AX

DATE	19th century
ORIGIN	Botswana

This elaborate battle-ax is likely to have been ceremonial in purpose. Its design, particularly the way in which the blade attaches to the shaft by a thin metal projection, would make it difficult for the battle-ax to withstand the rigors of combat. Tribal inscriptions decorate the bottom portion of the blade, which is also edged on the inside.

Double-edged
steel blade

Wooden balls
covered with gold

Tribal inscriptions
etched into metal

Ridged
handle

Reinforced
portion
of shaft

FULL
VIEW

CEREMONIAL SWORD

DATE   c. 1870

ORIGIN   Ashanti

This sword belonged to Kofi Karikari, ruler of the
West African Ashanti kingdom from 1867 to 1874.
It was an object of prestige rather than a weapon—
its iron blade is unsharpened. The golden balls,
representing seeds, are symbols of wealth and fertility.

Punched
decoration

Unsharpened
iron blade

Curved
metal blade

Double-pointed blade

FULL
VIEW

CONGOLESE THROWING KNIFE

DATE   c. 20th century

ORIGIN   Congo

Eccentrically shaped multibladed throwing knives are
found in many parts of Africa. This example is from
the Democratic Republic of Congo. When the knife
is thrown it turns on its center of gravity, causing the
blades to scythe dangerously through the air. No matter
which part of the knife made contact with the victim,
it would have inflicted serious injury.

POSTWAR BAYONETS

In the aftermath of World War II, it was widely recognized that bayonets had a limited role on the modern battlefield, at least in terms of combat. Yet as last-resort weapons, or for utility purposes, they still had a place. Postwar bayonets tend to be short (long bayonets would adversely affect the balance of assault rifles), and often combine the properties of fighting knife and bayonet in one. Many also incorporate special utility features such as wire cutters.

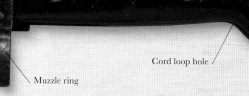

Bayonet shaft fits over flash hider

BRITISH L3A1 BAYONET

DATE	1990s	WEIGHT	c. 9 oz (250 g)
ORIGIN	UK	LENGTH	10 in (25 cm)

The bayonet supplied with the LA85 rifle has a shaft that fits over the flash hider of the muzzle, a device that reduces the visibility of burning gases emanating from the muzzle on firing. A lug on the bayonet's scabbard fits the slot in the blade and the ensemble becomes a pair of wire cutters, an idea borrowed from the Soviet AKM rifle.

Wire-cutting blade tip

Serrated top edge

Muzzle ring

Cord loop hole

IRAQI AK47 BAYONET

DATE	1970s	WEIGHT	11 oz (300 g)
ORIGIN	Iraq	LENGTH	10 in (27 cm)

This Iraqi copy of the AK47 bayonet has all the features of the original. A slot in the blade enables the bayonet to lock to the scabbard, turning the knife into a scissorlike wire cutter. The synthetic hilt does not conduct electricity, which means the knife is capable of cutting electrical cables.

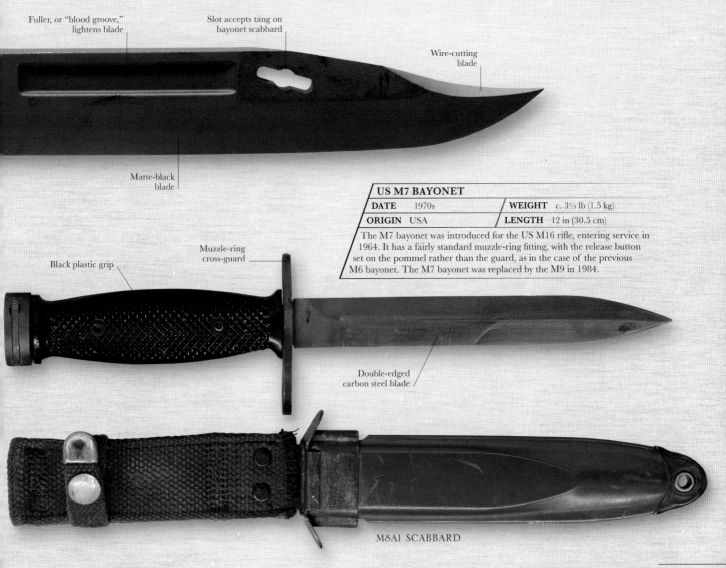

Fuller, or "blood groove," lightens blade

Slot accepts tang on bayonet scabbard

Wire-cutting blade

Matte-black blade

US M7 BAYONET

DATE 1970s	**WEIGHT** c. 3⅓ lb (1.5 kg)
ORIGIN USA	**LENGTH** 12 in (30.5 cm)

The M7 bayonet was introduced for the US M16 rifle, entering service in 1964. It has a fairly standard muzzle-ring fitting, with the release button set on the pommel rather than the guard, as in the case of the previous M6 bayonet. The M7 bayonet was replaced by the M9 in 1984.

Black plastic grip

Muzzle-ring cross-guard

Double-edged carbon steel blade

M8A1 SCABBARD

GLOSSARY

BARB A narrow, tapering projection at the end of an arrowhead, pointing backward. Barbs made it difficult to remove the arrow from the victim's flesh after penetration.

BASKET-HILT GUARD A hand guard of a sword that encases the wielder's hand like a basket.

BAYONET A blade designed to fit into, over, under, or around a rifle's muzzle. This allowed the soldier to use the gun as a stabbing weapon in close-quarters combat.

BLUEING A process of chemical treatment, using blue oxide, to prevent steel from rusting.

BODKIN A small, pointed multipurpose tool, often part of a hunting kit in 17th-century Europe.

BODKIN POINT A small arrowhead with a square cross-section, capable of penetrating armor.

BOLT A type of arrow fired from a crossbow. Bolts were shorter and thicker than arrows fired from bows.

BOSHI A line of bright steel at the point of a Japanese blade, created when forming the cutting edge of the blade during the process of tempering.

BOW NOCK A notch in a bow to attach the string; also a notch in an arrow to keep it in place as the bowstring is drawn.

BRAZING A process of joining metals together using a filler solder or alloy, such as brass.

BROADSWORD A double-edged cutting sword with a broad blade. Broadswords were extremely popular in medieval Europe.

CASTING A process of solidifying liquid metal to a given shape, in a particular mold.

CHAPE Protective metallic cap on the tip of a scabbard.

CLAYMORE A generic term applied to two types of Scottish sword used from the 16th to the 18th centuries—one was a two-handed sword with a cross-guard, the other was a broadsword with a basket hilt.

CLEAVER A heavy cutting weapon with a sharp, single-edged blade. Cleavers were an essential component of the medieval hunter's gear and were used for slicing through animal joints.

COLICHEMARDE A type of smallsword with a wide forte, often with multiple fullers. Typically, the blade narrowed after the fullers ended. Its light weight made the sword a useful parrying weapon.

COMPOSITE BOW A bow made of multiple layers, combining wood with bone, horn, or sinew.

CROSSBOW A mechanical bow used for shooting wooden or metal bolts. The user did not have to hold the bowstring manually in order to keep the crossbow loaded.

CROSS-GUARD A straight hand guard just below a sword's blade. It extended from both sides of the blade, which made the sword resemble a cross.

CROSS-SECTION The shape of a blade when viewed at a right angle to its long axis. It can be of various shapes. Blades with diamond or lozenge cross-sections were thick in the middle, and therefore rigid.

CUP-HILT GUARD A hand guard in the shape of a cup; it was popular in the 17th century, when many European rapiers featured cup hilts.

CUTLASS A heavy, curved sword, traditionally used by sailors.

DAISHO The Japanese term for the pairing of a long sword (*katana*) with a shorter sword (*wakazashi*).

ÉPÉE A fencing weapon developed in the 19th century. Similar in design to the smallsword, it had a blunt tip and was used for thrusting.

FALSE EDGE An additional bevel or surface on the back edge of the blade of a sword, which may or may not be sharpened. False edges were used for backhand strikes.

FERRULE A metal band used to secure the leather or wire wrapping on a sword's grip; also used as hilt decoration.

FIRE-WELDING A process of fusing pieces of metal using fire. Also called forge-welding, this was the only welding process followed until the end of the 19th century.

FLAKING A process of repeatedly striking a piece of flint with another stone, until a fine edge remains.

FLANGE A projecting rim or collar, typically seen on maces in the medieval period.

FLINT A type of hard stone, found in areas of chalk downland. It was extensively used to make weapons in the Paleolithic Age, about 2.5 million years to 20,000 years ago.

FLUKE A projecting spike or barb, sometimes hooked, on the head of a polearm or ax. Flukes could penetrate plate armor and were effective parrying weapons.

FOIL A light, flexible fencing weapon, with a blunt end. Introduced in Europe in the 18th century, it made fencing safer.

FORGE To shape metal by heating and hammering it. The term also refers to the hearth or smithy where forging takes place.

FORTE The strongest part of the blade just in front of the hilt. A forte may or may not be sharpened.

FULLER A groove running along the length of a sword blade, which both strengthens and lightens it.

HAMON A pattern of hardened steel on Japanese blades, created during tempering. *Hamon* varied from sword to sword, and were therefore often considered the signature of the swordsmith.

HANGER A type of sword named for the way it was hung from the belt of the user. Originally made for hunting, it became a standard military weapon by the 18th century.

HATCHET POINT A sword tip with a diagonally curved front edge.

HAUBERK A chain-mail coat or shirt, usually at least of thigh length.

HEAVY CAVALRY Heavily armed and armored mounted soldiers, primarily used to make attacks directly into enemy ranks.

HEAVY INFANTRY Heavily armed and armored foot soldiers, used mainly for fighting in close ranks against the main enemy lines.

HILT The portion of a sword or knife below the blade, including the grip, guards, and pommel.

JAVELIN A long, light spear used for throwing.

JOUST A medieval tournament game involving mounted, armored knights aiming to unseat each other with a lance strike.

KNAPPING See flaking.

KNUCKLE-DUSTER (BRASS-KNUCKLE) KNIFE A knife with studs protruding from its knuckle guard. The blade was designed for upward stabbing, and the studs were used to punch the opponent.

KNUCKLE GUARD An extension of a sword's guard running over the length of the grip; it protected the user's knuckles.

LANGET A metal strip securing the shaft of a staff weapon to its head. Also found on some swords, langets extend over both sides of the blade and fit tightly over the scabbard, keeping the sword securely sheathed.

LIGHT CAVALRY Lightly armed and armored mounted soldiers, used principally in raids and skirmishes and for reconnaissance.

LIGHT INFANTRY Lightly armed and armored foot soldiers, used primarily for skirmishes or raids.

LONGBOW A medieval bow up to 6½ ft (2 m) long, made of a single piece of yew or elm. It provided superior range and penetration compared to shorter bows.

LUG On a sword, lugs refer to projections from the blade that served to deflect or parry an enemy sword blow away from the user.

MACE A staff weapon, usually with a spiked or flanged head. Maces were popular weapons in the medieval period, with many ornate examples made in Europe and Asia.

MACHETE A heavy, single-edged cutting blade; ideal for operations in tropical and subtropical jungles, it can easily cut through thick foliage. It is also a popular household tool in Latin American countries.

MAIL (CHAIN-MAIL) ARMOR A type of armor made from small, riveted, interlocking iron rings and worn like a coat or shirt.

MAINGAUCHE Literally meaning "left hand" in French; also used to describe a dagger held in the left hand. It was a useful weapon for parrying enemy attacks.

MÊLÉE A free-for-all battle. The *mêlée* was a popular tournament game between mounted and dismounted knights until the 14th century.

MORTISE SLOT A slot or socket cut into a bayonet, designed to fit over a gun's muzzle.

MUZZLE The open front end of a gun's barrel to which a bayonet could be fixed.

PARRYING WEAPON A weapon used to deflect enemy blows or strikes. These could be of various types, including shields and sticks.

PATTERN-WELDING A technique of fusing different pieces of metal, and then folding or twisting the fused metal to form a pattern.

PIQUÉ A type of decoration, often with inlay work of metal, ivory, shell, or horn; seen on the hilts of some hanger swords in 17th-century Europe.

PLATE ARMOR Armor made of overlapping metal plates, which was more difficult to penetrate than chain-mail armor.

PLUG BAYONET A type of bayonet that was inserted into the muzzle of a musket.

POLEARM See staff weapon.

POMMEL A counterweight, often spherical, at the top of a sword grip, to provide balance.

PRESSURE FLAKING see flaking.

QUENCHING A process of hardening steel by heating and then rapidly cooling it.

QUILLON The extension of a cross-guard on either side of the blade. Found in various shapes and sizes, quillons protect the user's hand by blocking enemy blows.

QUOIT A sharpened metal ring designed to be thrown at the enemy.

RAPIER A thrusting sword with a long blade. Although used in combat, it was more closely associated with dueling.

RICASSO The unsharpened part of the blade, just above the hilt. It gave the user the option to hold the blade as well as the hilt for a better grip.

ROCOCO An 18th-century French style of elaborate ornamentation, also seen on some European sword hilts.

RONDEL Derived from the Old French *rond*, meaning "round." The rondel dagger took its name from its disk-shaped guard and pommel.

SABER A long, single-edged cutting sword with a curved blade.

SCIMITAR A generic name for curved swords of the Islamic world, including the *kilij* and the *shamshir*.

SEAX A single-edged blade used by the Anglo-Saxons and Franks as a weapon and as a tool. Saxons probably derived their name from this weapon.

SHELL GUARD A hand guard in the form of a circular or oval plate of steel.

SHURIKEN Literally the Japanese term for small blades that could be hidden in the hand. They could be of various shapes and were often tipped with poison.

SMALLSWORD A thrusting sword, typically with a stiff, triangular blade with unsharpened edges.

SOCKET BAYONET A type of bayonet which fits around the muzzle of a firearm, allowing the user to continue firing.

STAFF WEAPON A weapon in which a blade or club was attached to a long, commonly wooden, shaft. The long shaft gave a soldier extra reach in combat.

STILETTO A long, thin dagger, popular in Italy in the 16th and 17th centuries. It derives its name from the Latin *stilus*, meaning stake or spike.

SWEPT-HILT GUARD A hand guard so named because the bars of the guard sweep upward in a curve from the ricasso to the pommel.

SWORD BAYONET A type of bayonet with a long blade. It could be used as a sword or mounted on a firearm.

TANG The hidden portion of the blade that runs through the hilt and pommel.

TEMPERING The process of removing the brittleness accumulated in metal during quenching. The metal is reheated but at a lower temperature than when quenching, and then cooled slowly.

TILLER The stock, or main body, of a crossbow, which enabled the user to hold and aim the crossbow in the same manner as a firearm.

TOMAHAWK An ax used by native North American warriors.

WATERING See pattern-welding.

INDEX

"3-Line" rifle M1891 186
1809-pattern musket 141

A

adzes 15
Africa 119, 304–9, 342–9
aikuchi (dagger) 100–1
American Civil War 220–1, 236–43
Ancient World 6–59
Anglo-Saxons 36–7, 40–1, 56–7, 91
ankus (elephant goad) 300–1
anti-cavalry swords 98–9
Armenia 262–3
arming swords 92–3
armor
    medieval European 40–1, 62
    samurai 204–5
arrowheads
    African 311
    Bronze-Age 16, 53
    flint 8, 50–1
    medieval 112–3, 114–5
artillery swords 238–9
Ashanti kingdom 348–9
Asia *see* countries by name
Assam 292–3
Assyria 50–1
Austria 248–9
axes
    African 308–9, 348
    Anglo-Saxon 91
    Asian 110–1
    ax clubs 308
    ax match- and wheellock 217

B

Baker rifle 250–1
ballock daggers 80–1
bardiche 88–9, 174–5
baselard 70–1, 82–3
basket-hilted swords 125, 128–9,
    130
bastard sword 70–1, 114–5
battle-axes *see* axes
bayonets 119, 220, 221
    American 246–7, 332–3, 351
    Baker rifle 250–1
    Chassepot 245
bhuj 300–1
Bronze- and Iron-Age 26–7
carbine 216–7
Egyptian 18–9
Frankish 38–9
Greek hoplite 28–9
Indian 184–5, 292–3
long-handled 91
matchlock ax/dagger 214–5
Native American 258–9
poleaxes 86, 88–9, 172
skeg 43
Stone-Age 8, 10–1, 14–5
tabar 184–5, 302–3
tomahawk 258–9, 260–1
tongi 300–2
trench 324–5
Viking 42–3, 91
ayudha katti (scythe) 182
Aztecs 8, 63, 94–7

Elcho 246–7
Enfield rifle-musket 250–1
European 244–51, 320–1, 350–1
knife 321, 332–3, 351
musket 248–9
pistol 248–9
plug 119, 164–5
postwar 350–1
socket 119, 250–1, 252–3
sword 244–5, 250–1, 318, 334–5
tactics 252–3
trowel 246–7
World War I and II 318–22, 333–5
bearded ax 42–3
Belgium 248–9
Benin 346–7
bhuj (battle-ax) 300–1
Bhutan 211
bi shou (dagger) 106–7
bich'hwa (dagger) 208–9, 212–3,
    294–5
bills 173
bo shuriken (stick blade) 283
bodkins 151
bolts, crossbow 113
Botswana 348
Bowie knives 220, 256
bows 8
    Assyrian 50–1
    crossbows 112–3
    longbows 112, 114–5
brass knuckle knives 319, 330–1
breech-loading guns 221
Britain 84–5, 92–3, 223–7, 244, 246–7,
    250–1, 330–1, 334–9, 350–1

broad-bladed battle-ax 26
broadswords 125, 126, 128, 272–3
Bronze-Age 8–9, 22–3, 26–7, 52–3, 56
buck-horn weapons 298–9
Burma 221

C

carbine ax 216–7
carving knives 152
case sword 145
Castillon swords 74
cavalry swords
    American 220, 236–7, 242–3
    European 124, 126–7, 130–5, 220,
        222–5, 226–7, 318
    Indian 180–1
    medieval 76–7
    Ottoman 266–7
Celts 22–5
ceremonial weapons
    axes 18–9, 292–3
    daggers 16–7, 304–5, 319
    halberds 174–5
    knives 319, 342–3
    swords 228–32, 319, 348–9
chackram (quoit) 296–7
Chad 304–5
chain weapons 282
chalcedony knives 97
Chassepot bayonet 245
China 63, 98–9, 104–7, 110–1,
    272–9, 278–9
chokuto (sword) 63
cinquedea (sword) 72–3

claymore 120
cleavers 152–3
Clovis point spearhead 13
clubs
    African 308
    Aztec 96–7
    Maori 312–5
    maquahuitl 96–7
    Native-American 257–9
    patuki 312–3
    spiked 258
    taiaha 314–5
colichemarde-type swords 143
combination weapons 214–7, 221
Commandos, British 328–9
Congo, Democratic Republic of
    309, 342–3, 346–9
copper blades 8–9, 346–7
Cossack warriors 154–5
crossbows 112–3
Crusades 64–5
cumberjung (flail) 187
cup-hilt rapiers 139–41
cutlasses
    European 228–9
    Polynesian 312–3
    Union Navy 241
cutting and thrusting 188–9

D

dadao (sword) 63, 272–3
daggers
    African 304–5, 310–1, 346–7
    aikuchi 100–1

Anglo-Saxon 36
Asian 206–3
ballock 80–1
baselard 82–3
bi shou 106–7
bich'hwa 208–9, 212–3
Bronze-Age 22–3
Celtic 22–3
Chinese 106–7
dirks 160–1
dudgeon 158–9
Egyptian 20–1
European 78–83, 156–65
Fakir's Crutch 290
flint 12–13
Indian 206–3, 290, 294–6
Iron Age 22–3, 26–7
jambiya 310–1
Japanese 100–1, 192–3
kard 207
katar 207, 208–9
kris 119, 211
maingauche 156, 157
matchlock ax/dagger 214–5
medieval 78–83
Oceanian 312–13
Ottoman 188–9
parrying 296–7
pesh-kabz 294–5
piha kaetta 210
pirate 160–1
presentation 162–3
pugio 33
quillon 78–83, 156–63, 165
Roman 32–3

rondel 80–1
samurai 192–3
san-ku-chu 278–9
seax 36–7
stilettos 160, 165
Stone-Age 8, 12–3
Sumerian 16–7
sword-breaker 163
World War II 322–7
dao (sword) 63, 106–7, 272–3,
    292–3
Denmark 216
dha 221
dirks 161
double-edged swords
    Celtic 24–5
    medieval European 70–1
    Viking 44–7
dudgeon daggers 158–9
dueling 136–7, 234
düsack (sword) 127

E

eben (sword) 346–7
Egypt, Ancient 8, 17–9, 20–1,
    51–3
Elcho bayonets 246–7
Enfield rifle-musket bayonet 250–1
England 66–7, 70–1, 74–5, 78–83,
    125–7, 129–31, 141, 143–5, 147–9,
    157, 173
épée 234–5
Europe *see* countries by name
execution swords 118, 123, 292–3

F

Fairbairn-Sykes fighting knife
    319, 328–9
Fakir's Crutch (dagger) 290
fan dagger 192–3
fencing 234–5
fight books, medieval 92–3
fighting bracelets 344
fighting knives 318, 319, 328–9, 332–3
finger knives 344–5
firearms 119, 220, 221, 318
flails, with quoits 187
flint blades 8, 10–5, 50–1, 94–5
flintlock weapons 220
flute knife 192–3
flyssa swords 304–5
flyssa-style knives 344–5
foot soldiers, medieval 84–5
fouchard 63
France 66–7, 86, 130–3, 142–5, 148–9,
    162–3, 224–7, 230–1, 233, 245,
    248–51
Franks 36, 38, 56
fusil reglementaire 250–1

G

Gabon 345
gauntlet swords 178–9
Germanic tribes 22–3, 38, 217
Germany 70–1, 76–7, 87, 90, 113,
    121, 123, 126–7, 130–1, 138,
    148–51, 162–3, 165, 169, 172–5,
    174–5, 214–7, 320–7

Ghana 310–1
gladiators 34–5
gladius (sword) 9, 33, 34–5
glaive 63, 88–9, 173
gorz 184–5
greatswords 76–7
Greece, Ancient 28–31, 54–5
guan dao (halberd) 63, 104–5
guisarmes 63
Gulf War, Second 318
gunto (sword) 194–5
Gurkhas 338–9

H

Haida club 257
halberds 63, 87
  ceremonial 174–5
  double-barreled wheellock
    216–7
hammers *see* war hammers
hand-and-a-half sword 70–1
hanger swords 118, 129, 146–9, 220
harigata shuriken (stabbing blade) 283
Highland dirks 160–1
Highland swords 120–1
hilt design 8, 9, 47, 62, 118–9,
  202
Hitler Youth daggers 324–5
hoplites 28, 30–1, 54
horseman's hammers
  168–9
hunting crossbow 112–3
hunting knives 152–3
hunting swords 146–51

I

Ice-Age spearhead 13
iklwa (spear) 306–7
India 63, 108–11, 119, 178–87,
  206–15, 288–303
infantry swords
  American 220, 236–41
  European 125, 129, 220, 228–9
  medieval 84–5
Iran–Iraq War 318
Iraq 350
Iron-Age 9, 22–3, 26–7
Italy 64–5, 72–3, 89, 128–9, 139–41,
  146, 157, 160, 163, 165, 322–3

J K

jambiya (dagger) 310–1
Japan 62, 63, 98–103, 108–9, 119,
  190–205, 280–7, 318, 340–1
javelins 54–5
jian (sword) 63, 274–7
jousting 68–9
jungle operations 336–7
KA-BAR knives 319
kabuto (helmet) 204
kard (dagger) 207
Kasai copper daggers 346–7
kaskara (sword) 304–5
kastane (sword) 178–9
katana (sword) 63, 98–9, 100–1,
  190–1, 286–7, 318
katar (dagger) 207, 208–9
kenjutsu 286–7

khanda (sword) 288–9
kilij (sword) 262–3, 266–7, 270–1
kindjal (sword) 154–5
knights, medieval 68–9, 76–7
knives
  African 309, 342–9
  American 330–3, 336–7
  Aztec 94–5, 97
  bich-hwa 294–5
  Bowie 220, 256
  brass knuckle 319, 330–1
  cane 340–1
  carving 152
  cleavers 152–3
  cutlasses 312–3
  fighting 318, 319, 328–9, 332–3
  finger 344–5
  hunting 152–3
  Indian 294–7
  Japanese 192–3, 340–1
  KA-BAR 319
  knife bayonets 321, 332–3
  kukri 334–5, 338–9
  Native American 254–7
  pichangatti 297
  samurai 192–3, 196–7, 203
  sickle 346–7
  Stone Age 10–1
  throwing 345, 348–9
  trench 333
  World War I and II 330–3,
    336–41
kogatana (knife) 196–7, 203
kopis (scythe) 29
kris (dagger) 119, 211

kukri (knife) 334–5, 338–9
kung fu 105
kusarigama (chain and blade) 282

L

lancea (spear) 54–5
lances 68–9, 90
Landsknecht 166–7
Larim fighting bracelets 344
light cavalry swords 134–5
liuyedao (sword) 278–9
long swords
  Anglo-Saxon 36–7
  Egyptian 20–1
long-handled axes 91
longbows 112
Lowland swords 122
Luftwaffe daggers 322–3

M

maces
  Chinese 110–1
  European 170–1
  flanged 184–5
  Indian 108–9, 184–6, 303
  spiked 186, 303
  wheellock 214–5
machetes 336–7
mail coats 40, 62
maingauche (dagger) 156, 157
Malabar coast swords 178–9
Malaysia 211
Mammen axehead 42

Maoris 312–5
maquahuitl (club) 96–7
Martini-Henry socket bayonet 252–3
matchlock ax/dagger 214–5
Mesopotamia 16–7
Middle Ages 60–115
Modern World 316–51
Moguls 108–9, 180–1, 206–10
Mongols 111
morning star 175
Morocco 304–5, 342
mortuary swords 131
musket bayonets 248–9

N

naginata (staff weapon) 109
Native Americans 220, 254–9, 260–1
Nepal 334–5, 338–9
New Zealand 312–5
Nigeria 309
ninja 280–1, 282
ninjato (sword) 280–1
Normans 41

O P

obsidian blades 94, 313
Oceania 312–3
one-handed staff weapons 168–71
Ottomans 188–9, 221, 262–71
Paleolithic Age 10–1
Pappenheim-hilt rapier 138
Papua New Guinea 313
parade swords 121

parrying dagger 296–7
parrying shields 206, 298–9
parrying sticks 298–9
patuki (club) 312–3
Penobscot club 259
Persia 262–3, 270–1
pesh-kabz (dagger) 294–5
pichangatti (knife) 297
picks, fighting 310–1
piha kaetta (knife) 210
pikes and pikemen 176–7
pilum (javelin) 54–5
pioneer swords 224–5, 231
pipe tomahawk 258–9
pirate daggers 160–1
pistol bayonets 248–9
plate armor 62
plug bayonets 119, 164–5
poleaxes 86, 88–9, 172
Polynesia 312
pommels 9, 62
pouch daggers 193
presentation daggers 162–3
pugio (dagger) 33

Q R

quama (short sword) 269
quillon daggers 78–83, 156–63, 165
quillons 62, 119
rapiers 118–9, 136–41, 223, 228–9, 234
riding swords 66–7
Rome, Ancient 9, 32–5
rondel daggers 80–1
Russia 88–9, 154–5, 174–5, 222, 224–5

S

SA (*Sturmabteilung*) daggers 326–7
sabers 118, 130–1, 220, 222, 236–7,
    242–3, 264–5
saddle ax 184–5, 302–3
saif (sword) 268–9
saintie (spear) 63, 110–1
samurai 62, 63, 98–103, 119, 190–205
san-ku-chu (dagger) 278–9
Saxons *see* Anglo-Saxons
schiavona (sword) 129
Scotland 120–2, 128, 158–9, 160–1
seax (dagger) 36–7
shamshir (sword) 119, 180–1, 262–3, 270–1
Shaolin monks 104–5
shashka (sword) 154–5
shields
    Anglo-Saxon 40
    Viking 49
shin-gunto (sword) 340–1
short axes 91
short swords 20–1, 33, 37, 72–5, 191,
    220, 238–9, 269
shuangjian (sword) 278–9
shuriken (throwing weapons) 282–5
sickle knives 346–7
single-edged swords 63
skeg axes 43
smallswords 118, 142–5, 234
socket bayonets 119, 250–1, 252–3
sosun pattah (sword) 290–1
Spain 139, 228–9
Sparta 30–1
spearhead knives 254

spears
    African 306–7, 311
    Anglo-Saxon 56–7
    Aztec throwing 96
    Bronze-Age 52–3
    Egyptian 52–3
    Greek and Roman 54–5
    iklwa 306–7
    lancea 54–5
    Oceanian 313
    pilum 54–5
    saintie 110–1
    Stone-Age 13
    Viking 58–9
special weapons, Japanese 282–5
spiked *shuriken* 284
Sri Lanka 178–9, 210
SS (*Schutzstaffel*) daggers 319, 326–7
stabbing knives 309
staff weapons
    Asian 108–11, 184–7, 300–3
    European 86–91, 168–75
    Maori 314–5
    medieval 63, 86–91, 108–11
    one-handed 168–71
    two-handed 172–5
stilettos 160, 165
Stone-Age 8, 10–5, 50
Sudan 304–5, 310–1, 344, 346–7
Sumeria 16–7
Sweden 124, 134–5
swept-hilt rapiers 139, 141
Switzerland 87, 125
sword bayonets 244–5, 250–1, 334–5
sword-breaker daggers 163

swords
  African 304–5, 346–9
  American Civil War 220–1, 236–41
  Anglo-Saxon 36–7
  arming 92–3
  ayudha katti 182
  baselard 70–1
  bastard 70–1, 114–5
  broadswords 125, 126, 128, 272–3
  Bronze- and Iron-Age 22–3
  cased 145
  Celtic 24–5
  Chinese 98–9, 106–7, 272–9
  chokuto 63
  cinquedea 72–3
  claymore 120
  colichemarde-type 143
  curved 62–3
  cutlasses 228–9, 241, 312–3
  dadao 63, 272–3
  dao 63, 106–7, 272–3, 292–3
  decorated 142–5
  dha 221
  düsack 127
  eben 346–7
  Egyptian 20–1
  epée 234–5
  European 64–75, 124–35, 142–51,
      222–33
  execution 118, 123, 292–3
  flyssa 304–5
  gladius 9, 33, 34–5
  greatswords 76–7
  Greek 29, 30–1
  guan dao 104–5

gunto 194–5
hanger 118, 129, 146–9, 220
heavy cavalry 226–7
Highland 120–1
hunting 146–51
Indian 178–83, 288–93
infantry and cavalry 124–35,
    222–31, 318
Japanese 62, 63, 98–103, 190–1,
    194–203, 280–1, 286–7, 340–1
jian 63, 274–7
kaskara 304–5
kastane 178–9
katana 63, 100–1, 190–1, 286–7, 318
khanda 288–9
kilij 262–3, 266–7, 270–1
kindjal 154–5
kopis 29
liuyedao 278–9
Lowland 122
medieval European 64–75
mortuary 130–1
ninjato 280–1
Ottoman 262–71
pioneer 224–5, 231
quama 269
rapiers 118, 119, 136–41, 223,
    228–9, 234
Roman 32–5
Russian 154–5, 222, 224–5
sabers 118, 130–1, 220, 222, 236–7,
    242–3, 264–5
saif 268–9
schiavona 129
shamshir 119, 180–1, 262–3, 270–1

shashka 154–5
shin-gunto 340–1
shuangjian 278–9
single-handed, with shield 84–5
smallswords 118, 142–5, 234
sosun pattah 290–1
Sri Lankan 178–9
tachi 63, 102–3, 194–5
talwar 63, 180–3, 290–1
tanto 191
Tibetan 274–7
two-handed 120–3, 166–7
vechevoral 288–9
Viking 44–9, 62
wakazashi 63, 102–3, 196–203
xiphos 30–1
yataghan 221, 264–5
Zweihander broadswords 166–7

T

tabar (saddle ax) 184–5, 302–3
tachi (sword) 63, 102–3, 194–5
taiaha (staff weapon) 314–5
talwar (sword) 63, 180–3, 290–1
tanto (sword) 191
tetsubishi (spiked device) 285
throwing weapons
  axes 38, 42–3
  chakram 296–7
  Japanese 282–5
  knives 345, 348–9
  see also javelins; lances; spears
Tibet 274–7
Tlinglit knives 256–7

tomahawks, pipe 258–9, 260–1
tongi (ax) 300–2
tosei gusoku (armor) 204–5
tournament combat 68–9
trade knives 255
trench axes 324–5
trench knives 333
trident spearheads 52
trowel bayonets 246–7
Turkey *see* Ottomans
two-handed staff weapons 172–5
two-handed swords 63, 120–3, 166–7

U V W

Uganda 344–5
United States 13, 242–3, 246–7,
    330–3, 336–7, 351
  see also Native Americans
vechevoral (cutting tool) 288–9
Vietnam War 318
Vikings 42–9, 58–9, 62, 91
wakazashi (sword) 63, 102–3, 196–203
war hammers 168–9
  medieval European 89
  war hammer wheellock 214–5
wheellock pistols 214–7
World War I 318–21, 333–5
World War II 318–41

X Y Z

xiphos (sword) 30–1
yataghan (sword) 221, 264–5
Zulu warriors 306–7

ACKNOWLEDGMENTS

Dorling Kindersley would like to thank Jenny Baskaya for additional picture research; Richard Beatty and Debra Wolter for proofreading; Helen Peters for the index; and Aparna Sharma, Dawn Henderson, Arunesh Talapatra, Devika Dwarkadas, Alka Ranjan, Suchismita Banerjee, Steffenie Jyrwa, and Dipali Singh at DK Delhi.

Picture Credits

The publisher would like to thank the following for their kind permission to reproduce their photographs:

(Key: a-above; b-below/bottom; c-center; f-far; l-left; r-right; t-top)

akg-images: 77r, 137r; Peter Connolly 31r; Nationalmuseet, Copenhagen 25r; Nimatallah 177cr; Alamy Images: ephotocorp 189cr; Interfoto 49r, 286-287; Japan Art Collection (JAC) 281r; J Marshall - Tribaleye Images 205cr; Pictorial Press Ltd 227r; The Print Collector 235r; Viktor Todorov 60-61; V&A Images 218-219; Ancient Art & Architecture Collection: Interfoto / Hermann Historica 76-77c, 92-93, 114-115; R Sheridan 16-17 (Dagger and Scabbard); The Board of Trustees of the Armouries: 98-99c, 272-273t, 278-279b, 278-279c, 278-279t; The Art Archive: Musée de la Tapisserie Bayeux / Gianni Dagli Orti 41r; National Museum Copenhagen / Alfredo Dagli Orti 85r; Topkapi Museum Istanbul / Gianni Dagli Orti 267r; Image courtesy of Barringtons Swords, European suppliers of Hanwei Swords: 280-281; The Bridgeman Art Library: Biblioteca Nazionale, Turin, Italy / Index 69r; Bibliotheque Nationale, Paris, France 115cr; Egyptian National Museum, Cairo, Egypt 20-21c; Hermitage, St. Petersburg, Russia 167cr; Phoenix Art Museum, Arizona, USA 35cr; ChinaFotoPress: 104-105, 106cl, 106-107ca, 272-273c; Corbis: Bettmann 243r; Raymond Gehman 261r; Hulton-Deutsch Collection 329r; Anders Ryman 315r; Dorling Kindersley: 4hoplites 28bc, 28-29, 29bc, 29c, 30-31; The American Museum of Natural History 13c, 256-257b, 257cla, 257t, 258cb, 258clb, 259crb, 259r, 260-261, 261clb; The British Museum 16-17tc, 18-19, 20-21bc, 20-21tc, 22-23tc, 26,

32-33ca (Sword & Sheath), 51tr, 52-53bc, 53tr, 90c, 91cr, 97bc; CONACULTA-INAH-MEX. Authorized reproduction by the Instituto Nacional de Antropologia e Historia 94cb, 94-95c, 95bc, 95tc, 96bc, 96crb, 96-97tc; Confederate Memorial Hall, New Orleans 238-239b, 239bc, 240r, 240tr, 242-243, 256t (Knife & scabbard); Ermine Street Guard 32-33bc, 54-55ca; Exeter City Museums and Art Gallery 345r; Gettysburg National Military Park, PA 236-237b, 237clb, 238tr, 238-239c, 238-239t, 241t, 241tr; The History Museum, Moscow 174cr; The History Museum, Moscow 174-175tc; Master Kohaku Iwai 192tr, 192-193ca (Dagger and sheath), 192-193cb, 193; Judith Miller / Wallis and Wallis 130-131c, 131clb; Museum of Mankind / British Museum 258tr, 258-259tl; Museum of the Order of St John, London 223ca; The Museum of London 10-11tc, 14cr, 14fbr, 15bc, 15cl, 15cr, 24-25, 26-26tc, 26-27b, 42-43, 46ca, 46-47tc, 50-51tc, 56tl, 56-57cb, 91cl; National Maritime Museum, London 160-161ca; National Museum, New Delhi 210-211c; Natural History Museum, London 4tc; Pitt Rivers Museum, University of Oxford 1ca, 5tr, 180-181cb, 196-197ca, 210-211ca, 254, 255, 294-295b, 294-295t, 296cl, 296-297l, 300b, 300-301b, 308b, 308c, 309cl, 309l, 309r, 310-311c, 310-311t, 311cra (Arrows), 312b, 312-313b, 312-313t, 313cla, 313r, 338-339, 342c, 342-343b, 342-343t, 344tl, 344-345b, 344-345tc, 346-347b, 346-347c, 346-347t, 348-349br, 349cr; The Powell-Cotton Museum, Kent 348bl, 348br; RAF Museum, Hendon 330-331t; By kind permission of the Trustees of the Wallace Collection 4tr, 66-67tc, 68-69, 70-71tc, 72-73bc, 86cr, 87cr, 87tr, 89cr, 89tc, 110-111bc, 112cb, 112-113 (Crossbow & arrows), 121bc, 121cb, 136-137, 146cr, 162-163tc, 163bc, 163c, 164tl, 164-165cb, 164-165tc, 165br, 165cr, 170-171tc, 174-175bc, 178-179tc, 184bl, 184-185bc, 184-185tc, 186c, 186cr, 188-189, 194-195cb, 206br, 206tr, 262-263b, 262-263t (Sword & scabbard), 264-265b (Sword & scabbard), 264-265t (Sword & scabbard), 268-269b (Short sword & scabbard), 268-269r (Sword & scabbard), 348-349; Danish National Museum 42c, 44-45cb (Double edged swords); Imperial War Museum, London 153-154, 328-329; Royal Green Jackets Museum, Winchester 228-229cb,

229br, 250-251t (Rifle & bayonet); The Board of Trustees of the Royal Armouries 2-3, 5tc, 5tl, 19ca, 19cb, 22-23cb, 36-37c, 36-37tc, 38cl, 38tc, 39, 44-45tc, 46-47bc, 46-47cb, 50-51bc, 50-51ca, 51cl, 54-55bc, 58-59ca, 64-65bc, 64-65ca, 65tr, 66bl, 66crb, 66-67bc, 66-67ca, 70clb, 70-71bc, 70-71c, 71clb, 72cr, 72-73c, 74cl, 74tl, 74-75c, 75tr, 78-79bc, 78-79tc, 79tr, 80-81bc, 80-81c, 80-81tc, 82-83, 82-83bc, 83tr, 86-87, 88-89tc, 90cr, 98-99bc, 98-99tc, 100-101cb, 100-101tc, 102-103bc, 102-103ca, 106-107bc, 108br, 108cr, 108-109bc, 108-109ca, 110-111c, 110-111tc, 112r, 116-117, 120-121tc, 121tc, 122br, 122c, 123cb, 123cl, 123cr, 124br, 124tr, 125bc, 125ca, 125tr, 126bc, 126cr, 126-127, 127bl, 127c, 128cl, 128tc, 128-129, 129bl, 129ca, 129tl, 130-131tc, 132-133ca, 132-133cb, 136br, 138cr, 138tr, 138-139, 139br, 139cr, 139tl, 140bl, 140cl, 140-141cb, 141br, 141ca, 141tr, 142cr, 142cra, 142-143bc, 142-143tc, 143bl, 143tr, 144cl, 144crb, 144-145bc, 144-145tc, 145c, 145cb, 147c, 147cr, 148-149ca, 150-151cb, 151ca, 152c, 152-153bc, 152-153tc, 156cr, 156cra, 156-157, 157cl, 157cla, 157cr, 158-159bc, 158-159ca, 159crb, 160c, 160cl, 160-161cb, 162-163bc, 166-167, 168-169ca, 168-169cb, 169br, 169tl, 170-171bc, 170-171tc, 172cr, 172tr, 172-173bc, 173ca, 175ca, 176-177, 178-179ca, 178-179cb, 179bl, 180-181tc, 182br, 182tr, 182-183ca, 183bl, 183cb, 184-185tc, 187, 190-191bc, 194-195ca, 198-199ca, 198-199cb, 200c, 200-201bc, 200-201cb, 200-201tc, 202cb, 202tl, 202tr, 202-203tc, 203bc, 203cb, 204cr, 205cla, 206-207bc, 206-207ca, 206-207cb, 207tc, 208-209bc, 208-209ca, 210tc, 211bc, 212-213bc, 212-213c, 212-213ca, 214-215c, 214-215tr, 215bc, 215clb, 216-217bc, 216-217ca, 217br, 217fbr, 217tc, 222cr, 222fcr, 223bc, 224-225bc, 224-225c, 224-225ca, 225clb, 226-227, 228-229c, 228-229tc, 229cl, 230l, 230r, 230-231b, 230-231t, 231br, 231tr, 232bc, 232cb, 232-233b, 232-233t, 241b, 241clb, 244br, 244fcr, 244-245t, 245b, 245cr, 245tc, 246-247b, 246-247c, 246-247t, 248-249b (Musket & bayonet), 248-249c, 248-249t (Musket & bayonet), 250-251b, 250-251c (Rifle & bayonet), 251br, 252bl, 252-253, 253b, 266-267bc, 266-267cb, 270-271b, 270-271t, 271br, 271c, 271crb, 271t, 272-273b, 274-275b, 274-275t (Sword & scabbard), 275cb, 275tr, 276crb, 276-277b (Sword & scabbard), 276-277t

(Sword & scabbard), 288-289b, 288-289t, 289bl, 290-291b, 290-291t (Talwar & scabbard), 292c, 292-293b, 292-293cl, 292-293t, 297t (Knife & scabbard), 298-299b, 298-299t, 299tr, 300-301c, 300-301tr, 302cb, 302-303c, 302-303t, 303b, 303br, 304bl, 304-305b, 304-305c, 304-305ca, 304-305t, 306-307, 311br, 311crb, 316-317, 320-321c, 321t, 330-331b, 332b, 332-333t (Bayonet & scabbard), 334-335t, 350-351t; Vikings of Middle England 43bl, 43c, 48-49; Warwick Castle, Warwick 72-73c, 75br, 120bc, 148-149bc; The Science Museum, London 10-11bc; US Army Heritage and Education Center - Military History Institute 236-237t, 237tr; The Wardrobe: The Rifles (Berkshire and Wiltshire) Museum 320-321b, 322-323b, 322-323c, 322-323t, 324-325tr, 325cra, 326-327b, 326-327c, 326-327t, 334-335b, 334-335c, 336-337b (Knife & scabbard), 336-337t (Knife & scabbard), 340-341b, 340-341cb, 340-341t (Knife & scabbard); Robin Wigington, Arbour Antiques, Ltd., Stratford-upon-Avon 165cl, 165fcl, 290c, 290l, 294-295c, 296br, 296-297bc; Georg-August-Universität Göttingen / Institut für Ethnologie/ Cook-Forster Collection: Harry Haase 314-315; Getty Images: 105r, 339r; The Bridgeman Art Library 6-7, 58-59bc, 253r; The Bridgeman Art Library / Bronze Age 52tl; Paolo Negri 191ca; The Kobal Collection: Diamond Films 307r; MGM 155r; Shefton Museum of Antiquities, University of Newcastle: 54cl, 54tl; TopFoto.co.uk: HIP 93cr; Werner Forman Archive: Burke Collection, New York 287r.

Jacket images: Front: Dorling Kindersley: Pitt Rivers Museum, University of Oxford clb; By kind permission of the Trustees of the Wallace Collection br, ca, cb, cl; The Board of Trustees of the Royal Armouries bl, cr. Back: Dorling Kindersley: The Board of Trustees of the Royal Armouries ca, cr, crb, tr. Spine: Dorling Kindersley: By kind permission of the Trustees of the Wallace Collection. Back Flaps: Dorling Kindersley: By kind permission of the Trustees of the Wallace Collection.

All other images © Dorling Kindersley
For further information see:
www.dkimages.com